BLOOM'S

HOW TO WRITE ABOUT

Gabriel Garcia
Márquez

ERIC L. REINHOLTZ

Introduction by Harold Bloom

BLOOM'S
LITERARY CRITICISM
An imprint of Infobase Publishing

Library of Congress Cataloging-in-Publication Data
Reinholtz, Eric L.
    Bloom's how to write about Gabriel García Márquez/Eric L. Reinholtz; introduction by Harold Bloom.
        p. cm.—(Bloom's how to write about literature series)
    Includes bibliographical references and index.
    ISBN 978-1-60413-331-8 (acid-free paper). 1. García Márquez, Gabriel, 1928——Criticism and interpretation. 2. Criticism—Authorship. 3. Report writing. I. Bloom, Harold. II. Title. III. Title: How to write about Gabriel García Márquez. IV. Series.

PQ8180.17.A73Z9253 2009
863'.64—dc22   2009005490

Bloom's Literary Criticism books are available at special discounts when purchased in bulk quantities for businesses, associations, institutions, or sales promotions. Please call our Special Sales Department in New York at (212) 967-8800 or (800) 322-8755.

You can find Bloom's Literary Criticism on the World Wide Web at
http://www.chelseahouse.com

Text design by Annie O'Donnell
Cover design by Ben Peterson

Printed in the United States of America

MP MSRF 10 9 8 7 6 5 4 3 2 1

This book is printed on acid-free paper.

CONTENTS

SERIES INTRODUCTION

BLOOM'S How to Write about Literature series is designed to inspire students to write fine essays on great writers and their works. Each volume in the series begins with an introduction by Harold Bloom, meditating on the challenges and rewards of writing about the volume's subject author. The first chapter then provides detailed instructions on how to write a good essay, including how to find a thesis; how to develop an outline; how to write a good introduction, body text, and conclusion; how to cite sources; and more. The second chapter provides a brief overview of the issues involved in writing about the subject author and then a number of suggestions for paper topics, with accompanying strategies for addressing each topic. Succeeding chapters cover the author's major works.

The paper topics suggested within this book are open-ended, and the brief strategies provided are designed to give students a push forward in the writing process rather than a road map to success. The aim of the book is to pose questions, not answer them. Many different kinds of papers could result from each topic. As always, the success of each paper will depend completely on the writer's skill and imagination.

HOW TO WRITE ABOUT GABRIEL GARCÍA MÁRQUEZ: INTRODUCTION

by Harold Bloom

THERE IS a still strenuous principle, which I take from D. H. Lawrence: Trust the tale and not the teller. When the author of *One Hundred Years of Solitude* tells us that he invents nothing and merely describes the people and actions he beholds around him, simply shrug that aside.

What are very relevant to García Márquez's fictions are the forming influences of William Faulkner and Jorge Luis Borges, for García Márquez is inconceivable without them. The fecund way to write about him is to read them and bring that experience to García Márquez.

I recommend in particular Malcolm Cowley's *The Portable Faulkner* and the American collection of Borges entitled *Labyrinths*. If you carefully read through both, you will find the fictive realities that García Márquez has exploited throughout his work. Take Faulkner and Borges, turn them and turn them, for all of him is in them.

HOW TO WRITE
A GOOD ESSAY

By Laurie A. Sterling and Eric L. Reinholtz

WHILE THERE are many ways to write about literature, most assignments for high school and college English classes call for analytical papers. In these assignments, you are presenting your interpretation of a text to your reader. Your objective is to interpret the text's meaning in order to enhance your reader's understanding and enjoyment of the work. Without exception, strong papers about the meaning of a literary work are built upon a careful, close reading of the text or texts. Careful, analytical reading should always be the first step in your writing process. This volume provides models of such close, analytical reading, and these should help you develop your own skills as a reader and as a writer.

As the examples throughout this book demonstrate, attentive reading entails thinking about and evaluating the formal (textual) aspects of the author's works: theme, character, form, and language. In addition, when writing about a work, many readers choose to move beyond the text itself to consider the work's cultural context. In these instances, writers might explore the historical circumstances of the time period in which the work was written. Alternatively, they might examine the philosophies and ideas that a work addresses. Even in cases where writers explore a work's cultural context, though, papers must still address the more formal aspects of the work itself. A good interpretative essay that evaluates Charles Dickens's use of the philosophy of utilitarianism in his novel *Hard Times,* for example, cannot adequately address the author's treatment of the philosophy without firmly grounding this discussion in the book itself. In other words, any

1

analytical paper about a text, even one that seeks to evaluate the work's cultural context, must also have a firm handle on the work's themes, characters, and language. You must look for and evaluate these aspects of a work, then, as you read a text and as you prepare to write about it.

WRITING ABOUT THEMES

Literary themes are more than just topics or subjects treated in a work; they are attitudes or points about these topics that often structure other elements in a work. Writing about theme therefore requires that you not just identify a topic that a literary work addresses but also discuss what that work says about that topic. For example, if you were writing about the culture of the American South in William Faulkner's famous story "A Rose for Emily," you would need to discuss what Faulkner says, argues, or implies about that culture and its passing.

When you prepare to write about thematic concerns in a work of literature, you will probably discover that, like most works of literature, your text touches upon other themes in addition to its central theme. These secondary themes also provide rich ground for paper topics. A thematic paper on "A Rose for Emily" might consider gender or race in the story. While neither of these could be said to be the central theme of the story, they are clearly related to the passing of the "old South" and could provide plenty of good material for papers.

As you prepare to write about themes in literature, you might find a number of strategies helpful. After you identify a theme or themes in the story, you should begin by evaluating how other elements of the story—such as character, point of view, imagery, and symbolism—help develop the theme. You might ask yourself what your own responses are to the author's treatment of the subject matter. Do not neglect the obvious, either: What expectations does the title set up? How does the title help develop thematic concerns? Clearly, the title "A Rose for Emily" says something about the narrator's attitude toward the title character, Emily Grierson, and all she represents.

WRITING ABOUT CHARACTER

Generally, characters are essential components of fiction and drama. (This is not always the case, though; Ray Bradbury's "August 2026: There

Will Come Soft Rains" is technically a story without characters, at least any human characters.) Often, you can discuss character in poetry, as in T. S. Eliot's "The Love Song of J. Alfred Prufrock" or Robert Browning's "My Last Duchess." Many writers find that analyzing character is one of the most interesting and engaging ways to work with a piece of literature and to shape a paper. After all, characters generally are human, and we all know something about being human and living in the world. While it is always important to remember that these figures are not real people but creations of the writer's imagination, it can be fruitful to begin evaluating them as you might evaluate a real person. Often you can start with your own response to a character. Did you like or dislike the character? Did you sympathize with the character? Why or why not?

Keep in mind, though, that emotional responses like these are just starting places. To truly explore and evaluate literary characters, you need to return to the formal aspects of the text and evaluate how the author has drawn these characters. The 20th-century writer E. M. Forster coined the terms *flat* characters and *round* characters. Flat characters are static, one-dimensional characters who frequently represent a particular concept or idea. In contrast, round characters are fully drawn and much more realistic characters who frequently change and develop over the course of a work. Are the characters you are studying flat or round? What elements of the characters lead you to this conclusion? Why might the author have drawn characters like this? How does their development affect the meaning of the work? Similarly, you should explore the techniques the author uses to develop characters. Do we hear a character's own words, or do we hear only other characters' assessments of him or her? Or, does the author use an omniscient or limited omniscient narrator to allow us access to the workings of the characters' minds? If so, how does that help develop the characterization? Often you can even evaluate the narrator as a character. How trustworthy are the opinions and assessments of the narrator? You should also think about characters' names. Do they mean anything? If you encounter a hero named Sophia or Sophie, you should probably think about her wisdom (or lack thereof), since *Sophia* means "wisdom" in Greek. Similarly, since the name *Sylvia* is derived from the word *sylvan*, meaning "of the wood," you might want to evaluate that character's relationship with nature. Once again, you might look to the title of the work. Does Herman Melville's "Bartleby, the Scrivener" signal anything about Bartleby himself? Is Bartleby adequately defined by his job as scrivener?

Is this part of Melville's point? Pursuing questions like these can help you develop thorough papers about characters from psychological, sociological, or more formalistic perspectives.

WRITING ABOUT FORM AND GENRE

Genre, a word derived from French, means "type" or "class." Literary genres are distinctive classes or categories of literary composition. On the most general level, literary works can be divided into the genres of drama, poetry, fiction, and essays, yet within those genres there are classifications that are also referred to as genres. Tragedy and comedy, for example, are genres of drama. Epic, lyric, and pastoral are genres of poetry. *Form,* on the other hand, generally refers to the shape or structure of a work. There are many clearly defined forms of poetry that follow specific patterns of meter, rhyme, and stanza. Sonnets, for example, are poems that follow a fixed form of 14 lines. Sonnets generally follow one of two basic sonnet forms, each with its own distinct rhyme scheme. Haiku is another example of poetic form, traditionally consisting of three unrhymed lines of five, seven, and five syllables.

While you might think that writing about form or genre might leave little room for argument, many of these forms and genres are very fluid. Remember that literature is evolving and ever changing, and so are its forms. As you study poetry, you may find that poets, especially more modern poets, play with traditional poetic forms, bringing about new effects. Similarly, dramatic tragedy was once quite narrowly defined, but over the centuries playwrights have broadened and challenged traditional definitions, changing the shape of tragedy. When Arthur Miller wrote *Death of a Salesman,* many critics challenged the idea that tragic drama could encompass a common man like Willy Loman.

Evaluating how a work of literature fits into or challenges the boundaries of its form or genre can provide you with fruitful avenues of investigation. You might find it helpful to ask why the work does or does not fit into traditional categories. Why might Miller have thought it fitting to write a tragedy of the common man? Similarly, you might compare the content or theme of a work with its form. How well do they work together? Many of Emily Dickinson's poems, for instance, follow the meter of traditional hymns. While some of her poems seem to express traditional religious doctrines, many seem to challenge or strain against traditional conceptions of God and theology. What is the effect, then, of her use of traditional hymn meter?

WRITING ABOUT LANGUAGE, SYMBOLS, AND IMAGERY

No matter what the genre, writers use words as their most basic tool. Language is the most fundamental building block of literature. It is essential that you pay careful attention to the author's language and word choice as you read, reread, and analyze a text. Imagery is language that appeals to the senses. Most commonly, imagery appeals to our sense of vision, creating a mental picture, but authors also use language that appeals to our other senses. Images can be literal or figurative. Literal images use sensory language to describe an actual thing. In the broadest terms, figurative language uses one thing to speak about something else. For example, if I call my boss a snake, I am not saying that he is literally a reptile. Instead, I am using figurative language to communicate my opinions about him. Since we think of snakes as sneaky, slimy, and sinister, I am using the concrete image of a snake to communicate these abstract opinions and impressions.

The two most common figures of speech are similes and metaphors. Both are comparisons between two apparently dissimilar things. Similes are explicit comparisons using the words *like* or *as*; metaphors are implicit comparisons. To return to the previous example, if I say, "My boss, Bob, was waiting for me when I showed up to work five minutes late today—the snake!" I have constructed a metaphor. Writing about his experiences fighting in World War I, Wilfred Owen begins his poem "Dulce et decorum est," with a string of similes: "Bent double, like old beggars under sacks, / Knock-kneed, coughing like hags, we cursed through sludge." Owen's goal was to undercut clichéd notions that war and dying in battle were glorious. Certainly, comparing soldiers to coughing hags and to beggars underscores his point.

"Fog," a short poem by Carl Sandburg, provides a clear example of a metaphor. Sandburg's poem reads:

The fog comes
on little cat feet.

It sits looking
over harbor and city
on silent haunches
and then moves on.

Notice how effectively Sandburg conveys surprising impressions of the fog by comparing two seemingly disparate things—the fog and a cat.

Symbols, by contrast, are things that stand for, or represent, other things. Often they represent something intangible, such as concepts or ideas. In everyday life we use and understand symbols easily. Babies at christenings and brides at weddings wear white to represent purity. Think, too, of a dollar bill. The paper itself has no value in and of itself. Instead, that paper bill is a symbol of something else, the precious metal in a nation's coffers. Symbols in literature work similarly. Authors use symbols to evoke more than a simple, straightforward, literal meaning. Characters, objects, and places can all function as symbols. Famous literary examples of symbols include Moby Dick, the white whale of Herman Melville's novel, and the scarlet *A* of Nathaniel Hawthorne's *The Scarlet Letter.* As both of these symbols suggest, a literary symbol cannot be adequately defined or explained by any one meaning. Hester Prynne's Puritan community clearly intends her scarlet *A* as a symbol of her adultery, but as the novel progresses, even her own community reads the letter as representing not just *adultery,* but *able, angel,* and a host of other meanings.

Writing about imagery and symbols requires close attention to the author's language. To prepare a paper on symbolism or imagery in a work, identify and trace the images and symbols and then try to draw some conclusions about how they function. Ask yourself how any symbols or images help contribute to the themes or meanings of the work. What connotations do they carry? How do they affect your reception of the work? Do they shed light on characters or settings? A strong paper on imagery or symbolism will thoroughly consider the use of figures in the text and will try to reach some conclusions about how or why the author uses them.

WRITING ABOUT HISTORY AND CONTEXT

As noted above, it is possible to write an analytical paper that also considers the work's context. After all, the text was not created in a vacuum. The author lived and wrote in a specific time period and in a specific cultural context and, like all of us, was shaped by that environment. Learning more about the historical and cultural circumstances that surround the author and the work can help illuminate a text and provide you with productive material for a paper. Remember, though, that when you write analytical papers, you should use the context to illuminate the text. Do not lose sight of your goal—to interpret the meaning of the literary work. Use historical or philosophical research as a tool to develop your textual evaluation.

Thoughtful readers often consider how history and culture affected the author's choice and treatment of his or her subject matter. Investigations into the history and context of a work could examine the work's relation to specific historical events, such as the Salem witch trials in 17th-century Massachusetts or the restoration of Charles to the English throne in 1660. Bear in mind that historical context is not limited to politics and world events. While knowing about the Vietnam War is certainly helpful in interpreting much of Tim O'Brien's fiction, and some knowledge of the French Revolution clearly illuminates the dynamics of Charles Dickens's *A Tale of Two Cities,* historical context also entails the fabric of daily life. Examining a text in light of gender roles, race relations, class boundaries, or working conditions can give rise to thoughtful and compelling papers. Exploring the conditions of the working class in 19th-century England, for example, can provide a particularly effective avenue for writing about Dickens's *Hard Times.*

You can begin thinking about these issues by asking broad questions at first. What do you know about the time period and about the author? What does the editorial apparatus in your text tell you? These might be starting places. Similarly, when specific historical events or dynamics are particularly important to understanding a work but might be somewhat obscure to modern readers, textbooks usually provide notes to explain historical background. These are a good place to start. With this information, ask yourself how these historical facts and circumstances might have affected the author, the presentation of theme, and the presentation of character. How does knowing more about the work's specific historical context illuminate the work? To take a well-known example, understanding the complex attitudes toward slavery during the time Mark Twain wrote *Adventures of Huckleberry Finn* should help you begin to examine issues of race in the text. Additionally, you might compare these attitudes to those of the time in which the novel was set. How might this comparison affect your interpretation of a work written after the abolition of slavery but set before the Civil War?

WRITING ABOUT PHILOSOPHY AND IDEAS

Philosophical concerns are closely related to both historical context and thematic issues. Like historical investigation, philosophical research can provide a useful tool as you analyze a text. For example, an investigation into the working class in Dickens's England might lead you to a topic on the philosophical doctrine of utilitarianism in *Hard Times*. Many other works explore philosophies and ideas quite explicitly. Mary Shelley's famous novel *Frankenstein,* for example, explores John Locke's tabula rasa theory of human knowledge as she portrays the intellectual and emotional development of Victor Frankenstein's creature. As this example indicates, philosophical issues are somewhat more abstract than investigations of theme or historical context. Some other examples of philosophical issues include human free will, the formation of human identity, the nature of sin, or questions of ethics.

Writing about philosophy and ideas might require some outside research, but usually the notes or other material in your text will provide you with basic information, and often footnotes and bibliographies suggest places you can go to read further about the subject. If you have identified a philosophical theme that runs through a text, you might ask yourself how the author develops this theme. Look at character development and the interactions of characters, for example. Similarly, you might examine whether the narrative voice in a work of fiction addresses the philosophical concerns of the text.

WRITING COMPARISON AND CONTRAST ESSAYS

Finally, you might find that comparing and contrasting the works or techniques of an author provides a useful tool for literary analysis. A comparison and contrast essay might compare two characters or themes in a single work, or it might compare the author's treatment of a theme in two works. It might also contrast methods of character development or analyze an author's differing treatment of a philosophical concern in two works. Writing comparison and contrast essays, though, requires some special consideration. While they generally provide you with plenty of material to use, they also come with a built-in trap: the laundry list. These papers often become mere lists of connections between the works. As this chapter will discuss, a strong thesis must make an assertion that you want to prove or validate. A strong comparison/contrast thesis, then, needs to comment on the significance of the similarities and differences you observe. It is not enough merely to assert that the works contain similarities and differences. You might, for example, assert why the similarities and differences are important and explain how they illuminate the works' treatment of theme. Remember, too, that a thesis should not be a statement of the obvious. A comparison/contrast paper that focuses only on very obvious similarities or differences does little to illuminate the connections between the works. Often, an effective method of shaping a strong thesis and argument is to begin your paper by noting the similarities between the works but then to develop a thesis that asserts how these apparently similar elements are different. If, for example, you observe that Emily Dickinson wrote a number of poems about spiders, you might analyze how she uses spider imagery differently in two poems. Similarly, many scholars have noted that Hawthorne created many "mad scientist" characters, men who are so devoted to their science or their art that they lose perspective on all else. A good thesis comparing two of these characters—Aylmer of "The Birth-mark" and Dr. Rappaccini of "Rappaccini's Daughter," for example—might initially identify both characters as examples of Hawthorne's mad scientist type but then argue that their motivations for scientific experimentation differ. If you strive to analyze the similarities or differences, discuss significances, and move beyond the obvious, your paper should move beyond the laundry list trap.

PREPARING TO WRITE

Armed with a clear sense of your task—illuminating the text—and with an understanding of theme, character, language, history, and philosophy, you are ready to approach the writing process. Remember that good writing is grounded in good reading and that close reading takes time, attention, and more than one reading of your text. Read for comprehension first. As you go back and review the work, mark the text to chart the details of the work as well as your reactions. Highlight important passages, repeated words, and image patterns. "Converse" with the text through marginal notes. Mark turns in the plot, ask questions, and make observations about characters, themes, and language. If you are reading from a book that does not belong to you, keep a record of your reactions in a journal or notebook. If you have read a work of literature carefully, paying attention to both the text and the context of the work, you have a leg up on the writing process. Admittedly, at this point, your ideas are probably very broad and undefined, but you have taken an important first step toward writing a strong paper.

Your next step is to focus, to take a broad, perhaps fuzzy, topic and define it more clearly. Even a topic provided by your instructor will need to be focused appropriately. Remember that good writers make the topic their own. There are a number of strategies—often called "invention"—that you can use to develop your own focus. In one such strategy, called *freewriting*, you spend 10 minutes or so just writing about your topic without referring back to the text or your notes. Write whatever comes to mind; the important thing is that you just keep writing. Often this process allows you to develop fresh ideas or approaches to your subject matter. You could also try *brainstorming*: Write down your topic and then list all the related points or ideas you can think of. Include questions, comments, words, important passages or events, and anything else that comes to mind. Let one idea lead to another. In the related technique of *clustering*, or *mapping*, write your topic on a sheet of paper and write related ideas around it. Then list related subpoints under each of these main ideas. Many people then draw arrows to show connections between points. This technique helps you narrow your topic and can also help you organize your ideas. Similarly, asking journalistic questions—Who? What? Where? When? Why? and How?—can develop ideas for topic development.

Thesis Statements

Once you have developed a focused topic, you can begin to think about your thesis statement, the main point or purpose of your paper. It is imperative that you craft a strong thesis, otherwise, your paper will likely be little more than random, disorganized observations about the text. Think of your thesis statement as a kind of road map for your paper. It tells your reader where you are going and how you are going to get there.

To craft a good thesis, you must keep a number of things in mind. First, as the title of this subsection indicates, your paper's thesis should be a statement, an assertion about the text that you want to prove or validate. Beginning writers often formulate a question that they attempt to use as a thesis. For example, a writer exploring the theme of optimism in Gabriel García Márquez's *Nobody Writes to the Colonel* might ask, Why does the colonel continue to believe that his pension check from the government will soon arrive, even after years of frustration? While a question like this is a good strategy to use in the invention process to help narrow your topic and find your thesis, it cannot serve as the thesis statement because it does not tell your reader what you want to assert about hope. You might shape this question into a thesis by instead proposing an answer to that question: In No One Writes to the Colonel, the title character's unwavering faith in a better future is not a commentary on political naiveté but rather a statement on the power of the human spirit to endure injustice. It is precisely through his quixotic struggle to survive in the face of an absurd and cruel universe that the colonel emerges as a truly heroic figure. Notice that this thesis provides an initial plan or structure for the rest of the paper, and notice, too, that the thesis statement does not necessarily have to fit into one sentence. After discussing the colonel's steady faith that the government will pay him the money he has been promised, you could examine the other ways in which his optimism functions as a response to an ever-worsening situation and speculate on what García Márquez is saying about optimism and the human condition. You might then discuss how the colonel's own optimism in a corrupt and cynical world is an indictment of the oppressive society in which the story is set.

Second, remember that a good thesis makes an assertion that you need to support. In other words, a good thesis does not state the obvious. If you tried to formulate a thesis about optimism by simply saying The title character's optimism is a central theme in No One Writes to the Colonel, you have done nothing but rephrase the obvious. As the colonel's belief that he will soon receive his pension is the central point to the plot of García Márquez's novella, there would be no reason to spend three to five pages supporting that assertion. You might try, however, to develop a thesis from that point by asking yourself some further questions: What are the other symbols of the colonel's abiding optimism? What is the nature of the adversity he faces? How do other characters react to the colonel's optimism? Does the text ever suggest that the colonel knows that he is hoping in vain? Does it suggest that optimism is a heroic response that allows human beings to triumph over unjust circumstances, or is it ultimately a noble but tragic flaw? Such a line of questioning might lead you to a more viable thesis, such as the one in the preceding paragraph.

As the comparison with the road map also suggests, your thesis should appear near the beginning of the paper. In relatively short papers (three to six pages), the thesis almost always appears in the first paragraph. Some writers fall into the trap of saving their thesis for the end, trying to provide a surprise or a big moment of revelation, as if to say, "TA-DA! I've just proved that in García Márquez's *Chronicle of a Death Foretold,* honor is not defined by an intrinsic sense of right and wrong but rather by a preoccupation with maintaining the appearance of moral conformity." Placing a thesis at the end of an essay can seriously mar the essay's effectiveness. If you fail to define your essay's point and purpose clearly at the beginning, your reader will find it difficult to assess the clarity of your argument and understand the points you are making. When your argument comes as a surprise at the end, you force your reader to reread your essay in order to assess its logic and effectiveness.

Finally, you should avoid using the first person (*I*) as you present your thesis. Though it is not strictly wrong to write in the first person, it is difficult to do so gracefully. When using the first person, beginning writers often fall into the trap of employing self-reflexive prose (writing *about* their paper *in* their paper). Often, this leads to the most dreaded of opening lines: "In this paper I am going to discuss . . ." Not only does this self-reflexive voice make for very awkward prose, it frequently allows writers to announce a topic boldly while completely avoiding a thesis statement. An example might be a paper that begins as follows: Gabriel García Márquez's *Chronicle of a Death Foretold* tells the story of a murder that is committed even though an entire town is aware the crime is about to take place. In this paper, I am going to explore the concept of honor as it affects the events in the novel.

The author of this paper has done little more than announce a general topic for the paper. While the last sentence might be a thesis, the writer fails to present an opinion about the significance of honor in the text. To improve this "thesis," the writer would need to back up a couple of steps. First, the announced topic of the paper is too broad; it largely summarizes the events in the story, without saying anything about the ideas in the story. The writer should highlight what he or she considers the meaning of the story: What is the story about? The writer might conclude that characters who claim to be motivated by honor are more concerned about public opinion than with abiding by a moral code. From here, the author could select the means by which García Márquez communicates this contradiction and then begin to craft a specific thesis. A writer who chooses to explore these antithetical conceptions of honor, for example, might craft a thesis that reads: Chronicle of a Death Foretold is a novel that explores the nature of honor through the detailed recounting of a murder in a small town. While honor is frequently defined as an innate sense of duty governed by a moral code, Gabriel García Márquez subverts the honor paradigm to reveal it, not as a noble trait driven by an inner sense of right and wrong, but rather as a facade maintained for the sake of social reputation. Taking place in a paradoxical world in which the victim is culpable and the murderers heroic, Chronicle of a Death Foretold ultimately shows that while it is the Vicario brothers who stab Santiago Nasar to death, it is the society's twisted concept of honor that condemns him long before—and long after—the first stab of the knife.

Outlines

While developing a strong, thoughtful thesis early in your writing process should help focus your paper, outlining is an essential tool for logically shaping that paper. A good outline helps you see—and develop—the relationships among the points in your argument and assures you that your paper flows logically and coherently. Outlining not only helps place your points in a logical order but also helps you subordinate supporting points, weed out irrelevant points, and decide if there are necessary points that are missing from your argument. Most of us are familiar with formal outlines that use numerical and letter designations for each point. There are different types of outlines, however; you may find that an informal outline, for example, is a more useful tool for you. What is important, though, is that you spend the time to develop some sort of outline—formal or informal.

Remember that an outline is a tool to help you shape and write a strong paper. If you do not spend sufficient time planning your supporting points and shaping the arrangement of those points, you will most likely construct a vague, unfocused outline that provides little, if any, help with the writing of the paper. Consider the following example.

> *Chronicle of a Death Foretold* is a novel that explores the nature of honor through the detailed recounting of a murder in a small town. While honor is frequently defined as an innate sense of duty governed by a moral code, Gabriel García Márquez subverts the honor paradigm to reveal it, not as a noble trait driven by an inner sense of right and wrong, but rather as a facade maintained for the sake of social reputation. Taking place in a paradoxical world in which the victim is culpable and the murderers heroic, *Chronicle of a Death Foretold* ultimately shows that while it is the Vicario brothers who stab Santiago Nasar to death, it is the society's twisted concept of honor that condemns him long before—and long after—the first stab of the knife.

    I. Introduction and thesis

   II. Santiago Nasar's executioners: the Vicario brothers
      A. Seen as heroes

  III. Santiago's accomplices
      A. Angela Vicario
        1. Forced confession
        2. Condemned for life
      B. Bayardo San Román

IV. Religion and honor in the novel

V. Conclusion
   A. Santiago Nasar's murder is a crime and results from his murderers and accusers being more concerned with external appearances than with justice.

This outline has a number of flaws. First, the major topics labeled with Roman numerals are not arranged in a logical order. If the paper's aim is to show how Santiago Nasar's murder is the result of an honor code based more on reputation than on intrinsic values, then the first step is to establish the existence of such a code. Second, the principle of cause and effect dictates that it would be more logical to discuss the inciting event—the accusation—before the ensuing crime. Third, while religion is closely associated with the honor code, it is not a character (as are the subjects of the other sections) but a theme; it should not be discussed in its own section but rather incorporated into the other sections. Similarly, Bayardo San Román is an important figure in the text, but he is Angela's fiancé, not an "accomplice" to the adultery. His character should be assigned a separate section. A fourth problem is the inclusion of a section A in sections II and V. An outline should not include an A without a B, a 1 without a 2, and so forth. The final problem with this outline is the overall lack of detail. None of the sections provide much information about the content of the argument, and it seems likely that the writer has not given sufficient thought to the content of the paper.

A better start to this outline might be the following:

Chronicle of a Death Foretold is a novel that explores the nature of honor through the detailed recounting of a murder in a small town. While honor is frequently defined as an innate sense of duty governed by a moral code, Gabriel García Márquez subverts the honor paradigm to reveal it, not as a noble trait driven by an inner sense of right and wrong, but rather as a facade maintained for the sake of social reputation. Taking place in a paradoxical world in which the victim is culpable and the murderers heroic, *Chronicle of a Death Foretold* ultimately shows that while it is the Vicario brothers who stab Santiago Nasar to death, it is the society's twisted concept of honor that condemns him long before—and long after—the first stab of the knife.

I. Introduction and thesis

II. The honor code and Santiago Nasar's world
   A. The town
   B. The Nasar household
   C. Santiago Nasar on the morning of his death

III. Santiago's accomplice: Angela Vicario
   A. Forced into marriage
   B. Forced into confession
   C. Condemned to life in "solitary confinement" to expiate her sins

IV. Santiago's "victim": Bayardo San Román
   A. From a distinguished family with dubious past
   B. Believes his charm and wealth entitle him to whatever he wants
   C. Seen by the town as "poor Bayardo"

V. Santiago's executioners: Pablo and Pedro Vicario
   A. Unlikely guardians of honor
      1. Slaughter pigs for a living
      2. Pedro suffers from venereal disease
   B. Try to avoid their "duty"
   C. The murderers are celebrated as heroes

VI. Conclusion

This new outline would prove much more helpful when it came to write the paper.

The above outline, however, could be shaped into an even more useful tool by providing specific examples from the text to support each point and thus flesh on the argument. Once you have listed your main point and your supporting ideas, develop this raw material by listing related supporting ideas and material under each of those main headings. From there, arrange the material in subsections and order the material logically.

You might begin, for example, with one of the theses cited above: In *No One Writes to the Colonel*, the title character's unwavering faith in a better future is not a commentary on political naiveté but rather a statement on the power of the human spirit to endure injustice. It is precisely through his quixotic struggle to survive in the face of an absurd and cruel universe that the colonel emerges as a truly heroic figure. As noted above, this thesis already gives you the beginning of an organization. Start by supporting the notion that the colonel is not a naive character but rather one determined to maintain his dignity. Next, explain how García Márquez ennobles the colonel by contrasting his integrity and optimism with the corrupt world around him. You might begin your outline, then, with four topic headings: 1) The colonel's optimism reflects his pride and nobility of character, 2) The colonel's optimism is contrasted to the cynical and corrupt world around him, 3) The colonel never surrenders to the circumstances, and 4) The colonel's optimism, even in the face of defeat, transforms him into a hero. Under each of these headings, you could list ideas that support the particular point. Be sure to include references to parts of the text that help build your case.

An informal outline might look like the following:

In *No One Writes to the Colonel*, the title character's unwavering faith in a better future is not a commentary on political naiveté but rather a statement on the power of the human spirit to endure injustice. It is precisely through his quixotic struggle to survive in the face of an absurd and cruel universe that the colonel emerges as a truly heroic figure.

1. The colonel's optimism reflects his pride and nobility
   - Believes his health will return when the rainy season ends
     - Puts on his worn-out suit "as a transcendent act" and has "vitality" in his eyes" (6–7)
   - Believes the rooster will win
   - Expects his pension to come

2. The colonel's optimism is contrasted to the cynical and corrupt world around him through the metaphor of health
   - The colonel's wife, although a sympathetic character, is the major foil to her husband's optimism in her own pessimism
     - Her chronic asthma contrasts with the colonel's resiliency: "this thing I have is not a sickness but slow death" (59).
   - Don Sabas, the obese businessman, exploits his fellow citizens
     - His physical and economic status are the antithesis of the colonel's situation, as is his amoral attitude: "The only animal that feeds on human flesh is Don Sabas" (50).
     - While the colonel fought for his country, Don Sabas betrayed members of his own party in order to buy their land at a low price
   - The mayor represents everything the colonel fought against
     - Maintains the dictatorial state of siege
     - His toothache and undignified appearance reflect his ignoble character

3. The colonel never surrenders to his circumstances
   - The colonel maintains that the future will be better
     - ○ Their financial troubles will be over when the rooster begins fighting in January
   - The colonel stands up for what he believes in, even at his own expense
     - ○ Believes that a better world is worth fighting for: "Humanity doesn't progress without paying a price" (20).
     - ○ Remembers the rooster was the dream of his murdered son: "It's for Agustín" (30).
   - The colonel's dignity, even in the face of defeat, transforms him into a hero
     - ○ Continues to support the resistance
     - ○ Refuses to sell the rooster to Don Sabas even though he and his wife are on the verge of destitution
     - ○ Symbolism of the rooster in the cockfight: "His rooster didn't attack. He rebuffed every attack and landed in the same spot" (55).
   - Conclusion:
     - ○ The colonel is like a modern-day Job
     - ○ The colonel becomes "invincible," not in spite of having to eat "shit" (62), but because of it.

You would set about writing a formal outline with a similar process, although in the final stages, you would label the headings differently. A formal outline for a paper that argues the thesis about *Chronicle of a Death Foretold* cited above—the antithetical nature of the honor code and its role in the murder—might look as follows:

Chronicle of a Death Foretold is a novel that explores the nature of honor through the detailed recounting of a murder in a small town. While honor is frequently defined as an innate sense of duty governed by a moral code, Gabriel García Márquez subverts the honor paradigm to reveal it, not as a noble trait driven by an inner sense of right and wrong, but rather as a facade maintained for the sake of social reputation. Taking place in a paradoxical world in which the victim is culpable and the murderers heroic, *Chronicle of a Death Foretold* ultimately shows that while it is the Vicario brothers who stab Santiago Nasar to death, it is the society's twisted concept of honor that condemns him long before—and long after—the first stab of the knife.

I. Introduction and thesis

II. The honor code and Santiago Nasar's world
    A. Santiago's dream
    1. His dream deals with a deceiving appearance
       2. His mother insists she should have understood the dream's meaning
    B. The bishop's visit
       1. The town is preparing for the visit of the bishop
       2. The bishop's blessing is only perfunctory, from the boat
    C. The Nasar household
       1. Victoria Guzmán aggressively defends Divina Flor's honor from Santiago
       2. Victoria was the mistress of Santiago's father and has many illegitimate children
    D. Santiago Nasar on the morning of his death

1. Santiago gets up early to see the bishop and to have breakfast with his fiancée
2. Santiago has been out carousing and spends the morning harassing Divina Flor

III. Santiago's accomplice: Angela Vicario
    A. Does not really love the man she is marrying
    B. Blames Santiago Nasar although his guilt is dubious
    C. Believes she can restore her virginity

IV. Santiago's victim: Bayardo San Román
    A. Comes from a "good family" who are prominent supporters of the right-wing regime
    B. Charms Angela's family but reminds Angela of "the devil"
    C. Believes his wealth puts him above others but is pitied as "poor Bayardo" who has "lost everything"

V. Santiago's executioners: Pablo and Pedro Vicario
    A. Unlikely guardians of honor
        1. Slaughter pigs for a living
        2. Pedro suffers from venereal disease
    B. Try to avoid their "duty"
        1. Argue in the pigsty over who will commit the act
        2. Announce their intent to everyone
    C. The murderers are celebrated as heroes
        1. Priest tells them they are innocent "before God"
        2. Authorities fear they are in danger from Arab community

```
VI. Conclusion
      A. The official inquest
          1. The symbolism of the autopsy
          2. The literary tone of the magistrate
      B. "They've killed me": society as murderer
```

As in the previous example outline, this thesis provides the seeds of a structure, and the writer has been careful to arrange the supporting points in a logical manner, showing the relationships among the ideas in the paper.

Body Paragraphs

Once your outline is complete, you can begin drafting your paper. Paragraphs, units of related sentences, are the building blocks of a good paper, and as you draft, you should keep in mind both the function and the qualities of good paragraphs. Paragraphs help you chart and control the shape and content of your essay, and they help the reader see your organization and your logic. You should begin a new paragraph whenever you move from one major point to another. In longer, more complex essays, you might use a group of related paragraphs to support major points. Remember that in addition to being adequately developed, a good paragraph is both unified and coherent.

Unified Paragraphs

Each paragraph must be centered on one idea or point, and a unified paragraph carefully focuses on and develops this central idea without including extraneous ideas or tangents. For beginning writers, the best way to ensure that you are constructing unified paragraphs is to include a topic sentence in each paragraph. This topic sentence should convey the main point of the paragraph, and every sentence in the paragraph should relate to that topic sentence. Any sentence that strays from the central topic does not belong in the paragraph and needs to be revised or deleted. Consider the following paragraph about the use of symbolism to represent the protagonist's optimism in *No One Writes to the Colonel*. Notice how the paragraph veers away from the way in which the symbols in question help to establish the nobility of the colonel's character.

> From the outset of the story, the colonel's optimism
> reflects both his personal pride and his nobility of

character. Although "for nearly sixty years . . . the colonel ha[s] done nothing else but wait" (3), his unwavering optimism is illustrated through a range of symbolic acts. The very first sentence in the text is an example of how the protagonist views the glass, or, in this case, the coffee can, as half full. Seeing in the can that there is "only one little spoonful left" (3), he saves the last cup of coffee for his wife, lying to her that "there was a big spoonful left" (3), allowing enough for both. The colonel's wife is ill, so he wants her to have the warm beverage. A second significant act in the opening pages of the novella is the colonel's pride in his appearance as he dresses for a friend's funeral. Once again, the character's reality is a worn-out suit, a moth-eaten "circus clown's umbrella" (5), and a pair of ill-fitting shoes. Putting on his tattered clothes "as if it were a transcendent act" (6), he rises above his miserable circumstances. Noting "the vitality in his eyes" (7), even his pessimistic wife cannot help but admire her husband's undiminished dignity. A third symbol of the colonel's optimism, one that reappears throughout the novella, is the rooster. "A legacy" (11) from his son Agustín, who was murdered by the government, the rooster represents both economic salvation for the colonel if it wins in the upcoming cockfights and the opportunity for the colonel to honor the memory of a dead child. Again, the wife is negative about the rooster and constantly complains about it. George R. McMurray observes: "The cock, then, not only symbolizes hope, but ultimately emerges as a symbol of the absurd hero's (the colonel's) fight against fate" (83). By placing each of these symbols in the opening pages of the text, García Márquez leaves no doubt in the reader's mind that the colonel is not only the protagonist of the story but, indeed, its hero.

Although the above paragraph begins solidly and the second sentence provides the central idea of the paragraph, the author soon goes on a tangent. If the purpose of the paragraph is to illustrate how García Márquez uses symbolism at the beginning of the novella to accentuate the colonel's positive outlook on life, then the sentences about his wife's pessimism are tangential here. Such a comparison may find a place later in the paper, but it should be deleted from this paragraph.

Coherent Paragraphs

In addition to shaping unified paragraphs, you must also craft coherent paragraphs, paragraphs that develop their points logically with sentences that flow smoothly into one another. Coherence depends on the order of your sentences, but it is not strictly the order of the sentences that is important to paragraph coherence. You also need to craft your prose to help the reader see the relationship among the sentences.

Consider the following paragraph about the symbolism in *No One Writes to the Colonel*. Notice how the writer uses the same ideas as the paragraph above yet fails to help the reader see the relationships among the points.

From the outset of the story, the colonel's optimism reflects both his personal pride and his nobility of character. Although "for nearly sixty years . . . the colonel ha[s] done nothing else but wait" (3), his unwavering optimism is illustrated through a range of symbolic acts. The coffee can is one example of how he sees the glass as half full. Seeing in the can that there is "only one little spoonful left" (3), he saves the last cup of coffee for his wife, lying to her that "there was a big spoonful left" (3), allowing enough for both. The colonel's pride in his appearance as he dresses for a friend's funeral is another example. The character's reality is a worn-out suit, a moth-eaten "circus clown's umbrella" (5), and a pair of ill-fitting shoes. Putting on his tattered clothes "as if it were a transcendent act" (6), he rises above his miserable circumstances. Noting "the vitality in his eyes" (7), even the colonel's pessimistic wife cannot help but admire her husband's undiminished dignity. The rooster appears throughout the novella. "A legacy" (11) from his son Agustín, who was murdered by the government, the rooster represents both economic salvation for the colonel if it wins in the upcoming cockfights and an opportunity for the colonel to honor the memory of a dead child. George R. McMurray observes: "The cock, then, not only symbolizes hope, but ultimately emerges as a symbol of the absurd hero's (the colonel's) fight against fate" (83). Gabriel García Márquez leaves no doubt in the reader's mind that the colonel is not only the protagonist of the story but, indeed, its hero.

This paragraph demonstrates that unity alone does not guarantee paragraph effectiveness. The argument is hard to follow because the author fails both to show connections between the sentences and to indicate how they work to support the overall point.

A number of techniques are available to aid paragraph coherence. Careful use of transitional words and phrases is essential. You can use transitional flags to introduce an example or an illustration (*for example, for instance*), to amplify a point or add another phase of the same idea (*additionally, furthermore, next, similarly, finally, then*), to indicate a conclusion or result (*therefore, as a result, thus, in other words*), to signal a contrast or a qualification (*on the other hand, nevertheless, despite this, on the contrary, still, however, conversely*), to signal a comparison (*likewise, in comparison, similarly*), and to indicate a movement in time (*afterward, earlier, eventually, finally, later, subsequently, until*).

In addition to transitional flags, careful use of pronouns aids coherence and flow. If you were writing about *The Wizard of Oz*, you would not want to keep repeating the phrase *the witch* or the name *Dorothy*. Careful substitution of the pronoun *she* in these instances can aid coherence. A word of warning, though: When you substitute pronouns for proper names, always be sure that your pronoun reference is clear. In a paragraph that discusses both Dorothy and the witch, substituting *she* could lead to confusion. Make sure that it is clear to whom the pronoun refers. Generally, the pronoun refers to the last proper noun you have used.

While repeating the same name over and over again can lead to awkward, boring prose, it is possible to use repetition to help your paragraph's coherence. Careful repetition of important words or phrases can lend coherence to your paragraph by reminding readers of your key points. Admittedly, it takes some practice to use this technique effectively. You may find that reading your prose aloud can help you develop an ear for effective use of repetition.

To see how helpful transitional aids are, compare the paragraph below to the example paragraph on page 22. Notice how the author works with the same ideas and quotations but shapes them into a much more coherent paragraph whose point is clearer and easier to follow.

> From the outset of the story, the colonel's optimism reflects both his personal pride and his nobility of character. Although "for nearly sixty years . . . the colonel ha[s] done nothing else but wait" (3), his unwavering optimism is illustrated through a range of symbolic acts. The very first sentence in the text is an example of how the protagonist views the glass, or, in this case, the coffee can, as half full. Seeing in the can that there is "only one little spoonful left" (3), he saves the last cup of coffee for his wife, lying to her that "there was a big spoonful left" (3), allowing enough for both. A second significant act in the opening pages of the novella is the colonel's pride in his appearance as he dresses for a friend's funeral. The character's reality is a worn-out suit, a moth-eaten "circus clown's umbrella" (5), and a pair of ill-fitting shoes. Putting on his tattered clothes "as if it were a transcendent act" (6), however, he rises above his miserable circumstances. Noting "the vitality in his eyes" (7), even the colonel's pessimistic wife cannot help but admire her husband's undiminished dignity. A third symbol of the colonel's optimism, one that reappears throughout the novella, is the rooster. "A legacy" (11) from his son Agustín, who was murdered by the government, the rooster represents both economic salvation for the colonel if it wins in the upcoming cockfights and the opportunity for the colonel to honor the memory of a dead child. George R. McMurray observes: "The cock, then, not only symbolizes hope, but ultimately emerges as a symbol of the absurd hero's (the colonel's) fight against fate" (83). By placing each of these symbols in the opening pages of the text, Gabriel

García Márquez leaves no doubt in the reader's mind that the colonel is not only the protagonist of the story but, indeed, its hero.

Similarly, the following paragraph from a paper on the honor code in *Chronicle of a Death Foretold* demonstrates both unity and coherence. In it, the author argues that García Márquez uses the seemingly unrelated events at the beginning of the novel to illustrate the paradoxical nature of honor in Santiago Nasar's world.

The paradoxical nature of honor in *Chronicle of a Death Foretold* is made clear from the very beginning of the novel. Through seemingly unrelated events in Santiago Nasar's dreams, his town, his household, and his personal life, the text establishes the dichotomy between a superficial preoccupation with honor and an underlying contradiction. The first indication of the incongruity between appearances and reality is suggested by the description of Santiago's dream in the novel's opening scene. Having dreamt that he was walking through a forest while a "gentle drizzle was falling," he awakens with the sensation of being "completely splattered with bird shit" (3). The subsequent insistence of Santiago's mother, with her "well-earned reputation as an interpreter of other people's dreams" (4), that she should have correctly interpreted the "ominous augury" (4) is analogous to the town's absurd acceptance of its chimerical honor code. A second example of the contradiction between perception and truth is found in the much-anticipated visit from the bishop. While the community is "excited with the bishop's visit" and eager to receive the blessing of "God's medicine" (21), it is common knowledge that the bishop, "won't even get off the boat," because "he hates this town" (8). A further manifestation of this dichotomy is found within the Nasar household itself. The family servant, Victoria Guzmán, threatens Santiago with a kitchen knife when he makes unwanted advances on her daughter, Divina

Flor. Yet, the mother so zealous in defense of her child's virtue has none of her own. Having herself carried on an affair with Santiago's father "for several years in the stables of the ranch," she conducts her interview with the narrator "surrounded by the children of her other loves" (9–10). Finally, the contradiction evident in the promiscuous Victoria Guzmán's insistence on protecting her daughter's honor is analogous to a detail from Santiago Nasar's own behavior on the day of his murder. His sexual harassment of Divina Flor along with the hangover brought on by a night of "carousing" (18) are set against his sacrosanct attitude toward the above-mentioned visit by the bishop. After a night and a morning of sinning, Santiago gets "dressed up pontifical style in case he [has] a chance to kiss the bishop's ring" (8). Like his own dream, the blessing in question, and Victoria Guzmán's concern for her daughter's virtue, Santiago's religious devotion is a mirage. The text notes that the essence of his faith is mere artifice: "church pomp always had an irresistible fascination for him . . . like the movies" (8). But, when the boat passes without even stopping for the wood that Santiago has purchased for the steam engine, his religious devotion turns into a sense of "annoyance" and feeling "cheated" (17). Like the other dubious facades represented in the opening pages of *Chronicle of a Death Foretold*, this final deception alerts the reader to the reality of Santiago Nasar's world. Ironically, it is also this feigned concern with religious duty that leads the protagonist to the scene of his demise.

Introductions

Introductions present particular challenges for writers. Generally, your introduction should do two things: capture your reader's attention and explain the main point of your essay. In other words, while your introduction should contain your thesis, it needs to do a bit more work than that. You are likely to find that starting that first paragraph is one of the most difficult parts of the paper. It is hard to face that blank page or screen,

and as a result, many beginning writers, in desperation to start somewhere, start with overly broad, general statements. While it is often a
good strategy to start with more general subject matter and narrow your
focus, do not begin with broad sweeping statements such as Everyone
likes to be creative and feel understood. Such sentences
are nothing but empty filler. They begin to fill the blank page, but they do
nothing to advance your argument. Instead, you should try to gain your
readers' interest. Some writers like to begin with a pertinent quotation
or with a relevant question. Or, you might begin with an introduction
of the topic you will discuss. If you are writing about García Márquez's
representation of the honor code in *Chronicle of a Death Foretold,* for
instance, you might begin by talking about how honor functions as a
social construct. Another common trap to avoid is depending on your
title to introduce the author and the text you are writing about. Always
include the work's author and title in your opening paragraph.

Compare the effectiveness of the following introductions.

Many people do things because they feel obliged by
society's definition of honor. Sometimes you act in a
certain way because you have been taught that you have
to, even though you know it is not the intelligent,
or even the moral, thing to do. Although people think
honor is good, it can also cause tragedy, as in *Othello*.
Chronicle of a Death Foretold is a novel that explores
the nature of honor through the detailed recounting of
a murder in a small town. While honor is frequently
defined as an innate sense of duty governed by a
moral code, Gabriel García Márquez subverts the honor
paradigm to reveal it, not as a noble trait driven by
an inner sense of right and wrong, but rather as a
facade maintained for the sake of social reputation.
Taking place in a paradoxical world in which the victim
is culpable and the murderers heroic, *Chronicle of a
Death Foretold* ultimately shows that while it is the
Vicario brothers who stab Santiago Nasar to death,
it is the society's twisted concept of honor that

condemns him long before—and long after—the first stab
of the knife.

Honor is a cultural construct whose artistic
manifestations can be traced from the ancient Greeks
through the works of William Shakespeare to popular films
of the 20th century. As with other great themes, such as
love, beauty, and religion, honor is an amorphous idea
assigned specific values by a particular community at a
particular moment in its history. *Chronicle of a Death
Foretold* is a novel that explores the nature of honor
through the detailed recounting of a murder in a small
town. While honor is frequently defined as an innate
sense of duty governed by a moral code, Gabriel García
Márquez subverts the honor paradigm to reveal it, not
as a noble trait driven by an inner sense of right and
wrong, but rather as a facade maintained for the sake
of social reputation. Taking place in a paradoxical
world in which the victim is culpable and the murderers
heroic, *Chronicle of a Death Foretold* ultimately shows
that while it is the Vicario brothers who stab Santiago
Nasar to death, it is the society's twisted concept of
honor that condemns him long before—and long after—the
first stab of the knife.

The first introduction begins with a vague, overly broad sentence; cites
unclear, undeveloped examples; and then moves abruptly to the thesis.
Notice, too, how a reader deprived of the paper's title may be unclear
about the title of the work that the paper will analyze. The second introduction, meanwhile, works with the same material and thesis but provides more detail and is consequently much more interesting. It begins
by discussing the significance of honor as an artistic theme, gives specific
examples, and then speaks briefly about how honor may be understood as
a cultural construct. The paragraph ends with the thesis, which includes
both the author and the title of the work to be discussed.

The paragraph below provides another example of an opening strategy.
It begins by introducing the author and the text it will analyze and then

moves on by briefly introducing relevant details of the story so as to set up its thesis.

> Gabriel García Márquez's novella *No One Writes to the Colonel* is a tribute to the power of the human spirit to sustain hope, even in the cruelest of circumstances. The title character's "obstinate commitment to his own values" (Bell 26) is contrasted with the cynicism and pessimism of those around him. Chastised by both friends and enemies alike for being "naïve" (13) and for his "idiotic stubbornness" (37), the colonel maintains his optimism. The belief in a better tomorrow manifests itself not only in the expected arrival of a government pension check alluded to in the title but also in his attitudes toward his health, the fighting cock he inherited from his murdered son, and the political freedom he fought for many years ago. While the story ends without bringing relief to the colonel's suffering, the colonel is not overcome by his tragic circumstances, either. In *No One Writes to the Colonel*, the title character's unwavering faith in a better future is not a commentary on political naiveté but rather a statement on the power of the human spirit to endure injustice. It is precisely through his quixotic struggle to survive in the face of an absurd and cruel universe that the colonel emerges as a truly heroic figure.

Conclusions

Conclusions present another series of challenges for writers. No doubt you have heard the old adage about writing papers: "Tell us what you are going to say, say it, and then tell us what you've said." While this formula does not necessarily result in bad papers, it does not often result in good ones, either. It will almost certainly result in boring papers (especially boring conclusions). If you have done a good job establishing your points in the body of the paper, the reader already knows and understands your argument. There is no need to merely reiterate. Do not just summarize your main points in your conclusion. Such a boring and mechanical conclusion does nothing to advance your argument or interest your reader. Consider the following conclusion to the paper about the honor code in *Chronicle of a Death Foretold.*

> In conclusion, Gabriel García Márquez represents the honor code as the cause of Santiago Nasar's death. The Vicario brothers murder him, and the town allows the crime to be committed because everyone believes they must maintain the appearance of honor. Santiago's death indicates that even when we know something is wrong, sometimes we allow it anyway to save appearances. I am sure that many of us have been troubled by this sad tendency in those around us.

Besides starting with a mechanical transitional device, this conclusion does little more than summarize some, but not all, of the main points of the outline. It is incomplete and uninteresting, as well as a little too self-righteous.

Instead, your conclusion should add something to your paper. A good tactic is to build upon the points you have been arguing. Asking "why?" often helps you draw further conclusions. For example, in the paper on *Chronicle of a Death Foretold,* you might speculate on how the honor code speaks to what García Márquez is saying about the broader cultural values of the community with regard to gender, ethnicity, and social class. Scholars often discuss the novel in relation to the historical role of violence in Latin American society, and your paper could question whether this is a specifically Latin American or more universal theme. Another method for successfully concluding a paper is to speculate on other directions in which to take your topic by tying it into larger issues. You might do this by envisioning your paper as just one section of a larger paper. Having established your points in this paper, how would you build upon this argument? Where would you go next? In the following conclusion to the paper on *Chronicle of a Death Foretold,* the author reiterates some of the main points of the paper but does so in order to amplify the discussion of the story's central message and to connect it to other texts by García Márquez.

> By the end of the novel, virtually every member of the community has explained why he or she is not responsible for the murder. The magistrate's cryptic notations, "Give

me a prejudice and I will move the world" (100) and "Fatality
makes us invisible" (113), thus become comprehensible.
The prejudice (literally, the preconceived idea) of honor
has swept away all other rational considerations. The
culpability of murderers, accusers, witnesses, and self-
proclaimed innocent bystanders is thus erased by the
inexorable demands of honor. A mordant critique of a
society hiding its moral corruption behind a sacrosanct
veneer of outdated cultural mores, this theme is not
unique to *Chronicle of a Death Foretold*; it is revisited
by García Márquez in such works as *In Evil Hour* and
"A Very Old Man with Enormous Wings." And, while the
author, like the magistrate, seems inclined to enshroud
his criticism in enigma, his reader cannot avoid the
conclusion that this world of facades belies the most
disturbing of underlying realities.

Similarly, in the following example closing a paper on optimism in *No
One Writes to the Colonel,* the author draws a conclusion about what the
novella is saying about hope more broadly.

As much as *No One Writes to the Colonel* can be read
as a political commentary specific to life in Colombia
during La Violencia, it can also be understood in a
much more universal sense as a modern-day Book of Job:
Both Job and the colonel are deprived of their worldly
possessions, both endure the loss of a child, both are
deserted by friends, and both are reproached by wives
weary of sharing their husbands' misery. Similar to
the biblical archetype of the good man who refuses to
"curse God, and die" (Job 2:9) in the face of undeserved
suffering, the colonel embodies the humanist belief in a
better future even in an unjust world. But, whereas the
fortunes of the Old Testament protagonist are ultimately
restored by God, the end of García Márquez's novella
leaves the colonel trapped in an existential limbo.
Unlike the triumphant Job, to whom "The Lord gave . . .
twice as much as he had before" (42:10), the colonel

becomes "invincible" only through his insistence that he will survive even if he is forced to "eat . . . shit" (62). García Márquez is arguing, it would seem, that in an absurd, godless universe where the wicked (Don Sabas) prosper and the good are punished, optimism becomes the ultimate act of defiance. As the colonel tells his wife after a lightning bolt frightens her in the middle of a harangue, "I've always said that God is on my side" (42). This comic reference to a stereotypical convention is not exclusively parodic in nature. The colonel may never collect his pension, win the cockfight, or live to see democracy restored, but his uncompromising faith allows him to transcend his personal misfortune, transforming his character into a prophet of hope in an age of darkness.

Citations and Formatting

Using Primary Sources

As the examples included in this chapter indicate, strong papers on literary texts incorporate quotations from the text in order to support their points. It is not enough for you to assert your interpretation without providing support or evidence from the text. Without well-chosen quotations to support your argument you are, in effect, saying to the reader, "Take my word for it." It is important to use quotations thoughtfully and selectively. Remember that the paper presents *your* argument, so choose quotations that support *your* assertions. Do not let the author's voice overwhelm your own. With that caution in mind, there are some guidelines you should follow to ensure that you use quotations clearly and effectively.

Integrate Quotations

Quotations should always be integrated into your own prose. Do not just drop them into your paper without introduction or comment. Otherwise, it is unlikely that your reader will see their function. You can integrate textual support easily and clearly with identifying tags, short phrases that identify the speaker. For example,

The magistrate's report describes the Vicario brothers as "hard-looking, but of a good sort."

While this tag appears before the quotation, you can also use tags after or in the middle of the quoted text, as the following examples demonstrate:

```
"He was the man of my life," says Santiago's mother.

"Those two aren't about to kill anybody," Don Rogelio
tells his wife, "much less someone rich."
```

You can also use a colon to formally introduce a quotation:

```
Angela Vicario has little affection for the man she is
to marry: "I detested conceited men, and I'd never seen
one so stuck-up."
```

When you quote brief sections of poems (three lines or fewer), use slash marks to indicate the line breaks in the poem:

```
As the poem ends, Dickinson speaks of the power of the
imagination: "The revery alone will do, / If bees are
few."
```

Longer quotations (more than four lines of prose or three lines of poetry) should be set off from the rest of your paper in a block quotation. Double-space before you begin the passage, indent it 10 spaces from your left-hand margin, and double-space the passage itself. Because the indentation signals the inclusion of a quotation, do not use quotation marks around the cited passage. Use a colon to introduce the passage:

```
The narrator leaves little doubt as to the town's perception
of each character's respective innocence or guilt:

      For the immense majority of people there was only
      one victim: Bayardo San Román. They took it for
      granted that the other actors in the tragedy had
      been fulfilling with dignity, even with a certain
      grandeur, their part of the destiny that life
      had assigned them. Santiago Nasar had expiated
      the insult, the brothers Vicario had proved their
```

status as men, and the seduced sister was in
possession of her honor once more.

By transforming the crime into a "tragedy" and its
principals into "actors," the town replaces the reality of
Santiago Nasar's murder with the theatrical conventions
of a melodramatic honor play.

The whole of Dickinson's poem speaks of the imagination:

To make a prairie it takes a clover and
   one bee,
One clover, and a bee,
And revery.
The revery alone will do,
If bees are few.

Clearly, she argues for the creative power of the
mind.

It is also important to interpret quotations after you introduce
them and explain how they help advance your point. You cannot
assume that your reader will interpret the quotations the same way
that you do.

Quote Accurately
Always quote accurately. Anything within quotations marks must be the
author's exact words. There are, however, some rules to follow if you need
to modify the quotation to fit into your prose.

1. Use brackets to indicate any material that is not the author's
   exact wording. For example, if you need to add any words to the
   quotation or alter it grammatically to allow it to fit into your
   prose, indicate your changes in brackets:

   It is clear from the comments of witnesses that
   the Vicario brothers are, in fact, hoping to
   avoid their duty. To shopkeeper Clotilde Armenta

> "it seem[s] that the twins [are]n't as resolute
> as before."

2. Conversely, if you choose to omit any words from the quotation, use ellipses (three spaced periods) to indicate missing words or phrases:

> The hypocrisy underlying the town's sacrosanct
> facade is suggested by the "illusion" of the
> bishop's blessing: "the bishop [begins] to make
> the sign of the cross . . . and he [keeps] doing
> it mechanically . . . until the boat [is] lost
> from view."

3. If you delete a sentence or more, use the ellipsis after a period:

> When Angela seeks her friends' advice, the
> narrator makes plain that the social expectation
> of the bride's virginity is nothing more than an
> artificial convention designed to maintain the
> appearance of honor: "They insisted that even the
> most difficult of husbands resigned themselves to
> anything as long as nobody knew about it. . . .
> And they taught her old wives' tricks to feign
> her lost possession, so that on her first morning
> as a newlywed she could display open under the
> sun in the courtyard in front of her house the
> linen sheet with the stain of honor."

4. If you omit a line or more of poetry, or more than one paragraph of prose, use a single line of spaced periods to indicate the omission:

> To make a prairie it takes a clover and one bee,
> . . . .
> And revery.
> The revery alone will do,
> If bees are few.

Punctuate Properly

Punctuation of quotations often causes more trouble than it should. Once again, you just need to keep these simple rules in mind.

1. Periods and commas should be placed inside quotation marks, even if they are not part of the original quotation:

> Clotilde Armenta's plea to the brothers reinforces the town's twisted preoccupation with appearances: "Leave him for later, if only out of respect for his grace the bishop."

The only exception to this rule is when the quotation is followed by a parenthetical reference. In this case, the period or comma goes after the citation (more on these in the following section):

> Santiago Nasar understands his society's honor code: "He was aware of the prudish disposition of his world, and he must have understood that the twins' simple nature was incapable of resisting an insult" (101–2).

2. Other marks of punctuation—colons, semicolons, question marks, and exclamation points—go outside the quotation marks unless they are part of the original quotation:

> How is it possible that Angela Vicario "became a virgin again"?

> The entire town hears Santiago's cry of pain: "Oh, mother of mine!"

Documenting Primary Sources

Unless you are instructed otherwise, you should provide sufficient information for your reader to locate material you quote. Generally, literature papers follow the rules set forth by the Modern Language Association (MLA). These can be found in the *MLA Handbook for Writers of Research*

Papers (sixth edition). You should be able to find this book in the reference section of your library. Additionally, its rules for citing both primary and secondary sources are widely available from reputable online sources. One of these is the Online Writing Lab (OWL) at Purdue University. OWL's guide to MLA style is available at http://owl.english.purdue.edu/owl/resource/557/01/. The Modern Language Association also offers answers to frequently asked questions about MLA style on this helpful Web page: http://www.mla.org/style_faq. Generally, when you are citing from literary works in papers, you should keep the following guidelines in mind.

Parenthetical Citations

MLA requires parenthetical references in your text after quotations. When you are working with prose (short stories, novels, or essays) include page numbers in the parentheses:

> The Vicarios' plan is common knowledge: "Many of those who were on the docks knew that they were going to kill Santiago Nasar" (19).

When you are quoting poetry, include line numbers:

> Dickinson's speaker tells of the arrival of a fly: "There interposed a Fly-- / With Blue--uncertain stumbling Buzz-- / Between the light--and Me--" (12-14).

Works Cited Page

The parenthetical citations in your text are linked to a separate works cited page at the end of your paper. The works cited page lists works alphabetically by the authors' last name. An entry for the above reference to García Márquez's *Chronicle of a Death Foretold* would appear as follows:

> García Márquez, Gabriel. *Chronicle of a Death Foretold*. Trans. Gregory Rabassa. New York: Vintage, 2003.

The *MLA Handbook* includes a full listing of sample entries, as do many of the online explanations of MLA style.

Documenting Secondary Sources

To ensure that your paper is built entirely upon your own ideas and analysis, instructors often ask that you write interpretative papers without any outside research. If, on the other hand, your paper requires research, you must document any secondary sources you use. You need to document direct quotations, summaries, or paraphrases of others' ideas, as well as factual information that is not common knowledge. Follow the guidelines above for quoting primary sources when you use direct quotations from secondary sources. Keep in mind that MLA style also includes specific guidelines for citing electronic sources. OWL's Web site provides a good summary: http://owl.english.purdue.edu/owl/resource/557/09/.

Parenthetical Citations

As with the documentation of primary sources, described above, MLA guidelines require in-text parenthetical references to your secondary sources. Unlike the research papers you might write for a history class, literary research papers following MLA style do not use footnotes as a means of documenting sources. Instead, after a quotation, you should cite the author's last name and the page number:

> "The Nasars represent an upper class that distinguishes them from the rest of the town's citizenry by origins and by money" (Williams 138).

If you include the name of the author in your prose, then you would include only the page number in your citation. For example,

> Raymond L. Williams observes: "The Nasars represent an upper class that distinguishes them from the rest of the town's citizenry by origins and by money" (138).

If you are including more than one work by the same author, the parenthetical citation should include a shortened yet identifiable version of the title in order to indicate which of the author's works you are citing. For example,

Arnold M. Penuel notes: "The cult of virginity is an integral part of the cult of death" ("The Sleep of Vital Reason" 194).

Similarly, and just as important, if you summarize or paraphrase the particular ideas of your source, you must provide documentation:

A clear relationship exists between virginity and death (Penuel, "The Sleep of Vital Reason" 194).

Works Cited Page

Like the primary sources discussed above, the parenthetical references to secondary sources are keyed to a separate works cited page at the end of your paper. Here is an example of a works cited page that uses the examples given above. Note that when two or more works by the same author are listed, you should use three hyphens followed by a period in the subsequent entries. You can find a complete list of sample entries in the *MLA Handbook* or from a reputable online summary of MLA style.

WORKS CITED

Penuel, Arnold, M. *Intertextuality in García Márquez.* Rock Hill, SC: Spanish Literature Publications, 1994.

——. "The Sleep of Vital Reason in García Márquez's *Crónica de una muerte anunciada.*" *Critical Essays on Gabriel García Márquez.* Ed. George R. McMurray. Boston: G. K. Hall, 1987, 188–209.

Williams, Raymond L. *Gabriel García Márquez.* Twayne's World Authors Series. Boston: Twayne Publishers, 1984.

Plagiarism

Failure to document carefully and thoroughly can leave you open to charges of stealing the ideas of others, which is known as plagiarism, and this is a very serious matter. Remember that it is important to include quotation marks when you use language from your source, even if you use just one or two words. For example, if you wrote, The Nasars are distinguished by origins and by money, you would be guilty of plagiarism, because you used Raymond L. Williams's distinct language without acknowledging him as the source. Instead, you should write: Privileged "by origins and by money," the Nasars belong to the town's socioeconomic elite (Williams 138). In this latter case, you have properly credited Williams.

Similarly, neither summarizing the ideas of an author nor changing or omitting just a few words means that you can omit a citation. Michael Bell's monograph, *Gabriel García Márquez: Solitude and Solidarity*, contains the following passage about the climactic death scene in *Chronicle of a Death Foretold*:

> The killing is a public spectacle in the main square of the town. It implicitly involves the community as a whole, who are assembled like choric witnesses for this last act. Without ceasing to understand all this in modern ethical, social and psychological terms we also sense that some deeper nerve has been touched, some ancient stratum of feeling that might lie behind blood sacrifice, the earliest origins of tragedy, or indeed of the Mass or an "auto-da-fe" (99).

Below are two examples of plagiarized passages:

> The public nature of the death scene at the end of the novel evokes a Greek chorus in classical tragedy. It is an act of human sacrifice that harkens back to humanity's most ancient rituals.

> The killing is a public spectacle, involving the whole community. Along with its implications for modern society, the scene also evokes the earliest origins of both tragedy and ritual sacrifice (Bell 99).

While the first passage does not use Bell's exact language, it does list the same ideas he proposes without citing his work. Since this interpretation is Bell's distinct idea, this constitutes plagiarism. The second passage has shortened his passage, changed some wording, and included a citation, but some of the phrasing is Bell's. The first passage could be fixed with a parenthetical citation. Because some of the wording in the second remains the same, though, it would require the use of quotation marks, in addition to a parenthetical citation. The passage below represents an honestly and adequately documented use of the original passage:

> According to Michael Bell, the public nature of Santiago Nasar's death is highly significant. With the entire town "assembled like choric witnesses for this last act" (99), the scene transcends issues related to contemporary society. He argues that it evokes the same "ancient stratum" underlying both "blood sacrifice" and "the earliest origins of tragedy" (99).

This passage acknowledges that the interpretation is derived from Bell and appropriately uses quotation marks to indicate his precise language.

While it is not necessary to document well-known facts, often referred to as "common knowledge," any ideas or language that you take from someone else must be properly documented. Common knowledge generally includes the birth and death dates of authors or other well-documented facts of their life. An often-cited guideline is that if you can find the information in three sources, it is common knowledge. Despite this guideline, it is, admittedly, often difficult to know if the facts you uncover are common knowledge or not. When in doubt, document your source.

Sample Essay

Emily Lomander
Mr. Lopez
English II
February 10, 2010

THE POWER OF HOPE IN *NO ONE WRITES TO THE COLONEL*
Gabriel García Márquez's novella *No One Writes to the Colonel* is a tribute to the power of the human spirit to sustain hope, even in the cruelest of circumstances. The title character's "obstinate commitment to his own values" (Bell 26) is contrasted with the cynicism and pessimism of those around him. Chastised by both

friends and enemies alike for being "naïve" (13) and for his "idiotic stubbornness" (37), the colonel maintains his optimism. The belief in a better tomorrow manifests itself not only in the expected arrival of a government pension check alluded to in the title but also in his attitudes toward his health, the fighting cock he inherited from his murdered son, and the political freedom he fought for many years ago. While the story ends without bringing relief to the colonel's suffering, the colonel is not overcome by his tragic circumstances, either. In *No One Writes to the Colonel,* the title character's unwavering faith in a better future is not a commentary on political naiveté but rather a statement on the power of the human spirit to endure injustice. It is precisely through his quixotic struggle to survive in the face of an absurd and cruel universe that the colonel emerges as a truly heroic figure.

From the outset of the story, the colonel's optimism reflects both his personal pride and his nobility of character. Although "for nearly sixty years . . . the colonel ha[s] done nothing else but wait" (3), his unwavering optimism is illustrated through a range of symbolic acts. The very first sentence in the text is an example of how the protagonist views the glass, or, in this case, the coffee can, as half full. Seeing in the can that there is "only one little spoonful left" (3), he saves the last cup of coffee for his wife. He lies to her that "there was a big spoonful left" (3) that would allow enough for both of them. A second significant moment in the opening pages of the novella shows the colonel's pride in his appearance as he dresses for a friend's funeral. The character's reality is a worn-out suit, a moth-eaten "circus clown's umbrella" (5), and a pair of ill-fitting shoes. But, putting on his tattered clothes "as if it were a transcendent act" (6), he rises above his miserable circumstances. Noting "the vitality in his eyes" (7), even the colonel's pessimistic wife cannot help but admire her husband's undiminished dignity. A third symbol of the colonel's optimism, one that reappears throughout the novella, is the rooster. "A legacy" (11) from his son Agustín, who was murdered by the government, the rooster represents both economic redemption for the colonel if it wins in the upcoming cockfights and an opportunity for the colonel to honor the memory of a dead child. George R. McMurray observes: "The cock, then, not only symbolizes hope, but ultimately emerges as a symbol of the absurd hero's (the colonel's) fight against fate" (83). By placing each of these symbols in the opening pages of the text, García Márquez leaves no doubt in the reader's mind that the colonel is not only the protagonist of the story but also in every sense its hero.

In addition to the symbolic representations of the colonel's optimism, his character is also elevated by comparison to the other major characters in the novella. García Márquez achieves this comparison through an extended metaphor involving each character's health. The significance of health in *No One Writes to the Colonel* is suggested from the opening page of the text when the protagonist feels "the fungus and poisonous lilies . . . taking root in his gut" (3). Throughout the text, the colonel's willingness to suffer through his intestinal ailment, confident that " 'Everything will be different when it stops raining' " (29), is contrasted with the chronic illnesses affecting the other, flawed characters who surround him. The colonel's unhappy wife is convinced she will die from her asthma. While the colonel's wife can hardly be considered an antagonist, her pessimism remains a constant foil to his faith. Just as the colonel eventually notices that the cool December weather "has shriveled the flora in his gut" (53), so his hopeless spouse persists in counting rosary beads and lamenting that her asthma "is not a sickness but a slow death" (59). Similarly, the town's brutal mayor is shown with "his unshaven swollen cheek" (9) from a toothache—a physical manifestation of his moral decay.

Finally, the most marked contrast in health is made between the protagonist and the greedy Don Sabas, who has grown wealthy by betraying former friends to the mayor. Despite his wealth, the obese Sabas, dependent on insulin injections and saccharin tablets, has "the sadness of a toad in his eyes" (35). Furthermore, Sabas expresses his jealousy of the colonel's good fortune for having a "cast-iron stomach" in comparison to his own need for the vial of medication, which is "like carrying death in your pocket" (36). Subsequently, after the colonel's wife reproaches her husband for his futile optimism, saying, "You can't eat hope," his response brings the reader back to the underlying metaphor: "It sustains you . . . like my friend Sabas's miraculous pills" (39).

Like all heroes, the colonel's status is confirmed through the trials he must endure. His "fragile—but constant—dignity" (Williams 59) in the face of deprivations is evidenced most obviously by the long-awaited pension check. By showing the protagonist waiting for the letter in the post office, feigning disinterest "without taking his eyes off the postmaster" (12), the text presents the plight of maintaining dignity in the face of an uncontrollable destiny. Says Richard D. Woods, "Inspiring hope, but bringing frustration, the tantalizing letter synthesizes a life" (89). The colonel's assertion, "I wasn't waiting for anything. . . . Nobody writes to me" (13), captures both his pride and (in a clear reference to the title) his recognition of his unhappy circumstances. The colonel knows that he is waiting in vain, yet he still assures his wife, "Don't worry . . . the mail comes tomorrow" (20). Not only does the colonel endure the government's passive refusal to pay an overdue pension; he must also exist under its oppressive rule. As with the pension check, the hero speculates about the "hope of elections" (13). His friend, the doctor, chastises him: "Don't be naïve. . . .

we're too old to be waiting for the Messiah" (13). It is only later, in a second conversation, ostensibly on the advances in aviation, that the colonel's wisdom is made plain. The man who has lost both his fortune and his son to a corrupt government can still assert, "Humanity doesn't progress without paying a price" (20). Finally, the colonel's struggle to raise the rooster and find economic redemption in the January cockfights is an overarching challenge throughout the text. Harassed by his wife to sell the animal and tempted by Don Sabas's offers to buy it, the colonel must resist pressure from both sides. Although there is no certainty of the rooster's victory, the colonel will not part with the bird. His reason once again confirms that the hero is motivated by a higher power. Told by his wife to "Get rid of that rooster right now" (30), the colonel's true inspiration is finally explained: "The colonel had foreseen that moment. He had been waiting for it ever since the afternoon when his son was shot down, and he had decided to keep the rooster. . . . It's for Agustín" (30). Like so many other archetypal heroes, the colonel abides his suffering, not for his own sake, but for the memory of those he has lost.

Just as the hero must be willing to endure suffering, so his heroism is ultimately decided by a victory or a defeat. On the surface, the colonel is left utterly beaten at the end of the novella. On the verge of starvation, indebted to Don Sabas, dubious of the rooster's chances for success, and his wife "dying. . . a slow death" (59), the protagonist is in an even worse situation than at the outset of the story. In fact, however, it is in the colonel's very decision not to sell the rooster to Don Sabas, in spite of the consequences, that he achieves a victory. Declaring to his wife that they will return the down payment already spent "when the pension arrives" (57), the colonel effectively imposes his own optimism on the cynical Don Sabas. The rooster itself, always a symbol of the colonel's optimism, now becomes a metaphor for his unconventional heroism:

> He saw his rooster in the middle of the pit, alone, defenseless, his spurs wrapped in rags, with something like fear visible in the trembling of his feet. His adversary was a sad ashen rooster. . . . His rooster did not attack. He rebuffed every attack, and landed again in exactly the same spot. But now his feet weren't trembling (54–55).

The colonel has won by virtue of having "rebuffed every attack" and "landed in the same spot." The entire community cheers the colonel as he carries the bird home (57). Indeed, as his wife explains: "the rooster [does not] belong to us but to the whole town" (56). Like her husband, it has become a symbol of hope and dignity in a world of violence and greed.

As much as *No One Writes to the Colonel* can be read as a political commentary specific to life in Colombia during La Violencia, it can also be understood in a much more universal sense as a modern-day Book of Job. Both Job and the colonel are deprived of their worldly possessions, both endure the loss of a child, both are deserted by friends, and both are reproached by wives weary of sharing their husbands' misery. Similar to the biblical archetype of the good man who refuses to "curse God, and die" (Job 2:9) in the face of undeserved suffering, the colonel embodies the humanist belief in a better future even in an unjust world. But, whereas the fortunes of the Old Testament protagonist are ultimately restored by God, the end of García Márquez's novella leaves the colonel trapped in an existential limbo. Unlike the triumphant Job, to whom "The Lord gave . . . twice as much as he had before" (42:10), the colonel becomes "invincible" only through his insistence that he will survive even if he is forced to "eat . . . shit" (62). García Márquez is arguing, it would seem, that in an absurd, godless universe where the wicked—such as Don Sabas and the military regime—prosper and the good are punished, optimism becomes the ultimate act of defiance. As the colonel tells his wife after a lightning bolt frightens her in the middle of a harangue, "I've always said that God is on my side" (42). This reference to a stereotypical convention is not exclusively comic in nature. The colonel may never collect his pension, win the cockfight, or live to see democracy restored, but his uncompromising faith allows him to transcend his personal misfortune, transforming his character into a prophet of hope in an age of darkness.

WORKS CITED

Bell, Michael. *Gabriel García Márquez: Solitude and Solidarity.* New York: St. Martin's Press, 1993.

García Márquez, Gabriel. *No One Writes to the Colonel and Other Stories.* Trans. J. S. Bernstein. New York: Perennial Classics, 2005.

McMurray, George R. "The Threat of 'La Violencia.' " *Critical Essays on Gabriel García Márquez.* Ed. George R. McMurray. Boston: C. K. Hall, 1987. 79–85.

Williams, Raymond L. *Gabriel García Márquez.* Twayne World Authors Series. Boston: Twayne, 1984.

Woods, Richard D. "Time and Futility in the Novel *El coronel no tiene quien le escriba.*" *Critical Essays on Gabriel García Márquez.* Ed. George R. McMurray. Boston: C. K. Hall, 1987. 86–92.

HOW TO WRITE ABOUT GABRIEL GARCÍA MÁRQUEZ

READING TO WRITE

GABRIEL GARCÍA Márquez (born in 1928) enjoys a unique and almost unparalleled status in contemporary world literature. The Colombian-born writer first achieved international fame with his acknowledged masterpiece *Cien años de soledad* (1967; *One Hundred Years of Solitude*, 1970), which introduced millions of readers to magic realism and the fictional South American town of Macondo. The subsequent publication of *El otoño del patriarca* (1975; *The Autumn of the Patriarch*, 1976), *Crónica de una muerte anunciada* (1981; *The Chronicle of a Death Foretold*, 1983), and numerous short stories led to his selection for the 1982 Nobel Prize in literature. Over the following decades, he added to his preeminent standing with the widely acclaimed *El amor en los tiempos del cólera* (1985; *Love in the Time of Cholera*, 1988) and other novels such as *El general en su laberint* (1989; *The General in His Labyrinth*, 1990) and *Del amor y otros demonios* (1994; *Of Love and Other Demons*, 1995). As "the Spanish-speaking world's leading novelist" (Darraj 89), García Márquez is frequently described as a chronicler of Latin America. While there is no question that his novels and stories draw greatly from that region's culture and history, one of the principal challenges in writing about García Márquez is to avoid reading his work only from a cultural perspective. On a similar note, there is a tendency to see the formal aspects of García Márquez's writing exclusively in terms of magic realism. While the Nobel Committee rightly praised "novels and short stories in which the fantastic and the realistic are combined in a richly composed world of imagination, reflecting a continent's life and conflicts" (Gyllensten n.p.), it is important to remember that, like all great authors, García Márquez is a sophisticated and complex writer whose work cannot be reduced to only a handful of broadly defined elements.

One of the principal problems encountered by the readers of García Márquez is the temptation to confuse his characters and their worlds with the social and political reality of Latin America. Whether you are discussing Colonel Aureliano Buendía and the mythic village of Macondo in *One Hundred Years of Solitude* or Simón Bolívar of *The General in His Labyrinth* and 18th-century Cartagena in *Of Love and Other Demons*, it is important to see them first and foremost as fictional inventions. Any effort to separate fiction from reality must be predicated on a better understanding of Latin American history. You might begin, therefore, with a good general introduction, such as Edwin Williamson's *The Penguin History of Latin America* or Peter H. Smith and Thomas H. Skidmore's *Modern Latin America* (the latter offering an excellent chapter on modern Colombia). From there, you can consult more specialized works that provide more specific detail related to your essay topic. To familiarize yourself with García Márquez himself, Gene H. Bell-Villada's *García Márquez: The Man and His Work* is an extremely accessible biography. García Márquez's autobiography, *Living to Tell the Tale* (*Vivir para contarla*, 2002), is an engaging discussion of his life and literary influences as a young man growing up and living on eastern Colombia's Caribbean coast. Armed with a better understanding of Latin America, Colombia, and García Márquez himself, you will be able move on to your essay topic with a much higher degree of confidence in your ability to distinguish between cultural history and artistic fantasy.

The question of the often fantastic world of García Márquez's fiction is another potential double-edged sword of which you need to be cognizant. Few writers are so closely associated with a single genre or movement as is García Márquez with magic realism. The first challenge will be for you to get a solid grasp on the meaning of the term itself. While D. P. Gallagher has offered the rather succinct description of magic realism as "straightforward descriptions of the extraordinary" (146), the truth is that there is no definitive accepted denotation of magic realism. Instead, you may want to start with an Internet search for "magic realism" or "magical realism" where resources such as Alberto Ríos's appropriately titled site "Magical Realism: Definitions" (which cites some 25 different writers and critics on the topic) will help you formulate a more detailed working definition. You also need to keep in mind that many of García Márquez's works have little or nothing to do with magic realism. His early writings reflect the influence of Ernest Hemingway and William Faulkner, while many of his major works written after *One Hundred Years of Solitude*— such as *Chronicle of a Death Foretold, Love in the Time of Cholera*, and *The General in His Labyrinth*—explore distinct genres and styles with few magic realist elements. Ultimately, you will do well always to keep in mind Thomas Fahy's comment that "Even when García Márquez's realism is infused with the fantastic, he never neglects to show the ways in which human experience and feeling are affected by social realities such as war, disease, political corruption, and mortality" (65).

Once you have moved beyond some of the myths and misconceptions surrounding García Márquez and his work, you will be ready to begin exploring the texts themselves. No matter what kind of approach you take to the novel or short story you choose to study, the most important factor in determining your success will be your ability to dissect the author's language. As is frequently the case with modernist writers (think of Hemingway's "iceberg" principle), García Márquez's writing may seem rather opaque. Characters' dialogue may be deceptively simple. Narrative descriptions often seem rather pedestrian in tone and frequently incongruous with the fantastic or horrific subject at hand. Only through a close reading of these passages will you be able to penetrate the surface of the text and reach an insightful interpretation of the underlying meaning. Look closely at what characters say and what they do not say. By the same token, what is included in or excluded from the descriptions of people, places, and events? Finally, remember that García Márquez is also known for his humor. Is the tone of the passage serious, comic, ironic, or even sarcastic? You need to take all of the factors into account as you try to determine the significance of what you are reading.

Symbolism is another important part of textual interpretation. The difficulty with García Márquez is that his use of symbols can be ambiguous, so you need to read carefully and not make hasty assumptions. As you come across characters, animals, objects, or places, ask yourself whether they might have a metaphorical meaning. With which characters are they associated and in what way? Remember that there is no right or wrong interpretation of a symbol, provided you can substantiate your reading in the text. Consider the symbolism of the rooster in *No One Writes to the Colonel*. The title character cares for the rooster he has inherited from his murdered son with the hope of winning a fortune in the upcoming cockfights and saving himself and his wife from poverty. His wife hates the bird; the corrupt Don Sabas tries to exploit the colonel's desperate situation to buy it at a low price; the townspeople cheer for the animal; and the bird defends itself in the ring but is unwilling to attack its rival. What then is the rooster's significance? It might be seen as a symbol of the protagonist's stoic dignity and will to survive. Given the wife's attitude, it might signify the exact opposite: her husband's naive faith in an unforgiving world. Does it represent the struggle of the working class to resist exploitation by the socioeconomic elite? Is it a broad metaphor for hope? Given the symbolic meaning of the crowing cock in the biblical Passion story, is it suggesting that *No One Writes to the Colonel* should be read as an allegory for the martyrdom of Jesus? The validity of each of these interpretations depends, as it will with all of the symbolism you find in García Márquez, on your own attentive reading and thoughtful analysis of the text.

One final peculiarity you will face in writing about García Márquez lies in his penchant for recurring characters and settings in his novels and short stories. While the practice is hardly exclusive to García Márquez (it can be found in writers from Charles Dickens and Honoré de Balzac in the 19th century to Marcel Proust and William Faulkner in the 20th), the Colombian author has imbued it with a new complexity. His most famous character, Colonel Aureliano Buendía, only appears in *One Hundred Years of Solitude* but is mentioned as a historical figure in a number of other texts. If you write about this character, do you need to take these other, sometimes contradictory, references into account? On a similar note, what do you do with conflicting versions of the same incident, as is the case with an episode from *In Evil Hour* that is retold in the short story "One of These Days"? Even when characters in two texts have the same identity (such as the two principals from *The Incredible and Sad Tale of Innocent Eréndira and Her Heartless Grandmother* who also appear in *One Hundred Years of Solitude*), should we assume that they are one and the same and treat both texts as part of the same "biography"? Finally, it is important to address the matter of the mythical village of Macondo. Many critics and other readers have concluded that, like Faulkner's Yoknapatawpha County, the small town of Macondo serves as the setting for many of García Márquez's novels and stories. The author himself has stated, however, that *Leaf Storm, One Hundred Years of Solitude,* and a handful of stories "are the only books of mine that take place in Macondo" (González Bermejo 7). Can you still speak of a common setting for many of the texts based on their many similarities, or do you distinguish between Macondo and numerous small coastal villages when you discuss García Márquez's fictional universe?

None of the problems put forth here have either a single or a simple solution. Your success in navigating the many complexities surrounding the work of García Márquez will depend on two factors: your willingness to research the topic and your ability to think about the text in an original and critical manner. To this end, you need to consult the work of literary scholars to find out what has already been said about your subject: There is no merit in reinventing the proverbial wheel. At the same time, always keep in mind that this is your essay. Do not be afraid of taking a different perspective, even if it contradicts one, or more, of the accepted "authorities." If you are able to substantiate your thesis through textual documentation and outside scholarly sources—whether they be literary, historical, or biographical—you can be confident that you have written not only a solid essay but also one that makes a meaningful contribution to the study of an important world author.

TOPICS AND STRATEGIES

The remainder of this chapter will provide you with ideas to help you develop your essay on García Márquez. The first step, which is exclusively yours, is to choose the text or texts that you plan to analyze. You cannot write a short essay on all of García Márquez's novels and short stories, so you need to choose one or two that strike you as interesting or that relate to a topic you find particularly engaging. The potential topics you will find here should be considered more as examples than "ready-to-go" theses. No specific topic and no specific text combine to form the perfect essay. Nor is it a good idea to choose haphazardly based on what seems to be easy or convenient. Think about the length of the essay you need to write and how many works you could reasonably discuss in that amount of space. You also want to provide your reader with the rationale behind your choice although it may seem completely obvious to you. You might explain, for example, that you have chosen works with female protagonists in order to explore García Márquez's representation of women. Perhaps you have selected texts with nonlinear narratives to examine the concept of time. Even with a single short story or novel, it behooves you to clarify why the text in question represents a particularly compelling treatment of your topic. By being clear about your motives for selecting both the works and the particular focus, you can be assured that your reader will be much more likely both to follow and to appreciate the merits of your thesis. By contrast, an essay that fails to establish its purpose from the outset runs the risk of confusing its readers and frustrating their attempts to understand the entirety of its argument.

Themes

As is often the case with writers, García Márquez frequently revisits the same themes in many of his works. You could easily examine ideas such as the supernatural, political oppression, the effects of old age, or the nature of romantic love in a number of different texts. The great advantage of a thematic approach is that you have a vast array of possibilities from which to choose; the topics listed here are only a small fraction of those you will find in your reading. While you will want to focus your essay on one single theme, the work or works you include in your analysis will be limited only by your willingness to explore different texts. Whereas a longer novel might be sufficient in itself for thematic study, García Márquez's many novellas and numerous short stories offer an excellent opportunity for a comparative treatment of a theme. For example, *Love in the Time of Cholera* will offer you more than enough material for an essay on romantic love. The theme of revenge could be explored quite thoroughly in *Chronicle of a Death Foretold*. By contrast, you might examine the theme of solitude by avoiding the obvious choice of *One Hundred Years of Solitude* and choosing instead to compare several short stories. Having selected the theme and the text or texts you plan to study, you will want to reread each of them with particular attention to the passages that seem to focus on your topic. Conduct a close reading of these passages, being sure to take careful notes. Now you are ready to analyze your findings, comparing the treatment of the theme in different texts or how it evolves within a single work.

Sample Topics:

1. **Romantic love:** What does García Márquez's work have to say about the nature of romantic love and relationships?

While one does not usually think of García Márquez principally as a teller of love stories, romance figures prominently in many of his works. For this essay, select a text that includes a romantic relationship. You could study, for example, Cayetano Delaura's all-consuming passion for Sierva María in *Of Love and Other Demons*, focusing on the central theme of love as a "demon . . . the most terrible one of all" (118). Another possibility would be to explore the treatment of Simón Bolívar's romantic history in *The General in His Labyrinth*. At one point, one of his many lovers, Delfina Guardiola, reproaches him for his "inconstancy": "'You're a great man, General, greater than anyone. . . . But love is still too big for you'" (217). What separates some of García Márquez's characters who sacrifice everything for the sake of love from those who seem incapable of commitment? Thinking about these romantic relationships, as well as those in some of his other works, such as Eréndira and Ulises in *Innocent Eréndira* or Fermina Daza and Florentino Ariza in *Love in the Time of Cholera*, what is García Márquez's writing suggesting about the nature of love?

2. **Revenge and retribution:** Punishment for wrongdoing, both real and perceived, is a common theme in García Márquez's fiction. It is sometimes carried out by the aggrieved party in the form of revenge. On other occasions, it seems to come in the form of poetic justice or karmic retribution. What does the treatment of this theme seem to be suggesting about human beings and their need for justice—even when they take it into their own hands?

If you want to write on the topic of revenge and retribution, the first work that will probably come to mind is *Chronicle of a Death Foretold*. You might also consider, however, *In Evil Hour*, *One Hundred Years of Solitude*, or *The Autumn of the Patri-*

arch. When is a character punished? Is the act of retribution always justified? Consider the following conversation between the Vicario brothers and the village priest after the brutal honor killing of Santiago Nasar in *Chronicle of a Death Foretold*:

> "We killed him openly," Pedro Vicario said, "but we're innocent."
> "Perhaps before God," said Father Amador.
> "Before God and before men," Pablo Vicario said. "It was a matter of honor" (49).

What do the terms *God* and *men* suggest about the moral barometer for measuring an act of revenge? How do acts of retribution in other texts relate to this standard?

3. **Solitude:** García Márquez's name is almost synonymous with the theme of solitude. What do his works really say about the condition of being alone?

You have a vast array of texts from which to choose when writing on this topic. Almost every work by García Márquez has at least one character who seems to exist in his or her own world, isolated from the rest of the world. Figures reflecting this theme range from the supernatural (the "angel" in "A Very Old Man with Enormous Wings") to the historical (Bolívar in *The General in His Labyrinth*). Given the breadth of this theme in García Márquez's oeuvre, you will want to be sure to narrow your focus to one particular manifestation of solitude. For example, you could write on what the protagonist of *The Autumn of the Patriarch* describes as "the solitary vice of power" (254). Why do so many of García Márquez's political leaders, such as the mayor in *In Evil Hour* and Colonel Aureliano Buendía in *One Hundred Years of Solitude,* seem to be alienated from other characters in the text? Is it the leader's conscious decision to turn within, or is it the necessary consequence of power? What other forms of solitude could you explore? Is solitude always represented as a tragic condition, or does it have a positive aspect as well? Lastly, consider the hope expressed for Latin America in the last line of García Márquez's Nobel Prize acceptance address. He wished that "the lineal generations of one hundred years of solitude will have at last and for ever a second chance on earth" (211). Is solitude, as García Márquez represents it, a universal experience or one particular to the Latin American experience?

Characters

When you write about the characters in one or more texts, you need to begin by identifying the specific traits you plan to analyze so that your essay will have sufficient focus. In the case of García Márquez, you might decide to examine characters that represent political or religious authority. Another possibility would be to consider the characters who embody one of the author's philosophical or cultural interests. For example, you might explore solitary figures or those who represent the cultural preoccupation with honor. Whatever direction you take, you will want to reread all of the passages in the text in which your character appears, being sure to take thorough notes. Only after you have completed this detailed review should you begin to reflect on the pertinent characteristics that will allow you to draw informed conclusions. Drawing on your careful rereading of the texts, what thesis might you propose with regard to García Márquez's representation of religious or civil authorities? What might you say about the strong matriarchal figures who are found throughout his work?

Sample Topics:

1. **Priests:** Priests figure prominently in many of García Márquez's short stories and novels. How do these characters figure into the stories? Are they seen as servants of God, shepherds of their flocks, or purveyors of superstition in the employ of the forces of oppression?

   For this essay, you could compare the function of the priests from several different texts. For example, you could study Father Gonzaga ("A Very Old Man with Enormous Wings"), Father Amador (*Chronicle of a Death Foretold*), and Father Angel (*In Evil Hour*) with respect to their leadership in the community. How do these texts subvert the traditional role assigned to religious leaders? Consider the passage in "A Very Old Man with Enormous Wings" when Father Gonzaga attempts unsuccessfully to speak to the angel in Latin: "The parish priest had his first suspicion of an impostor when he saw that he did not understand the language of God or know how to greet His ministers" (219). What is the source of Father Gonzaga's criteria for assessing the angel's authenticity? What does this reveal about the priest's judgment? What is the effect on the reader of this humorous treatment of a religious figure? Are all of García Márquez's priests represented in a similarly derisive fashion, or are there exceptions? What does the treatment these characters suggest about the role of religion and/or religious figures in society?

2. **Despots:** Political leaders, frequently corrupt and cruel, appear throughout García Márquez's short stories and novels. How are these characters used for political commentary? What do they reveal about the darker side of human nature?

This topic offers numerous possibilities, given García Márquez's well-documented interest in social justice and Latin American history. As with priests, you can study these authoritarian political figures either with respect to García Márquez's ideology or as literary villains. You might choose to study the psychology of the monstrous dictator in *The Autumn of the Patriarch*. Another option would be to examine the way circumstances can tragically transform a leader with noble intentions, such as Colonel Aureliano Buendía in *One Hundred Years of Solitude*, into a despotic figure. Yet another option would analyze the derisive treatment of a petty tyrant, the mayor who appears in *No One Writes to the Colonel, In Evil Hour,* and "One of These Days." Do these characters suggest that tyrants are born or made? Are these figures universal, or are they meant to reflect the negative consequences of an authoritarian tradition in Latin America? What insights do these characters offer into the psychology of despots?

3. **Matriarchs:** It is often observed that many male writers have difficulty creating strong, convincing characters of the opposite

sex. In the case of García Márquez, many of the most memorable female characters are older women who seem to dominate the world, including the men, around them. Why has he included so many of these memorable matriarchs in his work, and what is their function?

If you choose to write about the strong older women in García Márquez's work, you will have ample choices. You might decide to examine the heroines who serve as a source of strength for their families: Úrsula in *One Hundred Years of Solitude* or the unnamed wife of the title character in *No One Writes to the Colonel*. Perhaps even more intriguing are the matriarchal antagonists such as the repugnant, debauched mother in *Of Love and Other Demons*, the "cruel grandmother" from *Innocent Eréndira*, and the darkly humorous, iron-fisted ruler of Macondo "eulogized" in "Big Mama's Funeral." Whether good or evil, García Márquez's matriarchs are characterized by their fortitude, as in the scene where Úrsula Buendía learns that her son has been condemned to death:

> Facing the impossibility of finding anyone to intervene, convinced that her son would be shot at dawn, Úrsula wrapped up all the things she wanted to bring him and went to the jail alone. "I am the mother of Colonel Aureliano Buendía," she announced. The sentries blocked her way. "I'm going in in any case," Úrsula warned them. "So if you have orders to shoot, start right in" (123).

What does this passage reveal about Úrsula? How does this contradict the norms of a patriarchal society? Why do you think powerful female characters like Úrsula tend to be older? What generalizations might you draw about García Márquez's representation of women?

History and Context

Reading García Márquez from a historical or cultural perspective presents a sizable challenge yet a tremendous opportunity for readers coming from a primarily Anglo-American tradition. While much of the author's work has been praised for its universality, it is also deeply rooted in the artistic, social, and political experience of Latin America, the Spanish-speaking Caribbean, and, specifically, his native Colombia. Any analysis that fails to take this into account runs the risk of falling into gross generalizations and, ultimately, a flawed interpretation. No one expects you to become an expert in Latin American history, sociology, or art, but you do need to familiarize yourself with the aspects of the region that are most relevant to your study. If you are examining the representation of political oppression, for instance, it will behoove you to learn as much as you can about the period of civil and political conflict in Colombian history known as La Violencia (ca. 1946–58). Similarly, a discussion of magic realism would benefit from a deeper understanding of the indigenous and African influences on the Latin American worldview. The more you choose to focus on the cultural or historical context of a work, the more you will need to conduct additional research: You would not want to compare, for example, the protagonist of *The General in His Labyrinth* to the real Simón Bolívar without first consulting several authoritative biographies of "The Liberator." Finally, you might elect to read a work in the context of the author's own life. Drawing on both biographical sources and García Márquez's autobiography, *Living to Tell the Tale,* you might investigate the relationship between the author's own life experiences and the fictional world he creates.

Sample Topics:

1. **Colombian history:** The history of Colombia serves as the backdrop for many of García Márquez short stories and novels. Do these texts act as a window on that history, or are they better seen as a lens that refracts historical reality and shapes it to reflect, not truth, but the author's own political perspective?

If you want to write on García Márquez's fiction within the context of Colombian history, you will need to begin by familiarizing yourself with the period you plan to study. For example, *In Evil Hour* is set during La Violencia. *One Hundred Years of Solitude* would oblige you to go back to the turn of the 20th century and the era of the Thousand Days War (1899–1902) and U.S. imperialism. *Of Love and Other Demons,* set in the 1700s, would require research into the colony then known as New Granada. Once you have done this initial work, you will want to compare the scholarly research with the vision of history projected by the literary text. Does the text reference specific individuals and events, or is it a more impressionistic treatment of its historical setting? How does the text attempt to alter the reader's understanding of history? Who are the heroes and villains? Do the themes suggest anything about the way García Márquez wants the reader to view this earlier time? Finally, what does the fictional work have to say about the way Colombia's past has affected its present?

2. **Indigenous and African cultures:** Non-European cultures have played an enormous part in the forming of modern Latin America, as well as in the genesis of magic realism. How are these cultures represented in García Márquez's works?

The presence of indigenous and African cultures in García Márquez's novels and short stories can make for a fascinating essay. Alejo Carpentier, often considered the first magic realist writer, attributed Latin America's "wealth of mythologies," in part, to the "presence of the Indian and the black man" and "its fecund racial mixing" (88). In this light, you might choose to write about the presence of African and indigenous culture in magic realist texts such as "A Very Old Man with Enormous Wings," "Nabo: The Blackman Who Made the Angels Wait," or *The Autumn of the Patriarch* with the indigenous general Saturno Santos, "who knew Indian secrets of how to change his form at will" (55).

Another possibility unrelated to magic realism would be to examine the representation of one these ethnicities within Latin American society. For example, you might analyze the representation of the African slaves who raise Sierva María in *Of Love and Other Demons*. Whatever topic you select, you will want to ask yourself a number of questions. How does the text portray indigenous, African, and other ethnicities? What qualities do they possess, and how do these traits distinguish them from characters of European descent? How does the work characterize the relations between different ethnic groups? What does it convey about the role of indigenous, African, and other non-European peoples in Latin America?

3. **The author's life:** Many of García Márquez's works draw on events in the writer's own life. How do reality and fiction intersect in his work?

When you read García Márquez's autobiography, *Living to Tell the Tale*, which chronicles his youth and early years as a struggling writer, you notice references to people, places, events, and family stories that seem to echo in his fiction. For instance, he recalls the portrait of Simón Bolívar displayed in his grandparents' home:

> . . . my grandfather hung in the dining room the picture of the Libertador Simón Bolívar at his [Bolívar's] funeral. It was difficult for me to understand why he did not have the corpse's shroud I had seen at wakes, but [rather] lay stretched out on a desk wearing the uniform of his day of glory. My grandfather cleared up my doubts with a categorical statement: "He was different." . . . It was my grandfather who taught me and asked me never to forget that [Bolívar] was the greatest man ever born in the history of the world (88–89).

How does this memory correspond to the fictional treatment of Bolívar in *The General in His Labyrinth*? In what way does the discrepancy between a child's impression and an adult's belief reflect the novel's representation of a dying man and a continent's vision of its hero? What other aspects of the writer's childhood seem to be present in his work? Does his close relationship with his grandparents find resonance in the presence of so many older protagonists (*No One Writes to the Colonel*, "A Very Old Man with Enormous Wings," *Love in the Time of Cholera, Memories of My Melancholy Whores*)? How does the mythical town of Macondo resemble the small town of Aracataca, where García Márquez grew up? Which legends and folklore from his youth manifest themselves in his later fiction? Lastly, what does the connection between García

Márquez's childhood and his writing suggest about the relationship between authors' early life experience and his work?

Philosophy and Ideas

An essay on the philosophy and/or ideas in the works of García Márquez might range from the writer's engagement with existentialism and Marxism to less explicitly ideological questions, such as the nature of evil or a cyclical versus linear concept of time. With regard to more formal philosophical constructs, you might wish to study the theme of solitude in terms of the existential concept of alienation or examine Marxist ideas about class conflict in terms of Macondo and García Márquez's other fictional towns. You could also explore the nature of evil in an analysis of any of the numerous murderous antagonists or twisted values that haunt many of his novels and short stories. Whichever direction you take, your first step should be to familiarize yourself with the philosophy or idea you plan to study. Once you are comfortable with the topic, you can proceed to your close reading of the texts and the process of refining the focus of your essay.

Sample Topics:

1. **Existentialism:** García Márquez's three-year self-imposed exile in Paris in the mid-1950s coincided with the zenith of French existentialism. How does this philosophical movement manifest itself in the writer's work?

   If you want to write an essay on existentialism in García Márquez's fiction, you will need to know the essential tenets of the philosophy. You might choose to begin with a book such as Thomas Flynn's *Existentialism: A Very Short Introduction.*
   You may want to focus on one particular existentialist concept, such as alienation, freedom, or bad faith. While you could study any of García Márquez's works, it is generally agreed that the influence of existentialism is more prominent in his earlier works: *Leaf Storm, No One Writes to the Colonel,* and *In Evil Hour.* Whichever text you choose, begin by asking yourself how its plot, characters, and/or themes relate to existentialist thought? For example, how might the protagonists's decision not to sell the rooster in *No One Writes to the*

Colonel be understood as an "authentic act"? Inversely, in what way might the honor killing in *Chronicle of a Death Foretold* be interpreted as an act of "bad faith"? Most compelling of all, can the solitude that defines so many of the writer's most memorable characters be viewed as existential alienation?

2. **Marxism:** García Márquez has long been associated with leftist politics in Latin America. How does his writing reflect Marxist ideology?

Michael Bell has noted García Márquez's "socialist convictions and his hostility to capitalist expansionism" (8). Many of the writer's works include an element of class conflict between a greedy bourgeoisie and courageous workers and peasants. You might choose to analyze this struggle in a text such as "Balthazar's Marvelous Afternoon" or *In Evil Hour* as a manifestation of Karl Marx's vision of historical progress. Another aspect of Marxist thought present in García Márquez's fiction is anti-imperialism. One option here would be to analyze the horrific episode that stems from the arrival of the "gringo" banana plantation in *One Hundred Years of Solitude.* You could also examine the representation of European and North American imperialism in *The Autumn of the Patriarch,* as in this passage where the title character learns of his country's plight:

> We're down to our skins general sir, we had used up our last resources, bled by the age-old necessity of accepting loans in order to pay the interest on the foreign debt ever since the wars of independence and then other loans to pay the interest on the back interest, always in return for something general sir, first quinine and tobacco monopolies for the English, then rubber and cocoa monopolies for the Dutch, then the concession for the upland railroad and river navigation to the Germans, and everything for the gringos . . . (210).

How does this passage convey the sense of imperialism as a historical problem for Latin America? What does it suggest as the solution to the chronic indebtedness of developing nations to developed ones? How does this reflect Marxist ideology with regard to imperialism? Considering Latin American revolutionary movements over the past 50 years, do you think the text is referring to a specific country (or countries), or is it operating on a purely hypothetical plane?

3. **The nature of evil:** What do García Márquez's short stories and novels have to say about the nature of evil?

Evil takes many forms in the work of García Márquez: men, women, individuals, groups, customs, beliefs, and so on. Your essay could explore the nature of evil either within a single text or in several works with regard to one of the aspects mentioned above. There are any number of antagonists you could analyze: *In Evil Hour*'s mayor, the title characters from *The Autumn of the Patriarch* or "Big Mama's Funeral," or the grandmother of *Innocent Eréndira*. Another option would be to choose an idea that García Márquez seems to represent as evil: for example, honor in *Chronicle of a Death Foretold*, greed in *No One Writes to the Colonel*, or religious fanaticism in *Of Love and Other Demons*. However you proceed, your first step will be to ask how and why the object of your analysis is evil. If you are studying a character, does he or she do something to wrong the innocent? If you select an idea or custom, in what way does it corrupt society? Is evil defeated in the text, or does it triumph? What does this resolution indicate about the fate of humanity?

Form and Genre

Essays on "form and genre" deal with the way in which a text is written rather than the text's subject matter. When you think about García Márquez, the first topic that probably comes to mind is "magic" or "magic realism" (also called "magical realism"). While he was not the inventor of this well-known subgenre of fiction, the author of *One Hundred Years of Solitude* is unquestionably its best-known practitioner. After investigating the tenets of magic realism, you could examine the way it functions in any number of García Márquez's novels or short stories. Ask yourself how the supernatural is introduced into the text and how the characters react to it. How is a magic realist text different from more traditional fantasy writing?

The close association between García Márquez and magic realism should not keep you from exploring other formal aspects of his work. One obvious example is his importance as a practitioner of the short story. In addition to numerous short stories, a number of his novellas—*No One Writes to the Colonel, Innocent Eréndira,* and *Memories of My Melancholy Whores,* for example—could be read as long short stories. How would you describe a García Márquez short story? What are its essential traits? How do his stories differ from those of such other well-known short story writers as Ernest Hemingway, Guy de Maupassant, or O. Henry?

Sample Topics:

1. **Magic realism:** García Márquez is unquestionably the most celebrated practitioner of magic realism in all of literature. What does it mean when we describe García Márquez as a magic realist, and what form does magic realism take in his writing?

   Any essay on magic realism needs to be predicated on a solid understanding of the essential aspects of the genre. A good starting point is Maggie Ann Bower's *Magic(al) Realism,* which discusses the origins of the movement and its many manifestations throughout the world. After you have researched the genre itself, you can move on to selecting the García Márquez text or texts on which you want to focus. Rather than simply examining magic realism in a work or works, you might want to narrow your essay and explore the way in which the genre manifests itself in relation to a specific topic. For example, you could write on magic realism and politics in *The Autumn of the Patriarch,* magic realism and religion in "A Very Old Man with Enormous Wings," or magic realism and the epic form in *One Hundred Years of Solitude.* How are fantastic events and characters introduced into the text? In what way is the fictional world of the text changed by the magical occurrence? In what way does it challenge and perhaps alter the reader's understanding of the work?

2. **The short story:** Analyze one or more of García Márquez's short stories with the purpose of identifying the essential traits of his writing in this genre.

If you choose to write on this topic, you will want to start by giving thought to the elements typically associated with the definition of a short story: one or two central characters with few, if any, secondary characters; single plot and theme; rapid exposition; and often a twist or surprise ending. Read a selection of García Márquez's short stories, both magic realist and not, and reflect on how his writing conforms to or differs from the accepted definition of the genre. Consider the example of "A Very Old Man with Enormous Wings," with its opaque title character, plethora of secondary characters, and this curious ending:

> Elisenda let out a sigh of relief, for herself and for him, when she saw him pass over the last houses, holding himself up in some way with the risky flapping of a senile vulture. She kept watching even when she was through cutting onions and she went on watching until it was no longer possible for her to see him, because then he was no longer an annoyance in her life but an imaginary dot on the horizon of the sea (225).

The conclusion reveals neither the identity nor the intent of the "angel." There is no surprise ending but rather an unexplained departure. How does this ambiguous ending defy the reader's expectations? Does this kind of ambiguity exist in other García Márquez short stories? What traits do his stories share with other well-known short story writers? A different kind of essay on this topic would discuss a work such as *No One Writes to the Colonel* or *Innocent Eréndira* with respect to its genre. Are these texts novellas, or are they better understood as long short stories?

Symbols, Imagery, and Language

When studying a writer with the creative imagination of García Márquez, you will find yourself with a wealth of symbolism and imagery to explore. Many texts have a character, animal, or object that clearly invites symbolic interpretation: the title character in "A Very Old Man with Enormous Wings," the rooster in *No One Writes to the Colonel*, the river in *Love in the Time of Cholera*. Another source of symbolic analysis is García Márquez's habit of using names with an underlying significance. You might explore the meaning of character names such as *Úrsula* (she-bear), *Aureliano* (wearing a halo), *Arcadio* (place of happiness), and *Greinaldo Márquez* (suspiciously close to *Gabriel García Márquez*) in *One Hundred Years of Solitude*. The language employed in these texts can similarly provide fertile ground, or you might examine the presence of extensive imagery of decay in *One Hundred Years of Solitude*, *The Autumn of the Patriarch*, or *In Evil Hour*. The key to a successful analysis of symbols, imagery, or language is a meticulous reading of the texts in question. You need to be sure that your interpretation of the metaphor or imagery in question takes into account every reference in the text and that it is consistent throughout. While there are numerous possible readings of a given symbol, the validity of the interpretation ultimately depends on your ability to develop a clear and well-documented explanation in your essay.

Sample Topics:

1. **Symbolism of names:** How does García Márquez use symbolic names to inform the reader's understanding of the text?

   Like many other writers, García Márquez frequently chooses names whose semantic association helps inform the reader's understanding of the character. You could elect to examine this symbolism in works such as *One Hundred Years of Solitude, In Evil Hour,* and *Chronicle of a Death Foretold*. With *Chronicle,* for example, you could explore the meaning of the name *Santiago Nasar: Santiago,* for example, is the patron saint of Spain, associated with the Reconquista of Muslim Andalusia; *Nasar,* an Arabic surname, is reminiscent of Gamal Abdel Nasser, the president of Egypt when García Márquez wrote the text and a leading voice of pan-Arab nationalism. What about this character and his status in the community makes the symbolism of this name so appropriate? What might be said about the connotation underlying the names of *Angela Vicario,* her brothers *Pedro (Peter)* and *Pablo (Paul),* and her aggrieved groom, *Bayardo San Román*? Are these symbolic names meant to reflect the characters' inner psychology or their status in the eyes of the community? Are they meant to be taken literally, or are they ironic?

2. **Images of decay:** Why are so many of García Márquez's works filled with images of death, disorder, and decay?

If you elect to write on this topic, you will effectively be writing on the "realist" part of magic realism. Alongside the mystical characters and events in García Márquez's fiction, there are numerous earthy images, many of which deal with some form of physical decay. What might this imagery serve as a metaphor for? Consider the following scene from *One Hundred Years of Solitude* in which Úrsula makes one final effort to restore the family home before her death:

> She did not need to see to realize that the flower beds, cultivated with such care since the first rebuilding had been destroyed by the rain and ruined by Aureliano Segundo's excavations, and that the walls and the cement of the floors were cracked, the furniture mushy and discolored, the doors off the hinges, and the family menaced by a spirit of resignation and despair that was inconceivable in her time (333–34).

Why is the house in such a state of decline? Is the decay natural, of human making, or both? How does the house become a metaphor for the Buendía family? What does the passage reveal about Úrsula's importance to the Buendías? Why is a dying woman so concerned with restoring the house and garden? What does her reaction to the ruin around her suggest about the Buendías' destiny?

Compare and Contrast Essays

If approached in the right way, compare and contrast essays can be among the most rewarding exercises in critical analysis. The key to success with this type of essay is to remember that your text needs not only to point out similarities between two works (or two elements with the same work) but also to explain why these similarities are significant. The best starting point for a comparison is to find a subject that strikes you as especially unique or compelling. For example, you might compare the title character from *No One Writes to the Colonel* with Simón Bolívar in *The General in His Labyrinth* with respect to what the two characters suggest about the tragic existence of the aging hero. Formal aspects can also make for an excellent compare and contrast essay, such as the use of multiple narrative points of view in *Chronicle of a Death Foretold* and *In Evil Hour*. You could also study one of García Márquez's novels or short stories with respect to the work of another writer. One such possibility would be the use of magic realism in *One Hundred Years of Solitude* and in Chilean writer Isabel Allende's *The House of the Spirits*.

Sample Topics:

1. **Comparing two García Márquez texts:** Compare a common theme, idea, technique, or other shared element in two different works by García Márquez.

   As with any comparative essay, your first step is to identify exactly what you intend to compare. You might examine two characters with common situations, such as the victimized ingénues Eréndira, from the story bearing her name, and Sierva María, from *Of Love and Other Demons*. Given García Márquez's propensity for using recurring characters, you could also compare and contrast the role of a single personage such as Don Sabas, who appears in both *In Evil Hour* and *No One Writes to the Colonel*. You could also compare themes such as unrequited love in *Chronicle of a Death Foretold* and *Love in the Time of Cholera*. Finally, stylistic comparisons dealing with imagery, structure, and narrative technique also offer numerous possible combinations. The most important question to ask yourself is why the comparison you chose is a compelling one. How do the texts relate to each other? Does the reader see a progression, a departure, or even a contradiction in García Márquez's writing?

2. **Comparing a García Márquez text to that of another writer:** Compare one of García Márquez's novels or short stories to the work of a writer who has influenced him, whom he has influenced, or with whose work he shares a common element.

If you choose this approach, one option would be to compare one of García Márquez's texts to one by his acknowledged stylistic "masters," Ernest Hemingway and William Faulkner. One example would be to explore the way the Colombian author utilizes Hemingway's "iceberg principle" in *No One Writes to the Colonel,* "Tuesday Siesta," "One of These Days," or another short story or novel. A second direction you might take would be to compare a García Márquez text with that of one of his contemporaries with respect to genre, theme, or underlying philosophies and ideas. If you are interested in Latin American literature, you might want to write an essay, for instance, about the subgenre of the dictator novel, comparing *The Autumn of the Patriarch* with Peruvian novelist Mario Vargas Llosa's *The Feast of the Goat.* Alternatively, you might compare and contrast García Márquez's use of magic realism with the work of another major writer with whom you are familiar: Toni Morrison's *Beloved,* Salman Rushdie's *Midnight's Children,* or Isabel Allende's *The House of the Spirits.* One word of caution on this type of essay: If your assignment is to write about the work of Gabriel García Márquez, be sure that you maintain the appropriate focus. Ask yourself how your essay contributes to the reader's understanding of García Márquez's work.

Bibliography and Online Resources

Bell, Michael. *Gabriel García Márquez: Solitude and Solidarity.* New York: St. Martin's Press, 1993.

Bell-Villada, Gene H. *García Márquez: The Man and His Work.* Chapel Hill: U of North Carolina P, 1990.

Bower, Maggie Ann. *Magic(al) Realism.* New York: Routledge, 2004.

Carpentier, Alejo. "On the Marvelous Real in Latin America." Trans. Tanya Huntington and Lois Parkinson Zamora. *Magic Realism Theory, History, Community.* Ed. Tanya Huntington and Lois Parkinson Zamora. Durham, NC: Duke UP, 1995. 75–88.

Darraj, Susan Muaddi. *Gabriel García Márquez.* New York: Chelsea House, 2006.

Fahy, Thomas. *Gabriel García Márquez's* Love in the Time of Cholera: *A Reader's Guide.* New York: Continuum, 2003.

Flynn, Thomas. *Existentialism: A Very Short Introduction.* London: Oxford UP, 2006.

Gallagher, D. P. *Modern Latin American Literature.* London: Oxford UP, 1973.

García Márquez, Gabriel. *The Autumn of the Patriarch.* Trans. Gregory Rabassa. New York: HarperPerennial, 2006.

———. *Chronicle of a Death Foretold.* Trans. Gregory Rabassa. New York: Vintage, 1982.

———. *The General in His Labyrinth.* Trans. Edith Grossman. New York: Vintage, 1990.

———. *Living to Tell the Tale.* Trans. Edith Grossman. New York: Alfred A. Knopf, 2003.

———. *Of Love and Other Demons.* Trans. Edith Grossman. New York: Penguin, 1994.

———. *One Hundred Years of Solitude.* Trans. Gregory Rabassa. New York: HarperPerennial, 2006.

———. "The Solitude of Latin America: Nobel Address 1982." Trans. Richard Cardwell. *Gabriel García Márquez: New Readings.* Ed. Bernard McGuirk and Richard Cardwell. Cambridge: Cambridge UP, 1987. 207–11.

———. "A Very Old Man with Enormous Wings." Trans. Gregory Rabassa. *Collected Stories.* New York: HarperPerennial, 1999. 217–25.

González Bermejo, Ernesto. "And Now, Two Hundred Years of Solitude." *Conversations with Gabriel García Márquez.* Ed. Gene H. Bell-Villada. Jackson: U of Mississippi P, 2006. 3–30.

Gyllensten, Lars. "Nobel Prize Presentation Speech." *Nobelprize.org.* 1982. 29 July 2008. <http://nobelprize.org/nobel_prizes/literature/laureates/1982/presentation-speech.html>.

Ríos, Alberto. "Magical Realism: Definitions." *Arizona State University.* 1999. 4 August 2008. <http://www.public.asu.edu/~aarios/resourcebank/definitions>.

Smith, Thomas E., and Peter H. Skidmore. *Modern Latin America.* New York: Oxford UP, 2004.

Williamson, Edwin. *The Penguin History of Latin America.* New York: Penguin, 1993.

NO ONE WRITES
TO THE COLONEL

READING TO WRITE

GABRIEL GARCÍA Márquez's *No One Writes to the Colonel* (1968; first published in Spanish as *El coronel no tiene quien le escriba* in 1961 but written in 1956–57) tells the story of the nameless colonel, an aging war hero who has spent the last 60 years waiting for a pension check from the government while he and his wife struggle against poverty and political oppression in their small town. Although the text itself is less than 100 pages in length and follows only three months of the protagonist's life, it is a penetrating study of the human psyche in an absurd and unjust world. A universal story of the good man beset by undeserved misfortune, the novella is also a telling commentary on 20th-century Latin American history revealed through a combination of realist detail, narrative flashbacks, and rich symbolism. Thus, the text offers a wide range of possible essay topics.

The classic exercise for identifying a potential essay topic, or for substantiating a thesis, is close reading. The idea behind close reading is to study a single passage from the text, reading it several times and giving careful attention to the author's use of language. Speculate on why García Márquez uses one word, or expression, rather than another. Think about how the sentences in the passage are organized and how different syntax might affect its meaning and/or its tone. Select a passage from *No One Writes to the Colonel* that you find interesting, such as the colonel's flashback while walking home from the cockfight:

> He had no regrets. For a long time the town had lain
> in a sort of stupor, ravaged by ten years of history. That

afternoon—another Friday without a letter—the people had
awakened. The colonel remembered another era.

He saw himself with his wife and his son watching
under an umbrella watching a show which was not
interrupted despite the rain. He remembered the party's
leaders, scrupulously groomed, fanning themselves to
the beat of the music in the patio of his house. He almost
relived the painful resonance of the bass drum in his
intestines.

He walked along the street parallel to the harbor and
there, too, found the tumultuous Election Sunday crowd
of long ago. They were watching the circus unloading.
From inside a tent, a woman shouted something about
the rooster. He continued to walk home, self-absorbed,
still hearing the scattered voices, as if the remnants of the
ovation in the pit were still pursuing him (56).

The representation of memory here makes the passage particularly
interesting from a formal perspective. The text addresses the relationship between the present and the past, as well as between the colonel's personal history and the collective history of the town. Although
the colonel is not bitter about the past, having "no regrets," he cannot
help but reflect on how both he and the town have been "ravaged" by
time. The frustrations of the present, "another Friday without a letter," are contrasted with a happier past when he, his wife, and his late
son enjoyed a moment as a family. Even the colonel's intestinal disorder functions as a link with a better time in his life. The anonymous
mention of the rooster brings the protagonist back to his current state.
Unlike the letter that never comes, however, the rooster symbolizes the
colonel's optimism for a more positive future, one anticipated by the
echoing "ovation" he can still hear from only a few moments earlier.
This passage suggests a number of questions that could lead to a good
essay topic. How does García Márquez construct the function of memory? What triggers our recollections of the past, and what does the
nature of our memories tell us about our attitudes toward the present
and the future? Finally, is the act of remembering an attempt to preserve the truth, or is it actually a means of rewriting the truth through
selective memory?

Much of what the colonel remembers is related to the town's political history. The celebration in question, attended by "the party's leaders," would seem to be the kind of popular gathering that (as the earlier funeral scene shows) is now forbidden. The description of the politicians as "scrupulously groomed" is in clear contrast to the corrupt mayor (also pictured earlier in the text), who appears on his balcony unshaven and wearing pajamas. A second reference to the country's lost democracy is the colonel's recollection of the "tumultuous Electoral Sunday crowd" with their anticipation of the "circus unloading" foreshadowing of the absurd government under which they now live. This political aspect of the passage raises an entirely different set of questions. Are the colonel's reminiscences merely nostalgia, or does he believe that democracy can be restored? As a war hero and former leader of the Liberal Party, how does the colonel understand his own role in his nation's history? Can the colonel be seen as an archetype for the forgotten hero who longs for his glorious past but hears only "the remnants of the ovation"? Lastly, is the novel's political content best seen as a commentary on the history of Colombia, on the history of Latin America, or, more universally, on the history of the human experience in the 20th century?

By now you can see how the close reading of a single passage can spawn numerous potential essay topics. After studying one passage and developing several possible theses, you will want to search for other passages that will allow you to distill your ideas. Repeat the same process of close reading with these other passages until you arrive at a premise that you believe would serve as a sound starting point for your essay.

TOPICS AND STRATEGIES

The following topics are merely a list of potential ideas for your essay. They should not be seen as the only possible subjects for your analysis but instead as a first step in the brainstorming process. To this end, you should not see these topics as a sequential checklist. To the contrary, try to be as creative as possible, utilizing the topics to help stimulate your own original ideas. After you put down your ideas on paper and conduct a close reading of pertinent passages, you can then begin to construct your thesis. With your thesis in place, you can return to your notes and begin the process of organizing them into a compelling critical essay.

Themes

A novel's themes are the major issues, the proverbial "big questions" that virtually all works of art address. While it is common to encounter the same themes in different works, each will offer its own treatment of the theme at hand. In your essay, the task will be to examine and explain not only what the theme is but also how it is unique to the text that you are discussing. *No One Writes to the Colonel* deals with many themes including, but not limited to, hope, death, solitude, and the nature of heroism. Start with one theme you find especially compelling, and think about how and where the novel deals with it. Now study the specific language used in those passages with an eye to building the argument that will serve as the basis of your thesis.

Sample Topics:

1. **Hope:** What is the novel saying about the human need for hope. Is hope always positive, or can it become a form of self-deception?

   Look at the colonel's conversations with his wife. How does her pessimism serve as a foil to his optimism? Are her points sometimes valid? Why does the colonel refuse to accept certain realities such as the futility of waiting for the letter? Does the novella ultimately represent the colonel's hopefulness as courageous or quixotic?

2. **Death:** Death appears in many forms in the text: the funeral at the beginning, the memory of Agustín's murder, the colonel's wife's insistence that she is "dying . . . a slow death" (59). To what extent can it be said that death is stalking the colonel?

   Return to the funeral scene. Why does García Márquez devote so much of the text to a funeral for an unnamed musician who has no apparent connection to the rest of the story? Analyze the passage and reflect on the significance of the sentence "He spun his head around and was face to face with the dead man" (8). Why does the colonel become so disoriented in this scene? Where else in the novella does the protagonist confront death, and how does he react? Is death something to be feared or to be defied?

3. **Solitude:** Although the colonel interacts with many other characters throughout the text, he is profoundly isolated from the world around him. What is the nature of his loneliness?

Michael Bell observes that *No One Writes to the Colonel* "makes us see through the eyes of solitude" (30). Why is the colonel isolated? How does the text convey his solitude? Is García Márquez saying that solitude is particular to the colonel's situation, or is he intimating that it is innate to the human condition? How does political oppression isolate the colonel and the other characters? What is the role of age and of economic status? Is the colonel forced into his isolation, or is it a conscious choice?

4. **Heroism:** Is the colonel a hero? If so, what makes him heroic?

Joseph Campbell observes: "A hero is someone who has given his or her life to something bigger than oneself" (151). Under this definition, can the colonel be considered a hero? Does the novel propose an alternative type of heroism? Does the colonel consider himself a hero? What about the town? Return to the passages where the colonel recalls his service to the country as a young man and how he has been (or, in this case, not been) repaid. Consider the scene in the lawyer's office when the colonel declares with regard to his pension, "It's not a question of doing us a favor. We broke our backs to save the Republic," to which the lawyer replies, "Human ingratitude knows no limits" (24). What is the text suggesting about the way we treat our heroes?

5. **Old age:** Examine the way in which the novella addresses the universal truth that we must all grow older and confront the inevitability of physical decay and death.

Robert G. Mead characterizes the novella as "a tale of dignity in old age" (30). In what ways does the text represent old age in the colonel and his wife? Do both characters have the same attitudes toward age? Are these attitudes represented through dialogue, behavior, or both? What is the novella saying about society's view of older people?

Characters

One of the most effective ways of exploring a work of narrative fiction is through its characters. Along with its complex protagonist, *No One Writes to the Colonel* has a number of other rich characters who merit further analysis. Begin your study by choosing a character you find compelling and reflect on the parts of the text where the character appears. Go back and highlight passages that shed light on either the character's nature or his/her function in the novella. Consider the narrator's description, as well as both internal monologue and dialogue with other characters. What are her motives (what does she want)? What are her priorities (what does she want first and foremost)? Is the character positive, negative, or ambiguous? What traits are you using as a basis for this judgment? Is he dynamic (he changes) or static (he remains the same) over the course of the novella? If the former, why does he change, and how does the novella portray the change? An obvious choice for character analysis is the colonel's wife. Is she an antagonist to her husband, or is it more accurate to see her as a victim of his absurd optimism? You could also compare two characters in a single category, such as contrast between the doctor and the lawyer as members of the professional class. You might also make the argument that the town itself functions as a character in *No One Writes to the Colonel.* Finally, you could use the analysis of a character to explore what the novel has to say about heroism (the colonel) or social class (Don Sabas).

Sample Topics:

1. **The colonel:** Return to the passages where the colonel is confronted by the reality of his situation. Does the novel show him to be heroic, naive, or both?

   The colonel is one of García Márquez's most complex figures. We hear his thoughts, see his actions, learn about his past through flashbacks, and observe the judgments of those around him, but he remains enigmatic. Does he truly believe that better days lie ahead, or is he merely maintaining a brave facade? If the latter, is this facade for his wife's sake, the community's, or his own? At the moment when the colonel utters the expletive at the very end of the novella, the text states: "It had taken the colonel seventy-five years—the seventy-five years of his life, minute by minute—to reach this moment. He felt pure, explicit, invincible. . . ." (62). García Márquez seems to be suggesting that his protagonist has either changed or come to a new awareness. What is the nature of this transformation?

2. **The colonel's wife:** Revisit the conversations between the colonel and his wife and try to decide whether she is better understood as one of his antagonists or as "a bedrock realist who understands her man" (Mead 30).

Is the colonel's wife at odds with her husband's worldview from the outset of the novella, or can we trace a gradual progression in her frustration. How are her attitudes different from her husband's with respect to the long-awaited pension? Their son? Her health? The future? Why does she hate the rooster so much? What does the bird represent to her? Does she still love her husband? If so, what is the nature of her feelings? As the only major female character in the novella, what does the way she is represented in the novella say about women in a male-dominated society?

3. **The doctor:** Analyze the doctor's physical description in the text, as well as his conversations with the colonel.

In many ways, the doctor is the most positive character in the novella. Sympathetic to political reform, he is also the only character who genuinely seems to care about the colonel and his wife. What is the doctor's function in the novella, besides being a friend to the colonel? What does the doctor's character suggest about the well-intentioned individuals who choose not to take action in an unjust world?

4. **Don Sabas:** Reread the conversations between the colonel and Don Sabas. Make special note of the way the text describes both the character's physical condition and his personal history.

Don Sabas and the colonel constantly refer to each other as "my friend." Why? What is the exact nature of their relationship, and how does its ambiguity reflect and reinforce the world García Márquez has created? The classic definition of an antagonist is a character who opposes the hero. Does Don Sabas fit this definition? If not, should he still be seen as an antagonist? With regard to the novella's political and social content, what does Don Sabas represent? How might his health and his desire to buy the rooster be connected to the character's ideological significance?

5. **The townspeople:** Study the scenes in which the colonel interacts with minor characters or unnamed members of the community, and consider how they function collectively as a character in the novella.

The colonel interacts with other residents of the town on a number of occasions, including during the funeral and after the cockfight. How do they treat him? Does the town consider the colonel a hero, a fool, or are both attitudes represented? When a group comes to take the rooster, they tell the colonel's wife that the animal belongs "to the whole town" (56). What is the significance of this comment? Finally, how do the colonel's memories of the town affect the reader's understanding about its current situation? Is there hope for the town?

History and Context

Although the town and its residents in *No One Writes to the Colonel* are fictitious, they are drawn from historical reality. In order to better appreciate the nature of the town and the characters who inhabit it, you may want to acquaint yourself with the social and political history of Colombia during the period in question. You do not need to attain an in-depth historical understanding, as this is a literary essay; rather, a basic familiarity with Colombia history from the end of the 19th to the middle of the 20th centuries will enrich your comprehension of the novella's plot, characters, and essential themes.

Sample Topics:

1. **La Violencia in Colombia:** Discuss La Violencia as a backdrop to the events in the novella.

The bloody period of political and social upheaval from 1946 to 1958, known to Colombians as La Violencia (the violence), is a common setting in the work of García Márquez. You should begin by reading a historical account of La Violencia. You might consult Forrest Hylton's *Evil Hour in Colombia* or Mary Roldán's *Blood and Fire: La Violencia in Antioquia, Colombia, 1946–1953.* With this new perspective, return to *No One Writes to the Colonel* and try to identify aspects of the text that seem to be drawn from history. Given García Márquez's well-known opposition to his county's conservative leadership, how can the novel be understood as a political commentary? Consider characters such as the mayor, the priest, and Don Sabas. Beyond their roles in the novella, do they have an ideological function as well?

2. **The colonel and García Márquez's grandfather:** Analyze the novella as a fictionalized portrait of the author's grandfather.

García Márquez has acknowledged on many occasions that the character of the colonel is based on the experiences of his own grandfather, Nicolás Márquez Mejía, who fought in the Thousand Days War but never received the pension he had been promised after the Treaty of Neerlandia. Reconstruct the history of Nicolás Márquez Mejía's life through his grandson's autobiography, *Living to Tell the Tale,* and statements from interviews such as those in Gene H. Bell-Villada's collection, *Conversations with Gabriel García Márquez.* To what extent can *No One Writes to the Colonel* be read as biography? Which elements are changed and why? Lastly, how do these changes affect our reading of the story?

3. **Governmental corruption in Latin America:** Consider the novella in a broader cultural sense as a critique of political corruption in Latin America.

In his acceptance speech for the 1982 Nobel Prize in literature, García Márquez said of Latin America: "The violence and disproportionate misery of our history are the result of secular injustice and infinite bitterness" ("The Solitude of Latin America" 210). How is this dialectic of "secular injustice and infinite bitterness" reflected in *No One Writes to the Colonel*? In what ways does the text confront the reader with "secular injustice"? Which characters reflect "infinite bitterness"? How can the main character's optimism be explained in light of the author's comments?

Philosophy and Ideas

No One Writes to the Colonel is a novella rich in philosophical and ideological content. These ideas range from age-old universal questions, such as "Why do bad things happen to good people?" to the moral and political obligations of citizenship and the presence of existentialist motifs in the novel. In order to prepare yourself for writing on one of these ideas, you need to return to the novella and search for passages that seem to address the philosophical concept you wish to examine. Undertake a close reading of the passages you have selected so that you can form a basis for the thesis you put forth in your essay. If you want to examine what the novella says about civic duty, for example, you will want to look at the way different characters confront the injustice they see in the town. For example, you might compare the attitudes and actions of the colonel, Don Sabas, the lawyer, and the doctor toward the government. How does the novella represent these four characters? Which ones are portrayed in a positive light and which ones in a negative light? What are the consequences of standing up or not standing up for justice? After studying the characters and reflecting on these questions, you might propose a thesis such as the following: In *No One Writes to the Colonel*, García Márquez demonstrates through the characters of the colonel, Don Sabas, the doctor, and the lawyer that political cynicism, self-interest, and fear will always outweigh a sense of civic duty. The dutiful colonel struggles to survive, while the traitorous Don Sabas prospers. The self-interested lawyer and the well-intentioned but apprehensive doctor represent the failure of civil society's leaders to challenge a system they know to be corrupt. The same analysis of the novella might lead you in the direction of this argument: In *No One Writes to the Colonel*, García Márquez calls the reader's attention to the importance of doing one's civic duty by contrasting the nobility of the colonel with the greed of Don Sabas, the cynicism of the lawyer, and the passivity of the well-intentioned doctor.

Sample Topics:

1. **Why do bad things happen to good people?** Think of how *No One Writes to the Colonel* addresses this age-old question in an original way.

   The colonel and his wife have led good lives, yet they are confronted by an endless array of misfortunes. What does the suffering of these fundamentally positive characters (and the apparent prosperity of negative characters such as Don Sabas) say about the moral structure of the universe? What is the novella suggesting about the presence/existence of God? Return to the passages where the colonel and his wife discuss their misfortunes. What does each one believe to be the cause of his or her suffering? Is there any indication in the novella that good people are ever rewarded or that evil ones are ever punished? At one point in the story, the colonel declares to his wife, "I've always said that God is on my side" (42). How should we interpret this assertion?

2. **Civic duty:** Analyze the novella as a commentary on the relationship between the individual and the state.

   Revisit the passages where the colonel recalls his service to the country as a young man. What does he say about his duty to the nation? Research the concept of the "social contract" in the writings of John Locke, Jean-Jacques Rousseau, or other prominent Enlightenment thinkers. What do they say about the mutual obligations of the citizen and the state? What is the status of this relationship in *No One Writes to the Colonel*? According to classic social contract theory, what is the recourse of citizens when the state fails to fulfill its obligations? How do the residents of the town respond to their government? Do they fail in their civic duty? Is the novella, as René Prieto argues, "an indictment of political injustice and, implicitly, an injunction to the men who, through their passivity, make it possible" (41)? Finally, what do you think the novella is suggesting about the town's political future? How might this relate to Latin American politics?

3. **Optimism versus pessimism:** Analyze the way in which these contradictory worldviews are represented in the novel.

The question whether the world is essentially a good or bad place has been debated in numerous works of literature. In *No One Writes to the Colonel,* this dialogue takes place principally between the optimistic colonel and his pessimistic wife. Return to the passages where they express their views and scrutinize the language to determine the essence of each character's beliefs. In what ways do the colonel and his wife embody their respective outlooks? How are their opposing points of view accentuated through narrative description and symbolism? Does the novella seem to paint one perspective as being truer than the other? What do the other characters (especially the doctor, who has the greatest interaction with both spouses) think? Is either position vindicated or repudiated at the end of the novella? Does *No One Writes to the Colonel* argue for an optimistic view on life, a pessimistic view, or neither?

4. **Existentialism:** Investigate existentialist philosophy, and examine the way it manifests itself in the novella.

Like many other 20th-century writers, from Franz Kafka to Ernest Hemingway, Gabriel García Márquez was heavily influenced by existentialism. Michael Bell, commenting on the writer's years in Paris—the time during which he wrote *No One Writes to the Colonel*—states: "[García] Márquez . . . doubtless assimilated the existentialist emphasis on solitude as fundamental to the human condition" (3). If you have never studied existentialism, you will want to familiarize yourself with its basic concepts of freedom, alienation, bad faith, and authenticity. Two good places to start are Thomas Flynn's *Existentialism: A Very Short Introduction* and Richard Kamber's *On Sartre*. Once you feel comfortable with these essential existentialist concepts, return to the novella and consider the ways in which it may be read as an existentialist text. Can the colonel's solitude be understood as existential alienation? Does he (or any of the characters in the novel) act authentically or in bad faith?

Form and Genre

Along with content areas such as theme, historical context, and philosophical ideas, a work of literature can also be analyzed in terms of its form, the way in which the author constructs the text. When doing this kind of formal analysis, you will want to ask yourself why the writer chose to tell the story the way he did. How does the structure of the novel affect the way we read it? When writing about *No One Writes to the Colonel*, you might choose to focus on the use of flashbacks. Another possible focus could be García Márquez's narrative technique.

Sample Topics:

1. **Use of flashbacks:** One possible essay topic would be for you to identify all of the flashback scenes in the novella and to analyze how the colonel's memories strengthen the sense of loss, decay, and isolation in the text.

   A flashback, called "analepsis" in critical discourse, typically provides the reader with information about events that took place prior to the beginning of the narrative. The location and content of a flashback, however, will often affect the reader's perception of the events in the narrative present. Consider the following passage in which the colonel is preparing to leave for the funeral:

   > He found an enormous old umbrella in the trunk. His wife had won it in a raffle held to collect funds for the colonel's party. That same night they had attended an outdoor show which was not interrupted despite the rain. The colonel, his wife, and their son, Agustín—who was then eight—watched the show until the

end, seated under the umbrella. Now Agustín was dead, and the
bright satin material had been eaten away by the moths (5).

What does this flashback tell the reader about the colonel's
past life compared to the present? What does the flashback
reveal with regard to the town? What is the significance of the
umbrella and the condition in which the colonel now finds it?
Explain the observation by Richard D. Woods that "Through the
technique of resuscitating the past the author creates an unbro-
ken line of uselessness which fuses with the present" (88).

2. **Narrative technique:** Reflect on how the realist technique
   employed in the narrative affects the reader's reaction to the
   events in the novella.

   García Márquez's "journalist-into-novelist" approach to writing has been compared to that of Ernest Hemingway (Kennedy
   63) in its use of extensive realist detail, terse dialogue, and
   minimal sentimentality. Return to the conversation that the
   colonel has with the doctor as they wait for the mail (20–21).
   Examine the description of the colonel's actions during his
   apparently mundane discussion that moves from aviation to
   newspaper headlines. What do these details reveal about the
   character's unstated feelings? How does the organization of
   the passage function to build the sense of anticipation and
   then disappointment? Look for similar passages in the novella
   where García Márquez uses realist narrative technique, and
   analyze the way in which this "journalistic" approach to sto-
   rytelling heightens the novella's dramatic effect.

Language, Symbols, and Imagery

The study of an author's use of language, symbols, and imagery in a work of
literature is an excellent starting point when looking for keys to interpreting the text. When searching for these elements, you should focus on the
mention of specific objects or ideas, especially when they appear more than
once in the text. When thinking about *No One Writes to the Colonel*, two
very clear symbols come to mind: the letter and the rooster. With regard to
imagery, the text makes repeated mention of the characters' health. Finally,

the expletive that ends the novella is an excellent example of a meaning-ful use of language. In formulating your argument, you want to illustrate how a particular symbol or image shapes our reading of the novella. For instance, you could make the case that the health of the respective charac-ters is symbolic of the sense of death and decay that dominates the novella. You could go on to make the case that while the colonel also suffers from ill health, his distinct optimism for an eventual recovery epitomizes the protagonist's heroic refusal to succumb to his grim circumstances.

1. **The rooster:** Analyze the multivalent symbolism of the rooster from the perspective of the colonel, his wife, and the town.

   The rooster has obvious symbolic value in *No One Writes to the Colonel,* but exactly what it symbolizes depends greatly on the reader's interpretation. Reread all of the passages where the rooster is mentioned. How does the narrator describe the animal? What do the colonel, his wife, and the other charac-ters say about it? First, consider the rooster's literal function. Why does the colonel have the bird in the first place, what are the consequences of the animal's presence, and how might the rooster affect the colonel's future? Now reflect on the rooster's symbolic value. Does it represent a person, an idea, or both? The colonel's wife calls it an "evil-omened bird" (52). Is she right, or does the rooster symbolize something very different?

2. **The letter:** Write an essay that discusses the symbolism of the letter referenced in the title.

   Revisit the sections of the novel where the letter containing the colonel's pension check is mentioned. You should include any references to the mail or to communication from the gov-ernment, as these are also indirect references. In attempting to determine the letter's symbolic value, ask yourself why the colonel continues to anticipate its arrival each day, even after so many years. Does his attitude ever change? What do other characters, especially his wife, say about the letter? Richard D. Woods observes: "Inspiring hope, but bringing frustration, the tantalizing letter symbolizes a life; in another sense it typifies the town" (87). Do you agree with this assessment, or do you believe the letter symbolizes something else?

3. **Health:** Analyze the symbolism of the colonel's health and that of other characters in the novella.

No One Writes to the Colonel is replete with references to health, or the lack thereof, beginning on the first page with the protagonist's "feeling that fungus and poisonous lilies were taking root in his gut" (3). Go through the novella and underline all of the references to health, as well as attitudes regarding health. How does the colonel's attitude compare with those of his wife and Don Sabas? The character of the doctor is clearly significant with regard to health. What are his prognoses for each character? What is the state of each character's health at the end of the novella? In what way can health be seen as symbolic of the social, moral, and spiritual position of each one?

4. **The colonel's final word:** Write an essay discussing the significance of the colonel's final word, *shit,* at the close of the novella.

A writer will frequently use the final words in a novel to leave readers with a message, a moral, or an explanation of the text they have just finished. In some cases, such as in *No One Writes to the Colonel,* this final message will be of an ambiguous nature, inviting the reader to speculate on its meaning. Return to the end of the novella. Thinking about the colonel's personality, why does this final expletive come as a surprise? To whom and/or what is he responding? Is the expletive a cry of desperation and an admission of defeat, or, as René Prieto argues, is "the excremental curse" a symbolic "drain[ing] of the thematic bottleneck" of the character's pent-up frustrations?

Compare and Contrast Essays

There are two essential types of compare and contract essays. You might choose to study two comparable elements within the novella, or you could choose to draw your comparison between similar aspects of this and another text. For example, you could compare the colonel and his wife to examine what the novella suggests about gender differences with regard to marriage and parenthood. Another possibility would be to compare the recurring characters (those who appear in more than one work of fiction) in *No One Writes to the Colonel* and García Márquez's novella *In Evil Hour*. This kind of comparison permits you to examine both the evolution of the characters and the author's treatment of certain themes at distinct points in his career. A different kind of intertextual comparison would be to examine the universal archetype of the good person who suffers in *No One Writes to the Colonel* and its best-known example in Western literature, the Book of Job in the Hebrew Bible. With this latter type of essay, you need to be especially sure that your comparison is meaningful. You not only need to be very familiar with the other text; you also have to be able to justify the relevance of your comparison.

Sample Topics:

1. **The colonel and his wife:** Compare the two characters with respect to gender roles in marriage, parenthood, and old age.

   As much as any other aspect of *No One Writes to the Colonel*, the nature of spousal relationships is explored throughout the text. What makes this relationship unique to most fictional spouses? How do the colonel and his wife communicate with each other? In what ways does the reader see that they still love each other? What are their principal points of conflict? How does each spouse express feelings about their dead son? García Márquez credits his grandparents with raising him (Guibert 47). In what way can the relationship between the colonel and his wife be seen as a tribute to older couples whose relationship transcends romantic love?

2. **Recurring characters in *No One Writes to the Colonel* and *In Evil Hour*:** Write an essay that traces the evolution of the characters who appear in both novellas.

   After reading *In Evil Hour*, identify the passages containing characters first introduced by García Márquez in *No One Writes to the Colonel*: Father Angel, Don Sabas, the doctor, and the mayor. How do the roles of these characters change from the first novella to the second? How does García Márquez use these characters to establish continuity between the two texts? How is the reader's understanding of the characters changed by reading both novellas? Do the nameless town and its population change from one novella to the other? Lastly, speculate on the way in which the use of recurring characters functions to help create a broader novelistic universe.

3. ***No One Writes to the Colonel* and the Book of Job:** Compare García Márquez's portrait of a good man who suffers unjustly with the archetypal character from the Hebrew Bible.

Read the Book of Job and think of the parallels between the two texts. How is Job's life prior to his affliction similar to the colonel's past as he remembers it in the flashbacks? What is the equivalent in *No One Writes to the Colonel* to God's agreement with Satan? Is there an analogous relationship for the colonel to Job's steadfast faith in God? How are the wives of the two characters alike? How does the end of the Book of Job differ from the novella? Job is often considered a didactic, or instructional, story. Is *No One Writes to the Colonel* also didactic? If Job is meant to offer hope for those who suffer inexplicably, does *No One Writes to the Colonel* have a comparable purpose?

Bibliography for *No One Writes to the Colonel*

Bell, Michael. *Gabriel García Márquez: Solitude and Solidarity.* New York: St. Martin's Press, 1993.

Campbell, Joseph. *The Power of Myth with Bill Moyers.* Ed. Betty Sue Flowers. New York: Anchor, 1991.

Flynn, Thomas. *Existentialism: A Very Short Introduction.* Oxford: Oxford UP, 2006.

García Márquez, Gabriel. *No One Writes to the Colonel and Other Stories.* Trans. J. S. Bernstein. New York: HarperCollins Perennial Classics, 2005.

——. "The Solitude of Latin America: Nobel Address 1982." Trans. Richard Cardwell. *Gabriel García Márquez: New Readings.* Ed. Bernard McGuirk and Richard Cardwell. Cambridge: Cambridge UP, 1987. 207–11.

Guibert, Rita. "Gabriel García Márquez." *Conversations with García Márquez.* Ed. Gene H. Bell-Villada. Jackson: U of Mississippi P, 2006. 31–58.

Hylton, Forrest. *Evil Hour in Colombia.* London: Verso, 2006.

Kamber, Richard. *On Sartre.* East Windsor, CT: Wadsworth Press, 2000.

Kennedy, William. "The Yellow Trolley Car in Barcelona: An Interview." *Conversations with García Márquez.* Ed. Gene H. Bell-Villada. Jackson: U of Mississippi P, 2006. 59–78.

Mead, Robert G. "For Sustenance: Hope." *Critical Essays on García Márquez.* Ed. George R. McMurray. Boston: G. K. Hall, 1987. 29–31.

Prieto, René. "Communication in *No One Writes to the Colonel.*" *Gabriel García Márquez: New Readings.* Ed. Bernard McGuirk and Richard Cardwell. Cambridge: Cambridge UP, 1987. 33–44.

Roldán, Mary. *Blood and Fire: La Violencia in Antioquia, Colombia, 1946–1953.* Durham, NC: Duke UP, 2002.

Woods, Richard D. "Time and Futility in the Novel *El coronel no tiene quien le escriba.*" *Critical Essays on García Márquez.* Ed. George R. McMurray. Boston: G. K. Hall, 1987. 86–93.

IN EVIL HOUR

READING TO WRITE

THE FIRST true literary success for Gabriel García Márquez, *In Evil Hour* (originally published in Spanish as *La mala hora* in 1962 and translated into English in 1979) is also widely considered to be his most overtly political work. A fictionalized account of life in rural Colombia during the turbulent decade (c. 1946–58) known as La Violencia, the novella is a more disturbing and brutal treatment of the period than *No One Writes to the Colonel*. While *In Evil Hour* has not received as much scholarly attention as some of the author's later works, such as *One Hundred Years of Solitude* and *Love in the Time of Cholera*, you should still be able to find ample critical material for an essay. If you have difficulty locating sources specifically on *In Evil Hour*, and you do not possess a reading knowledge of Spanish, you may want to expand your search to broader discussions of García Márquez's "early fiction." Before turning to the existing criticism on *In Evil Hour*, however, you will want to try to formulate your own ideas about the novella. The best way to get started is to select an interesting passage from the text and perform a close reading. For instance, you might examine this scene in the barbershop:

> The mayor didn't patronize the barbershop. At one time he'd seen the sign nailed to the wall: *Talking Politics Prohibited*, but it had seemed natural to him. That time, however, it caught his attention. "Guardiola," he called.
>
> The barber cleaned the razor on his pants and remained waiting. "What's the matter, Lieutenant?"

"Who authorized you to put that up?" the mayor asked, pointing to the notice.

"Experience," said the barber.

The mayor took a stool over to the back of the room and stood on it to remove the sign.

"Here the only one who has the right to prohibit anything is the government," he said. "We're living in a democracy."

The barber went back to his work. "No one can stop the people from expressing their ideas," the mayor went on, tearing up the pieces of cardboard (102–3).

The most notable aspect of this passage is its political content. Think about the way the text utilizes comic irony to serve its ideological purpose. While the mayor is a rather brutal figure who is known to have had a hand in a number of violent political reprisals, here he seems more a comical figure. What is this humorous scene meant to suggest about the mayor and, by extension, about the government? Now consider the barber's attitude toward the mayor's comments. How does his sarcastic, one-word response function to subvert the mayor's authority? What is the text saying about the relations between the residents of the town and the authorities?

Central to the political commentary in the passage is the statement being made about language. Why has Guardiola posted the sign? How does the apparent prohibition of political discussion actually make a political statement? How is the meaning of the word *democracy* altered by the context in which it is used? What about the mayor's assertion, "No one can stop the people from expressing their ideas"? Guardiola refers to the mayor as "Lieutenant." Why is it so significant that the barber uses the mayor's military rank rather than his civilian title? What does this indicate about the nature of government in the town? Finally, how does the use of language in this particular section relate to the anonymous lampoons that have instigated the crisis in the town?

From the questions you have asked about this passage, you might choose to write your essay on the relationship between language and politics in the novella. How does the government attempt to control free speech in the town? Who else is involved in restricting communication? Similarly, you might choose to write your essay about those characters who represent the "official voice" of the town. Father Angel and Judge Arcadio are part of the power structure, so why do they ultimately break with the mayor? What is the text intimating by this rupture? Yet another essay could deal with social class. Try to divide the characters according to their socioeconomic status to determine if the text is making a particular ideological statement. Lastly, you could focus on the lampoons themselves. Critics frequently see them as symbolic of the socially committed writer's function in politics. You might wish to analyze how the text defines that role.

The passage we have just studied offers a number of clear options for your essay. Should you opt for one of these, your next step will be to identify other parts of the work with similar content. Of course, you need not choose any of these options and instead pursue a different topic with a different set of passages. Either way, the textual evidence you glean from your close reading will allow you to take the next step in the writing process. After synthesizing your findings, you can generate the overarching argument that will serve as the thesis for your paper.

TOPICS AND STRATEGIES
Themes

Your search for the themes in a literary text begins by asking what are the major ideas or concepts that the work explores. *In Evil Hour* has no shortage of themes for you to examine. The list provided here is by no means exhaustive; rather, it is meant to stimulate your own reflections on the novella's themes. Whichever theme you choose to study, you will want to demonstrate how the text offers the reader a unique or unexpected perspective. It is most likely that you will not have a thorough understanding of the way the novel treats a given theme at the outset. Rather, you should think about how the text deals with a topic—solitude, for example—in a particularly engaging manner. From there, you can identify pertinent sections of the novella and then begin to refine your understanding of the theme.

Sample Topics:

1. **Violence:** What is the novella suggesting about the effect of violence on both society and the individual?

   Violence is omnipresent in the text. From César Montero's shooting of Pastor at the beginning of the novella to the death of Pepe Amador at the hands of the authorities, García Márquez paints a world in which brutality is a fact of daily life. How does this phenomenon manifest itself? Think of each individual character and decide if he or she is the victim violence, the perpetrator, or both? Does this behavior stem from the individual, the political system, the culture, or a combination of these factors?

2. **Solitude:** Explore the pervasive sense of isolation that seems to affect every character in the novella.

Contrasting the treatment of the solitude theme in *No One Writes to the Colonel* with that in *In Evil Hour,* Michael Bell observes that "Solitude remains a central theme [in *In Evil Hour*] but the emphasis is reversed: instead of focusing on the isolation of one individual, it studies a collective experience of a mutual solitude" (32). Identify the different characters who seem to be alone. How does the text illustrate their solitude? If "mutual solitude" is, by definition, a social phenomenon, what does the novella suggest to be the cause of this problem? Is a solution ever proposed, or does the text conclude that "mutual solitude" is an unavoidable consequence of the human condition?

3. **Resistance to oppression:** Analyze the many ways in which both individual characters and the town as a whole resist—and fail to resist—an oppressive government.

The novella presents various degrees of resistance to unjust government. Which characters seem to be involved with or sympathetic to the resistance movement? Why do some characters support the repression? Which characters are ambivalent about the situation? Why do they remain passive in the face of injustice? Noting "the absence of a protagonist," Regina Janes observes that there is "a sense that political heroism is problematic and that resistance is often futile though always necessary" (34). If this is the case, what is *In Evil Hour* saying about the willingness of human beings to accept political injustice? Moreover, what is required for individuals to stand up against their oppressors?

4. **The power of rumor and gossip:** Discuss the way rumor functions to push events forward in the novella. What is the text suggesting about the nature of gossip?

Robert Kirsner describes the effect of the malicious lampoons on the town in the following way: "Every family looks with terror at the possibility of having its dark secrets made public. Although . . . nothing more than common gossip, in its written form the canard becomes the incantation of demonic destruction" (72). Are the lampoons themselves the cause of the violence, or are they symptomatic of a deeper underlying conflict in the town? Which members of the community are targeted by the lampoons? How do they respond? In the story, Roberto Asís, a descendant of the town's founding family, observes that the lampoons "only tell what people are already saying" (30). If this is the case, why do the authorities attempt to suppress the lampoons? Should the reader understand the town's penchant for gossip mongering as a problem specific to this fictional town, or is the novella making a much broader statement about human nature and organized society?

5. **Morality:** Examine the town's contradictory moral code.

All societies, real or fictional, are governed by a moral code, a system of beliefs that defines good and bad behavior. Like other socially committed writers, García Márquez frequently uses irony to demonstrate the latent hypocrisy of small-town morality. Consider the following conversation between Father Angel and Judge Arcadio's common-law wife:

> "You should make him marry you and set up a home," he said "This way, the way you're living now, not only leaves you in a precarious situation, but it's a bad example for the town."
>
> "It's better to do things frankly," she said. "Others do the same thing but with the lights out. Haven't you read the lampoons?" (71).

Return to the passages where morality is mentioned or implied. To what extent is immoral behavior defined by perception rather than reality? Which instances of immoral behavior are ignored? How important is sexuality in the town's moral code as opposed to political, economic, and social justice? What is the novella saying about the town's moral priorities? In what way can this fictional morality also be understood as a commentary on the real world?

Characters

Examining a character or several characters in a text is both one of the most interesting and one of the most accessible approaches to literary study. While *In Evil Hour* may not have one clear protagonist, the many characters who inhabit the town offer a wide range of analytical options. Perhaps the most engaging character, the mayor, raises the issue of a villain-protagonist. Similarly, the ambiguous roles of Father Angel and Judge Arcadio offer the basis for a most engaging essay. Yet another possibility is an analysis of the mayor's nemeses: the doctor, the dentist, and the barber. Whichever character or combination of characters you choose to study, your first step will be to reconstruct a detailed biography and a psychological profile drawn from the text. Are these details drawn from the character's actions, his or her thoughts, or others' perceptions of the character? What do we know about the character's past? Does that character change over the course of the novella? If so, is it a positive change or a negative one? How does the character's journey relate to the broader themes and ideas in the work? Finally, after having given careful consideration to the character's function in the narrative, consider how it affects the way the reader understands the novella.

Sample Topics:

1. **The mayor:** Make a case for the character of the mayor as either the novel's antagonist or its protagonist.

While the mayor represents the oppressive military dictatorship in the town, he is an extremely complex character. Calling him "the novel's most interesting character," George R. McMurray observes: "in spite of his arrogance and corruption, the mayor occasionally elicits the reader's admiration and compassion" (*García Márquez* 33–34). Return to the passages dealing with the mayor. Is he always seen in a villainous light, or are there moments when he is earnestly attempting to do his duty? How does the mayor's toothache affect the reader's attitude and understanding of the character? In what way can the mayor be seen as a tragic figure? How might this character be understood as a statement about the consequences of political power?

2. **Father Angel:** Analyze Father Angel as his character relates to the broader conflict in the novella.

Revisit the parts of the text in which Father Angel figures prominently? Where does Father Angel stand in the social and political struggle that dominates the text? How does he approach his pastoral responsibilities to the people of the town? In what ways is he connected with the mayor and the town's ruling elite? How does his position change by the end of the novella? Why does the narrative begin and end with his character? Consider the following statement made to Father Angel by Dr. Giraldo: "One of these nights you'll put your hand on your heart and ask yourself if you're not trying to put bandages on morality" (165). What does the doctor mean, and how does it relate to the priest's dilemma?

3. **The doctor, the dentist, and the barber:** Explore the heroism of these three characters in a work seemingly devoid of heroes.

Gene H. Bell-Villada calls attention to "the clandestine roles played by the dentist, the doctor, and the barber, who in the end emerge as the book's subversive and nameless heroes" (147). Return to the passages in which these characters appear and analyze how they challenge the mayor's authority. What is the nature of their resistance? How are they alike and how are they different in their approach to politics in the town? Do any of the three ever confront injustice openly? What are the consequences for these three characters of their opposition to the government? How might the nature of their work—each as an independent professional—affect their ability to confront injustice? Finally, by creating these kinds of "heroes," what is the novella saying about the role of each citizen in the struggle against political oppression?

4. **Judge Arcadio:** Examine the judge's role in the novella.

Judge Arcadio's role in the novella is much more ambiguous than that of most of the other characters. A government official and the mayor's "best friend" (157), by the end of the story, he has become sympathetic to the rebel cause. Return to the sections of the text dealing with the judge. Why is he in the town? What is his attitude toward his work? How does he view the problem of the lampoons? What is his worldview? In Greek mythology, Arcadia is a utopian setting characterized by sensual pleasure and innocent bliss. How might this be fitting for the judge? Just before the barber Guardiola gives the judge a secret message about the resistance, he tells the judge, "Until now . . . I'd have thought that you're a man who knows that he's leaving and wants to leave" (157). What does Guardiola mean, and why does the judge accept the clandestine note? How can the judge's role in the novella be understood as a statement about the moral responsibility of the privileged and powerful?

5. **Mr. Carmichael:** Discuss this character who begins as a defender of the oppressive regime but ends as one of its victims.

Who is Mr. Carmichael? What is the nature of his relationship with the Montiel family? Why is it significant that he is of African descent and has an English surname? Reread the conversation with the barber in which Carmichael justifies his refusal to get involved with "your political hatreds": "No man can help being impartial with eleven children to feed" (44). Is his position defensible? Should Carmichael's fate at the end of the novella be seen as just punishment, the victimization of an innocent bystander, or a cautionary tale for those who eschew politics?

History and Context

Writers do not create in a vacuum. For this reason, their work often reflects or responds to events in the world around them. While you always want to remember that the text, not the context, is your focus, you can often write a fascinating essay about the relationship between a work of literature and the historical or biographical events that may have influenced its creation. An obvious topic with *In Evil Hour* is its representation of the Colombian conflict known as La Violencia. Another possibility would be for you to explore the way in which the author's early experience as a journalist, often at odds with the Colombian government, may have influenced the novella's representation of those in positions of social, economic, and for political power.

Sample Topics:

1. **La Violencia:** Discuss the novella in the context of Colombian history.

The fact that historian Forrest Hylton chose the title *Evil Hour in Colombia* for his monograph on the "prolonged, undeclared civil war called 'La Violencia'" (xvi) suggests the extent to which García Márquez captures the essence of that tragic chapter in his nation's history. Before returning to the text, reflect on the following statement made by García Márquez about the historical aspect of the novella:

> What counted for me was [*sic*] the motives and the root causes for the violence, and above all the consequences of the violence for the survivors. That's why you'll find that in *In Evil Hour* there are no massacres. The critical period in *la Violencia* is practically over. What you see in the book is that the pause is patched with cobwebs and the violence will come back, that it's not over because the causes aren't gone (González Bermejo 9).

What are the "causes" to which García Márquez refers? Are they linked with the insurrection that breaks out at the end of the novella? How does the text represent the uneasy "pause" in the violence? After consulting the work of historians such as Hylton and Marco Palacios (*Between Legitimacy and Violence:*

A History of Colombia, 1875–2002), evaluate *In Evil Hour* as a historical document. Lastly, is the novella best understood as a commentary specific to Colombian history, or does it also have a more universal resonance?

2. **García Márquez as journalist:** Trace the thematic and ideological origins of *In Evil Hour* in the journalistic writing of García Márquez.

With regard to the influence of García Márquez's early years as a journalist on his literary production, Aníbal González states: "One could consider García Márquez's journalism a kind of archive or 'author's notebook,' a source of information about how García Márquez developed certain themes, as well as an index to his intellectual background and preferences" (63).

Consulting García Márquez's autobiography, *Living to Tell the Tale,* as well as other works that examine his journalistic production, such as Robert L. Sims's *The First García Márquez: A Study of His Journalistic Writing from 1948 to 1955,* reconstruct the author's early formation as a reporter and political activist. What events might have inspired *In Evil Hour*? Was García Márquez a firsthand witness to such events, or did he experience them indirectly? At what point did he develop the ideological position advocated in the novella? García Márquez is a great admirer of Ernest Hemingway, another journalist-novelist whose early work deals with violent conflicts (World War I, the Spanish civil war). Do you think reporters-turned-authors are more drawn to particular themes and/or particular techniques in their writing?

Philosophy and Ideas

An interesting way of analyzing a work of literature is to examine the philosophical or ideological ideas it embodies. *In Evil Hour* raises a number of interesting issues for you to explore. The most salient of these is the role of the socially committed writer. With its numerous references to writing and reading and its anonymous lampoonist threatening the oppressive status quo, what is *In Evil Hour* saying about the role of the writer in the world? The novella also raises the issue of class conflict. Which characters constitute the ruling class, and how are they represented? What does this indicate about the novella's political intent? Yet a third topic is the novella's representation of the Catholic Church. What is the role of the church in the town? How does Father Angel feel about his duties? Is the novella anticlerical, antireligious, anti-Catholic, or a combination of these positions? What are the ideological implications of this position?

Sample Topics:

1. **The power of the written word:** Discuss the impact of the lampoons with regard to the role of the socially committed writer.

Before returning to the passages dealing with the pasquinades, reflect on Wolfgang A. Luchting's observation about their political function: "The pen is mightier than the sword then? Certainly its effects can be. . . . The lampoons' function is social criticism, just as literature's is—in the eyes of Hispanoamerican writers, anyway. It is the on-going critique of a given political reality" (99). Given that the lampoons are personal, rather than political, attacks, how do they contribute to the armed insurrection that seems to be under way at the end of the novella? In what ways can the anonymous author of the lampoons be compared to authors of politically motivated literature? Is Robert Coover correct in his assertion that *In Evil Hour* is a "parable . . . on the truth-provoking power of art" (35)?

2. **Class conflict:** Analyze the novella as a commentary on social class and the relationship between economics and politics.

Reflecting on the representation of social class in the novella, consider the following observation by Ricardo Gutiérrez Mouat: "The town's quandary is economic in the full meaning of the term. . . . The destruction caused by César Montero reflects the abuse of power and corruption practiced by a class grown rich in the climate of violence which will safeguard its privileges at any cost" (22). How can the conflict in the text be understood as a class struggle? Is it possible to reconstruct the town's socioeconomic organization? Which characters represent the ruling class? Who represents the working class? If the basis of the town's tension is, in fact, rooted in class conflict, does *In Evil Hour* project a Marxist worldview?

3. **Anticlericalism:** Discuss the novel's critique of the Catholic Church.

Anticlericalism is the criticism of religious institutions, as opposed to faith itself. Conduct a close reading of the passages in which Father Angel appears or that describe what is taking place in the church. Besides Father Angel, which other characters represent the church or its ideological positions? How does the text describe the physical state of the actual church building? Why is the problem of the mouse infestation mentioned repeatedly, and what might be its symbolic significance with regard to the institutional church? Consider the following statement made by Father Angel to the Catholic Dames: "Our church is the poorest in the apostolic prefecture. The bells are cracked and the naves are full of mice, because my life has been used up imposing moral standards and good habits" (38–39). What is the novella suggesting about the priorities of the Catholic Church and what its true mission should be?

Form and Genre

For many scholars, the formal aspects of a literary work supersede all other critical concerns. When examining issues of form and genre, ask yourself how and why the author structured the text as he did. *In Evil Hour* is not told from a single perspective, nor is the action linear, as in a traditional novel. What impact does this have on the way we read the novella? With regard to genre, one interesting topic might be the novella's relationship to classical tragedy. Is there a dramatic structure to the story? If so, is there also a tragic hero?

Sample Topics:

1. **Narrative montage:** Analyze the effect of the shifting narrative on the novella.

Commenting on the division of *In Evil Hour* into numerous short scenes, Raymond Williams has noted: "The use of these

sections and montage techniques make the novel an experience for the reader of organizing a story, rather than following
a linear story line" (60). In film, montage refers to the use of a
series of short sequences or images, typically either to condense
time or to create symbolic meaning. For example, consider the
first two sections of the novella: Trinidad ends the first section
with a "nervous little laugh" about the lampoons, while the second section begins "three houses down" with César Montero
preparing to commit the murder of Pastor, provoked by the
lampoon of his wife's infidelity with the musician (4). How do
the two scenes combine to affect the reader's understanding of
what is happening in the town? Look for similar instances of
montage in the text. How is meaning created by the sequence
of scenes? What effect does the constant shifting of perspective
have on the reader's interpretation of events?

2. **Tragedy:** Draw parallels between *In Evil Hour* and classical
tragedy.

Referring to Sophocles' ancient Greek tragedy *Oedipus Rex* as
"the most important book of my life," García Márquez once
related the following story to an interviewer: "Once, when I was
at a place on the Colombian coast, I came across a very similar
situation to that of the drama of *Oedipus Rex,* and I thought
of writing something called *Oedipus the Mayor*" (Guibert 41).
How great are the affinities between *In Evil Hour* and classical
Greek tragedy? To investigate this question, you will want to
review the basic principles of the genre as they were defined
by Aristotle. There are a number of good Internet sources,
such as "Aristotle on Tragedy" in Augusta State University's
Humanities Handbook. If you have never studied *Oedipus Rex*
or any other ancient Greek tragedy (by, for example, Aeschy-
lus, Sophocles, or Euripides), it will be useful for you to read
one of these plays before you begin. Once you are comfortable
with the fundamental concepts of classical tragedy, return to
In Evil Hour and look for corresponding elements in the text.
Is there a tragic hero? If so, what is his fatal flaw (hamartia)?
What other dramatic conventions are present? Is there a sense

of catharsis at the end of the text? Could the novel be titled *Oedipus the Mayor*?

Language, Symbols, and Imagery

If questions of form and genre examine the broad structural framework of a text, then an analysis of language, style, or imagery is looking at the smaller building blocks within it. A good example is the journalistic style employed in the narration, which, unlike narrative montage, functions at the level of language. Language is also central to the humor in the text. How and why does García Márquez employ comic elements in such a dark tale? Still another stylistic choice you might want to explore is the use of literary allusions. Ask yourself both why the novella has so many instances of characters in the act of reading and what significance there might be to the specific text being read. Finally, the novella contains repeated images of decay, decomposition, and death. Search out the passages with such imagery and explore its effect on both the specific scene and, ultimately, on the work as a whole.

Sample Topics:

1. **Journalistic style:** Analyze the way in which García Márquez's use of journalistic technique informs the reader's understanding of the novella.

   Consider the following comment made by García Márquez about the novella: "You'll find that the language in . . . *In Evil Hour* is more concise, drier, direct, picked up right from journalism" (González Bermejo 10). What are the characteristics of journalistic writing? Which elements are emphasized, and which ones are suppressed? How does the novella differ from objective journalism in its narration of the events? Return to the most violent and disturbing scenes in the text. Why doesn't the narrative express sorrow, anger, or horror at the events that transpire? What effect does this absence of emotion have on the reader's perception and personal reaction? Why do you think García Márquez chose this kind of technique for the subject matter he was addressing?

2. **Humor:** Identify and analyze the instances of humor in the
novella.

As grim as *In Evil Hour* may be, the text has many humorous moments. Writing on the rhetorical strategies employed
by García Márquez for comic effect, David William Foster
has identified the use of "pejorative or satiric situations": "The
text sardonically defines an alternate order by virtue of its not
being what is explicitly described" (111). One such example
can be seen in the conversation between Father Angel and the
upper-class society of Catholic Dames:

> "Nineteen years ago, when they assigned me to this parish,
> there were eleven cases of public concubinage among the
> important families. Today there is only one left and I hope for
> a short time only."
>   "It's not for us," Rebeca Asís said. "But these poor people
> . . ." (38).

What is the "official order" as perceived by Father Angel and
Rebeca Asís? How do the phrases "important families" and
"these poor people" function to create the kind of "satiric situation" described by Foster? Identify similar passages in the
work, and analyze the way in which satiric situations are created. Which characters tend to represent the "official order,"
and which topics of conversation tend to serve as the basis for
the satire?

3. **Literary allusions:** Analyze the symbolic meaning of the
numerous instances of characters reading.

Return to the scenes in the novella in which characters make
reference to reading or writing. For example, Dr. Giraldo and
his wife, who are reading a Dickens novella, debate whether it is
"a long short story" or "a short novel" (86). Judge Arcadio states
that the mystery of the lampoons is "like reading detective

stories" (104). Such references have prompted Michael Bell to comment: "In themselves, these fictional self-allusions remain rather puzzling. [García] Márquez seems to be promoting a consciousness of the fiction as one inseparable, and yet distinct from the lives of the character" (37–38). Why are there so many references to reading in the text? What does this reflexivity suggest about the way the characters perceive the events around them? Does it add a level of psychological realism to the novella, or does it constantly remind us that we are reading a work of fiction?

4. **Images of decay:** Identify and analyze the novella's images of decay, disintegration, and physical decline.

There are numerous references to decay, such as the mouse infestation, the mayor's tooth, the dead cow in the river, and Don Sabas's diabetes. Return to the text and identify those passages describing states of physical disintegration. Why are there so many instances of decay in the text? Who and what are described this way? Who is trying to prevent the decay from taking place? Are they successful? If this imagery is symbolic, what is it meant to symbolize? Is this symbolism only negative, or does the novella suggest a positive consequence to this state of decomposition?

Compare and Contrast Essays

One of the most creative ways you can write about literature is to seek out the affinities that exist between the work in question and other texts. These comparisons can be made between two texts by the same author or between those of two different writers. If you pursue the former strategy, you will want to look for common narrative or thematic elements that tie the two works together. For example, you might want to study the roles played by characters from *In Evil Hour* who have a recurrent role in other works by García Márquez. Another possibility would be to analyze the treatment of either a concept, such as solitude, or a common cultural or historical context. One such possibility would be to study the representation of La Violencia in both *In Evil Hour* and *No One Writes to the Colonel.* If you want to compare *In Evil Hour* to a text written by a different author, you need to be sure there is a logical connection between the two works.

Sample Topics:

1. **Recurring characters in *In Evil Hour* and García Márquez's other works:** Trace the evolution of characters from *In Evil Hour* in other works by García Márquez.

   A number of the characters in the novella play an important role in other García Márquez texts. Don Sabas figures prominently in *No One Writes to the Colonel*. The wife of the late José Montiel appears in "Balthazar's Marvelous Afternoon" and is the protagonist of "Montiel's Widow." Trinidad and Mina, who work for Father Angel, are the principal characters in "Artificial Roses." Finally, the encounter between the dentist and the mayor is retold in "One of These Days." Read one or more of these short texts and compare the portrayal of the characters in question. What additional details are revealed about the characters? Do they play similar roles in both texts, or does each text portray them in a different light? If we were to map García Márquez's fictional universe, what would be the significance of these characters? Lastly, how is our reading of a text affected when we reencounter the same character from a previous work?

2. **La Violencia in *No One Writes to the Colonel* and *In Evil Hour:*** Compare the representation of Colombia's mid-20th-century political and social upheaval in the two novellas.

   Writing on García Márquez's portrayal of La Violencia, George R. McMurray has observed of *No One Writes to the Colonel* and *In Evil Hour* that "these two books in some respects constitute a single novel, both having the same anonymous pueblo as their setting and several of the same characters" ("Threat" 79). If you wanted to support or refute this opinion, you would want to begin by returning to both texts and identifying those passages dealing with politics. What are the social and political conflicts in each work? What is the nature of the relationship between the town's government, especially the mayor, and the other characters? Do both novellas portray La Violencia as an omnipresent reality in the life of the town, or is there a variance with regard to the citizens' collective awareness of the brutality that surrounds them? Finally, how does the focus on a single, sympathetic figure in *No One Writes to the Colonel* (as opposed to *In Evil Hour*'s multiple, more ambiguous characters, led by the mayor) affect the reader's feelings about the political situation in each work?

3. **García Márquez's *In Evil Hour* and Kafka's "In the Penal Colony":** Compare the representation of injustice in the two works.

García Márquez frequently cites Franz Kafka (1883–1924) as one of his most important influences, praising the Czech writer for writing "the wildest things, in the most natural way" (*El Manifiesto* 82). While best known for his novella *The Metamorphosis*, Kafka's "In the Penal Colony" is a similarly surreal short story about an unnamed town governed by a twisted system of justice. Read "In the Penal Colony," and consider points of comparison with *In Evil Hour*. What does Kafka seem to be attacking in his short story? How is this similar to or dissimilar from what García Márquez condemns in his novella? In what way is Kafka's officer like García Márquez's mayor? What role does official language play in each text's twisted concept of justice? How does each text use humor to achieve its ideological purpose? Writing on the "banality of evil" in the context of *In Evil Hour*, Michael Bell comments: "Tyranny not only enters the tissues of everyday life, it gets treated as if it were itself an everyday fact. Evil often arises from a moral blankness which it in turn exacerbates" (34). In what way could this statement be equally pertinent to both *In Evil Hour* and "In the Penal Colony"?

Bibliography and Online Resources for *In Evil Hour*

"Aristotle on Tragedy." *The Humanities Handbook*. 28 January 2001. 10 May 2009. <http://www.zellus=lit.com/upload/files/1/Aristotle%20%Tragedy.doc>.

Bell, Michael. *Gabriel García Márquez: Solitude and Solidarity*. New York: St. Martin's Press, 1993.

Bell-Villada, Gene H. *Gabriel García Márquez: The Man and His Work*. Chapel Hill: U of North Carolina P, 1990.

Coover, Robert. "The Gossip on the Wall." *Critical Essays on Gabriel García Márquez.* Ed. George R. McMurray. New York: Frederick Ungar, 1977. 33–36.

El Manifiesto. "Journey Back to the Source." *Conversations with Gabriel García Márquez.* Ed. Gene H. Bell-Villada. Jackson: U of Mississippi P, 2006. 79–92.

Foster, David William. "The Double Inscription of the Narrataire in 'Los funerales de la Mamá Grande." *Critical Essays on Gabriel García Márquez.* Ed. George R. McMurray. New York: Frederick Ungar, 1977. 102–13.

García Márquez, Gabriel. *In Evil Hour.* Trans. Gregory Rabassa. New York: Harper-Perennial, 1991.

González, Aníbal. "The Ends of the Text: Journalism in the Fiction of Gabriel García Márquez." *Gabriel García Márquez and the Powers of Fiction.* Ed. Julio Ortega. Austin: U of Texas P, 1988. 61–73.

González Bermejo, Ernesto. "And Now, Two Hundred Years of Solitude." *Conversations with Gabriel García Márquez.* Ed. Gene H. Bell-Villada. Jackson: U of Mississippi P, 2006. 3–30.

Guibert, Rita. "Gabriel García Márquez." *Conversations with Gabriel García Márquez.* Ed. Gene H. Bell-Villada. Jackson: U of Mississippi P, 2006. 31–58.

Gutiérrez Mouat, Ricardo. "The Economy of the Narrative Sign in *No One Writes to the Colonel* and *In Evil Hour.*" *Gabriel García Márquez and the Powers of Fiction.* Ed. Julio Ortega. Austin: U of Texas P, 1988. 17–33.

Hylton, Forrest. *Evil Hour in Colombia.* New York. Verso: 2006.

Janes, Regina. *Gabriel García Márquez: Revolutions in Wonderland.* Columbia: U of Missouri P, 1971.

Kafka, Franz. *Franz Kafka: The Complete Short Stories.* Ed. Nahum Glatzer. New York: Schocken Books, 1971.

Kirsner, Robert. "Four Colombian Novels of 'La Violencia.'" *Hispania* 49.1 (1966): 70–74.

Luchting, Wolfgang A. "Lampooning Literature in *La mala hora.*" Critical Essays on Gabriel García Márquez. Ed. George R. McMurray. New York. Frederick Ungar, 1977. 93–102.

McMurray, George R. *Gabriel García Márquez.* New York: Frederick Ungar, 1977.

———. "The Threat of 'La Violencia.'" *Critical Essays on Gabriel García Márquez.* Ed. George R. McMurray. New York: Frederick Ungar, 1977. 79–86.

Palacios, Marco. *Between Legitimacy and Violence: A History of Colombia 1875–2002.* Trans. Richard Stoller. Durham, NC: Duke UP, 2006.

Sims, Robert L. *The First García Márquez: A Study of His Journalistic Writing from 1948 to 1955.* Lanham, MD: UP of America, 1992.

Williams, Raymond. *Gabriel García Márquez.* Boston: Twayne, 1984.

ONE HUNDRED
YEARS OF SOLITUDE

READING TO WRITE

*O*NE *HUNDRED Years of Solitude* (1970; originally published in 1967 as *Cien años de soledad*) is not only Gabriel García Márquez's acknowledged masterpiece, it is also regarded by many as one of the great novels of the 20th century. The Chilean poet and Nobel laureate Pablo Neruda described it as "the greatest revelation in Spanish since the *Don Quixote* of Cervantes (Kennedy, "The Yellow Trolley" 62)." Pulitzer Prize–winning author William Kennedy praised it as "the first piece of literature since the Book of Genesis that should be required reading for the entire human race" ("The Great Novel of the Americas?" 11). Given the novel's lofty standing, you will have no difficulty in finding a broad range of critical sources; to the contrary, your greatest challenge may be in selecting a single essay topic out of the many elements within this rich literary work. As Raymond Williams states, *"One Hundred Years of Solitude* is an utter joy to read yet, paradoxically, an elusive book to write about"* (69). If you decide to take on this rewarding but challenging enterprise, the first step in this process is, of course, to reflect on those passages in the text that you found most compelling and conduct a close reading. One of the most unquestionably powerful of these scenes is the description of the massacre of the banana workers, told from the perspective of a young boy rescued by José Arcadio Segundo:

Many years later the child would still tell, in spite of people thinking he was a crazy old man, how José Arcadio Segundo had lifted him over his head and hauled him, almost in the air, as if floating on the terror of the crowd, toward a nearby street. The child's privileged position allowed him to see the moment that the wild mass was starting to get to the corner and the row of machine guns opened fire. Several voices shouted at the same time:

"Get down! Get down!"

The people in front had already done so, swept down by the wave of bullets. The survivors, instead of getting down, tried to get back to the small square, and the panic became a dragon's tail as one compact wave ran against another which was moving in the opposite direction, toward the other dragon's tail in the street across the way, where the machine guns were firing without cease. They were penned in, swirling about in a giant whirlwind that little by little was being reduced to its epicenter as the edges were systematically being cut off all around like an onion being peeled by the insatiable and methodical shears of the machine guns. The child saw a woman kneeling with her arms in the shape of a cross in an open space, mysteriously free of the stampede. José Arcadio Segundo put him up there at the moment he fell with his face bathed in blood, before the colossal troop wiped out the empty space, the kneeling woman, the light of the high, drought-stricken sky, and the whorish world where Úrsula Iguarán had sold so many little candy animals (305–306).

What you first notice in this passage is its point of view: The event is recounted by an old man who, as a boy, had been saved by José Arcadio Segundo. This framing device accomplishes several narrative goals. First, it contextualizes the massacre beyond the scope of the Buendía family saga into an act of historical infamy that has been repressed by those responsible: No one believes the "crazy old man." Second, it establishes José Arcadio Segundo as a heroic figure for having placed the life of an unknown child before his own, allowing the boy to live to tell the tale. Finally, the reader cannot help but be stunned by the description of human carnage through the eyes of a little boy "floating on the terror of the crowd."

Another notable aspect of this scene is its description of the rapid succession of events. Words like *wave, panic, swirling,* and *whirlwind* sweep the reader up in the chaotic spontaneity of the attack. The metaphorical references to a "dragon's tail" and a pair of "methodical shears" underscore the cruelty of the slaughter. Moreover, the comparison between the machine guns cutting down the innocent bystanders and the peeling of an onion adds a disturbingly mundane aspect to the scene, as if the murder of hundreds of innocent people were nothing more than a routine assignment for the perpetrators who proceed "systematically" with the slaughter with geometric precision.

The passage concludes with a shift from the panoramic view of the desperate multitude to a focus on the pitiless death of a single individual. Eerily detached in an almost filmic close-up, "mysteriously free of the stampede," a lone woman places a human face on the atrocity. Her kneeling posture connotes both a prayer for divine intervention and supplication to her murderers for mercy. Her "arms in the shape of a cross" evoke both the biblical Crucifixion and Francisco de Goya's iconic painting of political martyrdom, *The Third of May,* which portrays a Spanish partisan standing in a similar Christ-like position before a French firing squad. Her subsequent death becomes part of the apocalyptic end of the scene after the "colossal" (the word *colossal* evokes the Colossus, an enormous statue from the ancient world, and perhaps another Goya painting of a monstrous giant who stalks the countryside) military force has "wiped out" not only humanity but, indeed, nature ("the light of the high, drought-stricken sky") itself. The narrative also connects the slaughter with the destiny of the Buendía clan. First, it leaves the fate of José Arcadio Segundo in doubt. The reader is uncertain whether the character, who has fallen "with his face bathed in blood," is dead or alive. Perhaps even more poignant are the final words that refer back to an earlier, simpler time when José Arcadio Segundo's grandmother Úrsula first sold confections to help support the young Buendía family. In the wake of the horrendous crime that the reader has just witnessed, that innocent time is now forever lost, replaced by a "whorish world" of greed, corruption, and brutality.

As much as this passage offers points of departure for a range of essays—narrative technique, political oppression, the character of José Arcadio Segundo, the theme of destiny—it only scratches the surface of the topics you may wish to explore in *One Hundred Years of Solitude.* The direction you choose will ultimately depend on your own close reading of the text, your ability to synthesize your findings, and the thesis that you are able to formulate from these initial steps.

TOPICS AND STRATEGIES
Themes

If you are thinking about writing a thematic essay on *One Hundred Years of Solitude*, you have one obvious topic—the one mentioned in the novel's title. Whether described as solitude, isolation, or loneliness, it is unquestionably the most widely discussed theme in the work and one that will offer you no shortage of textual or critical material. On the other hand, there are numerous other themes in *One Hundred Years of Solitude* that would also make for excellent essay topics. Incest is another of the most prevalent themes in *One Hundred Years of Solitude*. The novel makes constant reference to the incestuous relationships within the Buendía family and the generational preoccupation with the consequences of this forbidden love. Yet another thematic essay could be written on the question of fate, not what the characters strive for, but their inevitable destiny. Still another theme seen in many of García Márquez's works is that of old age as the ultimate, unavoidable destiny. This list is, of course, far from definitive. Ask yourself what the novel is saying about the human condition. What themes stand out to you? Where in the text are these themes most prevalent? Return to those passages, and try to determine not only what the novel is saying about the theme but also how and why it treats the theme the way it does.

Sample Topics:

1. **Solitude:** Why is the novel entitled *One Hundred Years of Solitude*? Analyze the development of this theme throughout the text.

   Should you choose this topic, your first task will be to define the word *solitude* as it is conceived in the novel. Is it simply isolation or loneliness, or is it more existential in nature? You must ask, moreover, whether the theme is more prevalent in certain characters or is paradoxically a collective state of solitude: For example, does it exist among the members of the Buendía family or among the residents of Macondo, the "races condemned to one hundred years of solitude" (417), as lamented in the novel's last sentence? Regina Janes concludes that the text "represents solitude not as a psychological state but as a physical condition and reminds of it on every page" (61). Given Janes's assessment, you may want to limit your analysis of the solitude theme to a particular aspect of the novel. You could, for example, write about the solitude of old age or the solitude of a loveless existence. Perhaps you want to explore the solitude of a single character, such as Amaranta or José Arcadio Segundo. Whichever aspect of the theme you select, your close reading should focus on those passages where a character or characters are isolated or isolate themselves. What causes the character to seek a solitary existence? Is it a personality trait or caused by external factors? Besides physical isolation, in what other ways is solitude represented? Do characters ever escape from their solitude and return, at least for a time, to a communal existence? What allows them to do so? Finally, thinking of the final line in the novel, does the solitude theme have a broader meaning? García Márquez concluded his Nobel Prize acceptance speech with the following words:

> ... It is not too late to undertake the creation of a minor utopia: a new and limitless utopia for life wherein no one can decide for others how they are to die, where love can really be true and happiness possible, where the lineal generations of one hundred years of solitude will have at last and for ever a second chance on earth (211).

In the context of the author's statement, in what way does the solitude theme take on a broader, more universal significance?

2. **Incest:** Trace the theme of incest and its consequences throughout the novel.

Rubén Pelayo argues that, along with solitude, "incest comprises [one of] the central themes of *One Hundred Years of Solitude*" (101). Which members of the Buendía family engage in incestuous behavior? Return to the beginning and the end of the novel where Úrsula refuses to have sex with her cousin-turned-husband for fear they will "suffer the shame of breeding iguanas" or have a child with "a pig's tail" (20). How are these fears ultimately borne out? Thinking about the cultural taboo on incest and its manifestation in ancient Greek tragedies such as Sophocles' *Oedipus Rex* and Euripides' *Hippolytus*, how does García Márquez's treatment of the incest theme resemble or differ from these classical texts? Is the text concerned literally with incest, or does this theme have metaphorical or allegorical implications?

3. **Fate:** What does the novel have to say about whether human beings are in control of their own destinies?

Fate is one of the most prevalent themes in *One Hundred Years of Solitude.* In the opening line of the novel, the text plays with the idea of fate in placing Colonel Aureliano Buendía before a firing squad that will never shoot him. Some 400 pages later, however, the reader, along with Aureliano Babilonia, discovers that "fate was written in Melquíades' parchments" (415) and that "everything written in them was unrepeatable since time immemorial" (417). Look for passages in the novel where predestined events are discussed (such as the birth of a child with a pig's tale). What is the novel saying about fate? Is it unavoidable? If not, is it at least possible for human beings to understand their destiny? Is it correct to talk about individual destiny, or is the text suggesting that the fate of humanity is inexorably intertwined?

4. **Old age:** Many of the characters in the novel live to an advanced, sometimes mythical, age. What does the novel have to say about the way in which human beings deal with the inevitable process of growing old and confronting death?

Old age is a common theme in many of García Márquez's works, such as *No One Writes to the Colonel, The Autumn of the Patriarch, Love in the Time of Cholera,* and *The General in His Labyrinth.* None of these texts, however, has as many portraits of old age as does *One Hundred Years of Solitude.* Úrsula; her husband, José Arcadio Buendía; their son, the famous Colonel Aureliano; their daughter, the tragic Amaranta; and the prostitute Pilar Ternera, who mothers the next generation of

Buendías, all reach an advanced age. The way each of them experiences these later years, though, is quite distinct. Return to the parts of the novel that describe how the characters confront this period of life. Do they remain active figures in the novel, or do they withdraw from life? Is their physical decline reflected in a mental one as well? What attitude does each exhibit in dealing with the inevitability of death? How are they treated by the younger people around them? What is the novel ultimately saying about old age?

Characters

The characters in *One Hundred Years of Solitude* are both numerous and meticulously woven into a complex intergenerational tapestry. Indeed, one of the challenges for most first-time readers of the novel is to keep track of the many same- or similarly named Buendías. Choosing a single character to trace throughout the course of the book, however, can be an extremely rewarding exercise. There are obvious choices, such as Colonel Aureliano Buendía or his mother, Úrsula, the long-lived matriarch of the clan. There are also many other figures in the novel who, if not as overarching as the two already mentioned, are no less intriguing. The ethereal Remedios the Beauty, who floats away, is one of the most original and memorable personages in all of García Márquez's oeuvre. The diametric opposite of the airy Remedios is her morbid great aunt, Amaranta, the embodiment of bitterness and the archetype of the unhappy spinster. Finally, you might choose the magical Gypsy Melquíades, who literally haunts the entire story and whose magical books reveal the destiny of the Buendías. The list of other characters for potential essays could go on for pages. If you want to write this type of essay, a good rule of thumb would be for you to think about which characters you personally found most engaging. Return to the parts of the book where that character appears. As you conduct your close reading, try to construct a physical and psychological portrait based on what the character says and does, as well as how he or she is perceived by other characters. What does your character want most? Why does she or he achieve or not achieve this goal? How do his or her actions affect the other characters in the novel? Finally, how does the existence of this character affect the novel as a whole?

Sample Topics:

1. **Colonel Aureliano Buendía:** Examine the role in the novel of García Márquez's best-known character.

Colonel Aureliano Buendía is a legendary figure whose name reappears as an element of fictionalized history in texts such as *No One Writes to the Colonel* and "Big Mama's Funeral." As the character named in the celebrated opening sentence of *One Hundred Years of Solitude*—"Many years later, as he faced a firing squad, Colonel Aureliano Buendía was to remember that distant afternoon when his father took him to discover ice" (1)—he is usually understood as the novel's protagonist. One interesting question you will want to ask, as does Rubén Pelayo, is whether the character is best understood less as the novel's hero and more as "the leading thread of the plot" (92). Pelayo elaborates:

> Some readers may choose him as the central protagonist of the novel, although he dies—of old age, defeated, without any honors, ignored by the crowds and in complete solitude—while the novel continues. His own family is not aware that he is dead until the next day at eleven in the morning. His whole life seems like one big failure. He loses all the wars he fights, and none of his eighteen sons continues his bloodline (92).

Is Aureliano Buendía the hero? Is he better understood as an antihero? If he is neither of these, what is his role in the text? Why is it significant that he is always referred to as *Colonel Aureliano Buendía*? What might the novel be saying about our notion of heroes? What particular meaning might the inclusion of the military title, appropriated by the character at the outset of his first revolt, have with regard to Latin American history? Isolated by power, his inability to find love, and finally old age, can the character be seen as the embodiment of the novel's solitude theme? Lastly, what is the significance of the small gold fish figurines whose crafting becomes the colonel's obsession in his later years?

2. **Úrsula Iguarán:** Write an essay discussing the omnipresence of Macondo's seemingly ageless matriarch and her importance in *One Hundred Years of Solitude.*

When discussing the implausibly long life of Úrsula's character, García Márquez told an interviewer: "When you work it out she must be 200 years old. While I was writing *One Hundred Years,* I realized frequently that she had lived too long, and I tried to have her die. However, she continued. I always needed her for something" (Dreifus 122). By the author's own admission, Úrsula is, in many ways, the most pivotal character in the novel. Why does García Márquez attribute her such a crucial role? What is Úrsula's principal goal or desire? Does she have a fatal flaw? What does Úrsula's resilience and quiet courage in contrast to the ambitious and profligate men who surround her suggest about the reality of a woman's position in a patriarchal society? Can it be argued that Úrsula, rather than her sons or grandsons, is actually the novel's true protagonist in her capacity as the figurative (and perhaps literal) mother of Macondo?

3. **Remedios the Beauty:** Write an essay on this most original and enigmatic character.

Remedios the Beauty is unquestionably a unique character in all of García Márquez's fiction. A young woman "becalmed in a magnificent adolescence, more and more impenetrable to formality, more and more indifferent to malice and suspicion, happy in her own world of simple realities" (229), this ethereal character's unexplained disappearance by floating up into the sky underscores her magical opacity. Given the mystery that surrounds Remedios, what do you think is the purpose of her character in the novel? What is the significance of her sobriquet beyond its literal meaning? What is the purpose of her magical disappearance? What aspect of the human experience might be embodied in her character?

4. **Amaranta:** Analyze this complex and tragic character.

If solitude and incestuous passion are indeed the central themes in *One Hundred Years of Solitude,* perhaps no character embodies both more than the lonely spinster Amaranta. D. P. Gallagher observes of Colonel Aureliano Buendía's sister that "incestuous leanings certainly spell an especially bitter fruitlessness and loneliness, for it is hard for her to share her passions with anyone" (161). What is the source of Amaranta's solitude? How are her passions frustrated? Return to the sections of the novel dealing with Amaranta's rivalry with her adopted sister, Rebeca, over Pietro Crespi, and her incestuous flirtation with her nephew Aureliano José. Is Amaranta's unhappiness caused by fate or her own actions? What is the significance of the burn on her hand and the black bandage she wears throughout her life? Why does she spend the latter part of her life weaving her funeral shroud? What does Amaranta's character suggest about the fate of many women in a patriarchal society? Is Arnold M. Penuel right in seeing in Amaranta a critique of Hispanic cultural values that "demythologizes . . . a dark side to the cult of virginity" (558)?

5. **Melquíades:** Examine the role of this mystical figure who dies in the first chapter but whose presence persists until the final page of the novel.

Michael Bell sees Melquíades as not only important to *One Hundred Years of Solitude* but key in understanding the entirety of García Márquez's oeuvre:

> Artistic self-consciousness and the solitude theme are combined in Melquíades. He seems partly a trickster yet also a reminder of the lonely God of *In Evil Hour.* Whereas the divine Creator was necessarily lonely, Melquíades as a human being adopts his solitude for a creative purpose (68).

As you reread the principal parts of the novel dealing with Melquíades—as a living character in chapter 1 to his supernatural return to save Macondo from the insomnia plague and as the spirit inhabiting the Buendía home up to the final cataclysmic page—consider his allegorical meaning in the text. Is he a godlike figure? Is he the embodiment of the novelist? What other importance does he have in the saga of the Buendías?

History and Context

While *One Hundred Years of Solitude* is a fictional work, it is frequently hailed as a powerful portrait of Latin America's historical experience in the 19th and early 20th centuries. Several of the events in the story clearly refer to actual historical events. Should you choose to write an essay on history and context, your first step must be to familiarize yourself with the broader period as well as the details of the specific incident you plan to explore. One such topic is the arrival of the North American banana plantation, which is quite obviously based on the exploitative practices of the United Fruit Company in Colombia and other areas of Latin America. A second historical reality fictionalized in the campaigns of Colonel Aureliano Buendía is Colombia's turn-of-the-century civil conflict known as the Thousand Days War. A different kind of essay on context would be an examination of the effects of industrialization—the introduction of new technologies such as the train and the automobile—on Latin American society. Your chief concern when writing on one of these or other essays relating to history and context is to keep your primary focus on the literature, not the history. While you need to be sure about your historical "facts," your essay needs to explore how the novel takes those facts and transforms them into fiction. Whose view of the events does the text represent as "truth"? What does it want the reader to conclude about the history in question? Perhaps most important, what formal elements does it use to achieve its desired vision of the past?

Sample Topics:

1. **The United Fruit Company and U.S. imperialism:** Study the tragic episode of the "gringo" banana company and the slaughter of the plantation workers in the context of the United Fruit Company's exploitation of Latin America in the early 20th century and the actual 1928 massacre.

Eduardo Posada-Carbó has observed that "critics and historians have accepted as history García Márquez's rendition of the events of the 1928 strike, and the impact of the banana industry on the region, in general" (399). In refuting the veracity of many of the fictional aspects of what he terms the *bananeras* (events related to the banana companies), Posada-Carbó raises an interesting question about the relationship between history and fiction. Read Posada-Carbó's article and other historians' work on the subject, and then reread the episode in the novel. How does García Márquez alter historical fact? How does the text's treatment of history affect the reader's understanding of the events and those responsible for them? Conversely, why do you think García Márquez chose this particular historical event for inclusion in the novel?

2. **The Thousand Days War:** Analyze Colonel Aureliano Buendía's 32 futile uprisings in the context of this turn-of-the-century Colombian conflict.

If you select this topic, you will need to begin by conducting some basic research in the history of the conflict in question. A good starting point is Marco Palacios's *Between Legitimacy and Violence: A History of Colombia, 1875–2002.* Once you have familiarized yourself with the history of the war, return to the novel and reread the passages involving Colonel Aureliano Buendía's military campaigns. Pay special attention to the character's comments on why he believes he must rise up against the government. What is the cause of the war? Is Colonel Aureliano Buendía justified in his rebellion? Why does he go to war so many times? What do you think the text is suggesting about the Thousand Days War's impact on Colombian history? Based on your research, is García Márquez's historical portrayal accurate, or has he altered the facts? If so, to what end do you think he changes the story of the war? Could the events of 1899–1902 described in the novel have any allegorical relationship to events in modern Colombian history?

3. **Industrialization and technology:** What is the novel saying about society's belief in progress through technological advancements—particularly in Latin America?

Sandra M. Boschetto observes: "In *One Hundred Years* the assumptions of the industrial revolution emerge as just that—a set of assumptions" (62). José Arcadio Buendía "laments" upon realizing that his newly founded town is completely isolated, "We're going to rot our lives away here without receiving the benefits of science" (13). What are the new technologies introduced into Macondo during the course of the novel, and what impact do they have? Are these inventions and innovations shown to be beneficial or harmful to the community? Return to a passage relating to new technologies, such as the curiosities brought by Melquíades and the Gypsies at the beginning of the story or Aureliano Triste's railroad. What do you make of Boschetto's assertion that "With the appearance of advanced science, the spirit of social initiative in Macondo disappears" and, consequently, that "Faith in progress is betrayed" (63)?

Philosophy and Ideas

Essays dealing with the philosophy and ideas that are explored in *One Hundred Years of Solitude* can present you with both considerable challenges and considerable rewards as a writer. The challenge lies in reconstructing an understanding of the novel's philosophical or ideological position based on the textual evidence. This can be complicated, as it requires you to make value judgments about the characters who voice such views. Is the character in question (including the narrator) reliable? What conclusions can you draw from a negative character who advocates in favor of a particular idea? What if two protagonists have opposing positions? While such issues can be problematic, and may sometimes oblige you to conclude that the text is ambiguous on certain points, there is a tremendous sense of satisfaction to be had from exploring the "big ideas" underlying a work of literature. In this case, one of the most provocative concepts that you can study is the way the novel challenges our widely held concept of linear time. Does history always move forward in the novel, or is there a sense that time is cyclical? A less metaphysical but no less thought-provoking idea in the text is the absurdity and uselessness of warfare. Colonel Aureliano Buendía fights, and loses, 32 wars. What is gained from his years of combat?

Sample Topics:

1. **A linear versus circular notion of time:** Trace the flow of narrative time in the novel. How does it challenge the traditional Western concept of temporality?

Time does not move linearly in *One Hundred Years of Solitude*, as is suggested by a flashback in the opening sentence on the part of a character who has not yet been born: "Many years later, as he faced the firing squad, Colonel Aureliano Buendía was to remember that distant afternoon when his father took him to discover ice" (1). Commenting on this aspect of "García Márquez's treatment of time," one early review noted: "The future, is thus history, the end is the beginning, and the reader is tempted to start again" ("Orchids and Bloodlines" 96). Where in the text is circular representation of narrative time most prevalent? How does it challenge the reader's expectations about the way the plot will unfold? In turn, in what way does this circular structure oblige the reader to reconsider traditional Western assumptions about time as a forward progression? On the other hand, do you agree with Regina Janes, who argues that despite its "repetitive, cyclic pattern . . . in *One Hundred Years of Solitude*, time is linear, the town passes through chronological phases that reduce it to the nothingness from which it began, everyone dies (or disappears), and the book ends" (65)? Does the novel, in fact, imply that time, while suggesting repetition, remains essentially linear?

2. **The futility of war:** What does the novel, especially the fruitless military campaigns of Colonel Aureliano Buendía, imply about the pointlessness of war?

Having survived the massacre of the banana company workers, José Arcadio Segundo has a revelation:

> Years before Colonel Aureliano Buendía had spoken to him about the fascination of war and had tried to show it to him

> with countless examples drawn from his own experience. He
> had believed him. But the night the soldiers looked at him
> without seeing him while he thought about the tension of the
> past few months, the misery of jail, the panic of the station,
> and the train loaded with dead people, José Arcadio Segundo
> reached the conclusion that Colonel Aureliano Buendía was
> nothing but a faker or an imbecile (312).

Based on this citation, why does José Arcadio Segundo repudiate his grandfather's beliefs? Return to the passages dealing
with Colonel Aureliano Buendía's military exploits. Are these
conflicts justified? Does the text distinguish between fighting a
just war and an unjust war, or is it a broad rejection of all armed
conflicts?

Form and Genre

As interesting as its content is, the most critically celebrated aspect of
One Hundred Years of Solitude is almost certainly its form. Questions
of form and genre refer, of course, to the way a text is understood with
respect to other works of literature and within the history of literary
movements. In the case of García Márquez's masterpiece, the clearest
example of this type of topic is its relationship to and use of magic realism. An essay on the novel in the context of magic realism will leave you
with no shortage of critical sources; in fact, one of your most difficult
tasks with this topic will be to sort out the massive amount of material
that has been written on the subject. A somewhat less studied topic in
the area of form and genre is the novel's relation to epic literature. How
is the epic defined as a genre, and in what ways does *One Hundred Year
of Solitude* conform to and differ from that definition?

Sample Topics:

1. **Magic realism:** Analyze the way in which magic realism is
   incorporated into the novel.

   Perhaps no other work of modern literature has been so closely
   associated with magic realism as has been *One Hundred Years
   of Solitude.* To write this essay, you will have to begin by learning more about magic realism. You might begin by reading the

first two chapters of Maggie Ann Bowers's *Magic(al) Realism,* which define and trace the evolution of the genre. Once you feel confident with your understanding of the term, return to the novel and try to identify as many instances as you can of magic realism. What common traits do they share? How do the characters in the novel react to these supernatural phenomena? Is the reader's action the same or different? What effect do these repeated instances of the fantasy-turned-reality have on the reader's expectations? What does this suggest about the Western tradition of rationalism and alternative philosophical worldviews? What did García Márquez, intimating about the cultural component of magic realism, mean when he stated, "I am a realist . . . because I believe in Latin America everything is possible, everything is real" (Bowers 92)?

2. **Epic:** Explore García Márquez's novel in the context of this ancient genre.

Most students of literature first consciously encounter the epic genre when studying Homer's *Iliad* and *Odyssey.* Other works from the Bible to *Beowulf* to John Milton's *Paradise Lost* also fall under the classification: a long narrative beginning in medias res (in the middle of the story) that recounts the events in the life of a hero, a family, or a community. Many epics contain supernatural elements. Conduct some research to find out more about the genre. What is the purpose of an epic? What is it meant to explain or to illustrate? Is it merely a story about the past, or is it intended to have significance to the readers of its time as well? Next, consider how well *One Hundred Years of Solitude* fits into your definition of epic literature? Who is the hero? What is the community? How do the text's magic realist elements compare with earlier examples of the genre? Is the novel a true epic, or is it better understood, like *Don Quixote,* as an epic parody, as Michael Bell comments: "Profiting from Cervantes' example, Márquez has built a similar ambivalence into his tale more consciously and thematically" (67). Finally, what "message" does it have for 21st-century readers? Is it a universal epic, or is it better understood as an epic of Latin America?

Language, Symbols, and Imagery

If genre and form examine literature at a broad level, issues of language, form, and imagery look at the underlying structures, the proverbial building blocks of the text. This type of essay is dependent, more than any other, on your ability to read the text for slight nuances in connotation. It also allows you to study the text in a creative fashion as you define the potential relationships between the images and symbols that form the novel's metaphorical meaning. One interesting essay would be to analyze the symbolic meaning of character names and how these names correspond to the characters' role in the story. You could also select a single symbol that plays a key function in the development of the narrative. One possibility is to explore the allegorical nature of the Gypsy Melquíades's cryptic books with regard to the relationship between literature and life. With either of these symbols, as well as with any of the many others found in the novel, you should begin by searching out every reference you can in the text. Where does the object come from and what ultimately happens to it? Which characters and events are associated with the symbol in question? Most important, what concept, idea, or theme seems to be embodied in the symbol?

Sample Topics:

1. **Symbolism of character names:** Analyze the names of the character in relation to their underlying semantic meanings?

    Like other writers, García Márquez frequently gives his characters names that are symbolic of their personalities or their roles in the story. Even if you have but a rudimentary knowledge of Spanish (and a good Spanish-English dictionary), you might choose to explore the symbolism of character names in *One Hundred Years of Solitude*. For example, *Aureliano* seems to be derived from *aureola*, the Spanish word for "halo." What might this suggest about Colonel Buendía? *José*, the Spanish equivalent of *Joseph*, is a biblical name meaning "increase" or "may God multiply." *Arcadio* is the adjectival form of the mythical Arcadia, a rustic utopia of shepherds and farmers living in ignorant bliss. How might this be a commentary on the founder of Macondo, José Arcadio Buendía, or on his decadent, carefree great-grandson, José Arcadio Segundo, who grows

wealthy because of his livestock's amazing capacity to reproduce? Search for the symbolism of other character names such
as Úrsula, Amaranta, and Remedios, and explore the possible
related character traits. To what extent does the reader's understanding of this kind of symbolism affect or even prejudice his
or her understanding of the characters and their actions?

2. **Melquíades's books:** Write an essay on the symbolism of
   Melquíades's mystical writings, or, in the words of critic Scott
   Simpkins, why *"One Hundred Years of Solitude* is 'about' a book
   titled *One Hundred Years of Solitude"* (156).

Literary reflexivity—when a text comments on its own status
as literature—is a concept dating back to Miguel de Cervantes's
Don Quixote (1605). García Márquez appropriates the idea of
reflexivity to *One Hundred Years of Solitude* in the form of
the writings of the Gypsy Melquíades. These cryptic Sanskrit
documents—locked away for 100 years before José Arcadio
Segundo, and later Aureliano Babilonia, undertake the task of
deciphering them—are revealed in the final pages of the text
to be the story of the Buendía family—the novel the reader is
about to finish. Lois Marie Jaeck observes:

> Aureliano's reading of Melquíades's manuscript within the
> book that his family has been living (and which its author has
> been writing) is the moment in which the living book (the
> Buendía race) and the book (Melquíades's manuscript) rec-
> ognize themselves as doubles, causing the living presences to
> which the written one refers to lose themselves in a play of
> reflected doubles, and to leave an abyss which must be sup-
> planted by the infinite "redoubling" of interpretations about
> the event of "doubling" itself (51).

What does Jaeck mean by "a play of reflected doubles," and
what is its implication for the act of reading the novel? Return
to the passages where Melquíades is first seen writing, when
José Arcadio Segundo first unlocks the Gypsy's room and
begins to translate, and especially when Aureliano Babilonia

brings both the translation and the novel to their simultaneous conclusion. As you conduct your close reading of these passages, reflect on that exercise in relation to the translations performed by José Arcadio Segundo and Aureliano Babilonia. How are your goals and challenges as a reader similar to theirs? Thinking about the interrelationship between the author, the text, and the reader, what allegory might be constructed around Melquíades's manuscripts? How can it be said that the intentional reflexivity in *One Hundred Years of Solitude* holds true for every work of literature?

Compare and Contrast Essays

Compare and contrast essays are frequently among the most popular choices for essay topics as they provide the writer with an almost limitless number of possibilities. The danger with these kinds of essays is, however, that they run the risk of making a comparison for its own sake rather than with the goal of offering greater insight into the work in question. Comparing *One Hundred Years of Solitude* to Miguel de Cervantes's *Don Quixiote* because they are frequently cited as the two greatest novels written in Spanish is, for example, a rather flimsy premise for a comparison. When you are considering potential topics, you need to think about which specific element you want to compare. For example, perhaps you could compare *One Hundred Years of Solitude* with *The House of the Spirits* by Isabel Allende, another major Latin American writer who uses magic realism, in this case, to recount the epic story of a family's rise and fall. Another type of comparison you might pursue would be between elements common to *One Hundred Years of Solitude* and other García Márquez texts. While such an analysis might involve themes, historical context, or stylistic elements, one interesting possibility would be to examine the iconic town of Macondo as it is represented in other novels and short stories.

Sample Topics:

1. ***One Hundred Years of Solitude* and *The House of the Spirits*:** Compare García Márquez's novel with Isabel Allende's magic realist epic of a Latin American family.

   Chilean writer Isabel Allende's 1982 best-selling novel has frequently been compared to *One Hundred Years of Solitude* for its multigenerational story and magic realist idiom. Some critics have argued that Allende's novel is far too derivative of *One Hundred Years of Solitude,* while others, such as P. Gabrielle Foreman distinguish its feminist voice and an "ultimate allegiance to the political and historical [that] marks her text's difference from García Márquez's" (294). Read Allende's novel and compare it to *One Hundred Years of Solitude.* You might examine the way magic realism is manifested in each work. Another possibility would be to compare two characters such as the two matriarchs, Clara Trueba and Úrsula Buendía, or the two problematic patriots, Senator Esteban Trueba and Colonel Aureliano Buendía. Finally, you could choose to compare a thematic or philosophical aspect. Is Foreman correct when she says that, unlike García Márquez, Allende "both feminizes and politicizes the magical mode" (294)? Whatever direction you choose to take with this comparison, remember that you are not attempting to decide which is the "superior" novel but rather what light the reading of one novel can shed upon the understanding of the other.

2. **Macondo in *One Hundred Years of Solitude* and other works:** Compare the mythical town of the Buendía family with its reincarnations in García Márquez's other works.

Although the mythical Macondo is most closely associated with *One Hundred Years of Solitude,* that is neither the first nor the only García Márquez text in which the town is featured. The setting for the novella *Leaf Storm* and for short stories including "Big Mama's Funeral" and "Monologue of Isabel Watching It Rain in Macondo," the town is also referenced in the novella *In Evil Hour.* Finally, one may speak of the many nameless towns, such as the village in *No One Writes to the Colonel,* that bear great resemblance to Macondo. An interesting exercise would be to reread passages in *One Hundred Years of Solitude* that describe the town and its history and then compare your findings with the representation of Macondo in one or more of these other texts. A good starting point for your essay is the essay "García Márquez: From Aracataca to Macondo," written

by the celebrated Peruvian novelist Mario Vargas Llosa. What
is the inspiration for the town? Is Macondo the same in every
text, or are there noticeable differences? How, if at all, are the
inhabitants connected to the characters and events in *One
Hundred Years of Solitude*? What is the artistic value of setting
so many texts in a single place? Finally, should Macondo's inclusion in so many works be understood primarily as a unifying
literary device, or does it also have an allegorical significance
for the historical and cultural experience of Latin America?

Bibliography for *One Hundred Years of Solitude*

Bell, Michael. *Gabriel García Márquez: Solitude and Solidarity.* New York: St.
Martin's Press, 1993.

Boschetto, Sandra M. "*One Hundred Years of Solitude* in Interdisciplinary
Courses." *Approaches to Teaching García Márquez's* One Hundred Years of
Solitude. Ed. María Elena Valdés and Mario J. Valdés. New York: Modern
Language Association of America, 1990. 57–68.

Bowers, Maggie Ann. *Magic(al) Realism.* New York: Routledge, 2004.

Dreifus, Claudia. "*Playboy* Interview: Gabriel García Márquez." *Conversations
with Gabriel García Márquez.* Ed. Gene H. Bell-Villada. Jackson: U of Mississippi P, 2006. 93–132.

Foreman, P. Gabrielle. "Past-on Stories: History and the Magically Real, Morrison and Allende on Call." *Magical Realism: Theory, History, Community.*
Ed. Lois Parkinson Zamora and Wendy B. Faris. Durham, NC: Duke UP,
1995. 285–303.

Gallagher, D. P. *Modern Latin American Literature.* London: Oxford University
Press, 1973.

García Márquez, Gabriel. *One Hundred Years of Solitude.* Trans. Gregory
Rabassa. New York: HarperPerrenial, 2006.

———. "The Solitude of Latin America: Nobel Address 1982." Trans. Richard
Cardwell. *Gabriel García Márquez: New Readings.* Ed. Bernard McGuirk
and Richard Cardwell. Cambridge: Cambridge UP, 1987. 207–11.

Jaeck, Lois Marie. "*Cien años de soledad*: The End of the Book and the Beginning
of Writing." *Hispania* 74.1 (1991): 50–56.

Janes, Regina. *Gabriel García Márquez: Revolutions in Wonderland.* Columbia:
U of Missouri P, 1981.

"Orchids and Bloodlines." *Time* 16 March 1970: 96.

Kennedy, William. Introduction. "The Great Novel of the Americas?" *One Hundred Years of Solitude*. By Gabriel García Márquez. New York: Harper-Perennial, 2006. 8–12.

———. "The Yellow Trolley Car in Barcelona: An Interview." *Conversation with Gabriel García Márquez*. Ed. Gene H. Bell-Villada. Jackson: U of Mississippi P, 2006. 59–78.

Palacios, Marco. *Between Legitimacy and Violence: A History of Colombia, 1875–2002*. Trans. Richard Stoller. Durham, NC: Duke UP, 2006.

Pelayo, Rubén. *Gabriel García Márquez: A Critical Companion*. Westport, CT: Greenwood Press, 2001.

Penuel, Arnold M. "Death and the Maiden: The Demythologization of Virginity in García Márquez's *Cien años de soledad*." *Hispania* 66.4 (1983): 552–560.

Posada-Carbó, Eduardo. "Fiction as History: The *Bananeras* and Gabriel García Márquez's *One Hundred Years of Solitude*." *Journal of Latin American Studies* 3.2 (1998): 395–414.

Simpkins, Scott. "Sources of Magic Realism/Supplements to Realism in Contemporary Latin American Literature." *Magical Realism: Theory, History, Community*. Ed. Lois Parkinson Zamora and Wendy B. Faris. Durham, NC: Duke UP, 1995. 145–59.

Vargas Llosa, Mario. "García Márquez: From Aracataca to Macondo." *Gabriel García Márquez*. Ed. Harold Bloom. New York: Chelsea House, 1989. 5–19.

Williams, Raymond. *Gabriel García Márquez*. Boston: Twayne, 1984.

"A VERY OLD MAN WITH ENORMOUS WINGS"

READING TO WRITE

IN ADDITION to being one of the best known of Gabriel García Márquez's many short stories, "A Very Old Man with Enormous Wings" ("Un señor muy viejo con unas alas enormes," 1968) is also one of the most frequently cited examples in all literature of the genre known as magic realism. While you very well may want to examine the magic realist aspect of "A Very Old Man with Enormous Wings," you will also find numerous other potential essay topics to explore in this rich text. As you consider the many possibilities, begin by choosing a passage for a close reading. As always, you should give special attention not just to what happens in the passage, but also the way the events are related. Think about the way the author's choice of words creates a particular tone and the impression with which the reader is left with regard both to the miraculous phenomenon and the people who experience it. For example, consider the following section of the story that takes place shortly after the strange visitor is first discovered:

> On the following day everyone knew that a flesh-and-blood angel was held captive in Pelayo's house. Against the judgment of the wise neighbor woman, for whom angels in those times were the fugitive survivors of a celestial conspiracy, they did not have the heart to club him to death. Pelayo watched over him all afternoon from the kitchen, armed with his bailiff's club, and before going to bed he dragged him out of the mud and

locked him up with the hens in the wire chicken coop. In the middle of the night, when the rain had stopped, Pelayo and Elisenda were still killing crabs. A short time afterward the child woke up without a fever and with a desire to eat. Then they felt magnanimous and decided to put the angel on a raft with fresh water and provisions for three days and leave him to his fate on the high seas. But when they went out into the courtyard with the first light of dawn, they found the whole neighborhood in front of the chicken coop having fun with the angel, without the slightest reverence, tossing him things to eat through the openings in the wire as if he weren't a supernatural creature but a circus animal (218).

Although the text establishes that all of the characters are convinced the creature in their midst is, in fact, an angel, it emphasizes how their attitudes and actions are completely incongruous with the wondrous circumstances. The passage is replete with violent images and language: "captive," "club to death," "bailiff's club," "dragged," "locked up," "killing crabs." In the presence of this "supernatural creature," not a single human evidences the slightest humanity. The "wise neighbor woman" advocates murdering the angel, the mob treats him like a "circus animal," and the couple who first found him would prefer to "leave him to his fate on the high seas." Why do they all regard the angel with suspicion and fear? What is the text saying about human nature and our impulses with regard to that which we do not understand?

The issue of not understanding the exact nature of the angel is another important aspect of the passage. This use of intentional narrative ambiguity leaves the reader with more questions than answers. The entire populace is convinced that the creature is a "flesh-and-blood angel." The most authoritative observer, the "wise" neighbor woman, maintains that its origins are purely diabolical. Lastly, it is suggested that Pelayo and Elisenda believe the creature to be of a more benign nature, having seemingly brought about an improvement in their son's medical condition. In the absence of an omniscient narrator, however, all of these opinions remain conjecture. Why does the text refuse to provide a definitive explanation for the existence of this "supernatural creature"? What effect do the characters' varied interpretations have on the reader's ability to draw conclusions about the nature of the angel? What does this narrative technique imply about our desire as human beings to achieve an absolute understanding of the world around us, as well as the feasibility of such an objective? Does the language of the text suggest that such an enterprise is heroic, tragic, or absurd?

You can certainly see how a close reading of even a small portion of the text can inspire a broad range of fruitful questions. Repeating this process with other passages will allow you to expand upon these points of inquiry and raise new ones as well. Once you find a question that seems to resonate throughout the short story, you will then be ready to develop the thesis for your essay.

TOPICS AND STRATEGIES

The topics discussed here constitute only a point of departure for exploring the many potential theses that you could formulate about "A Very Old Man with Enormous Wings." Keep an open mind as you consider possible topics, and let yourself be guided first by your own reading rather than any outside source. Write down a list of ideas based on your initial reading. Since you are working with a short story (as opposed to a 400-page novel), you have the additional advantage of rereading the text more than once before selecting passages for closer examination. Only then should you set about the task of formulating a thesis, organizing your notes, and beginning the actual process of writing your critical essay.

Themes

When studying the themes in a work of literature, you are analyzing its treatment of broad concepts common to the human experience. Beyond merely identifying a theme, you will want to explore how the text deals with it in a unique and interesting manner. "A Very Old Man with Enormous Wings" deals with a number of essential literary themes. For example, you might write about the way the text represents supernatural phenomena and the way human beings react when they encounter them. What do we mean when we describe something as "supernatural"? Do the reactions of the characters in "A Very Old Man with Enormous Wings" reflect or contradict those typically associated with supernatural encounters? Another theme is that of the outsider, the Other, who is misunderstood and often mistreated by the community. What does the text suggest about our acceptance of difference both as individuals and as a society?

Sample Topics:

1. **The supernatural:** Write an essay that examines the encounter between humans and the otherworldly.

One of the central themes in the short story is the presence of inexplicable phenomena in our world. Thinking about literature you have read dealing with the supernatural (for example, the short stories of Edgar Allan Poe, Mary Shelley's *Frankenstein*, Bram Stoker's *Dracula*, Charles Dickens's *A Christmas Carol*), how is García Márquez's story different in its treatment of the theme? Do the characters in "A Very Old Man with Enormous Wings" react to the supernatural in the same way as in these other texts? These earlier texts each explain the cause and purpose of the supernatural phenomena. How does the ambiguity of the García Márquez story affect the reader's perception of the supernatural? Some works suggest that the supernatural is to be feared (*Dracula*); others represent it as a positive force (*A Christmas Carol*); still others pose it in the form of a cautionary tale (*Frankenstein*). Why do you believe "A Very Old Man with Enormous Wings" rejects all of these thematic options? What is the story suggesting about the realm of the supernatural in the modern world?

2. **The Other:** Explore the status of the outsider through the town's treatment of the old man.

The *Other* is a philosophical term used in opposition to the *Same* to characterize our individual and collective tendency to see the world in dualistic terms. The Other, defined by difference, is typically seen, therefore, as inferior, dangerous, or evil. Rubén Pelayo observes that "the winged old man is viewed as an object, not a human being" because "he does not speak the same language, ignores the town's social and cultural codes, and is the only one of his kind in the town" (84). What is the story saying about humans with respect to those who are different? Does it suggest that such behavior is innate or learned? Finally, does the text offer any hope that humanity can move beyond the rejection of the Other?

Characters

Unlike novels, which typically provide a more in-depth portrait of their characters, short stories usually require the reader to make more inferences based on only a few details. While this can present something of a challenge, it also allows for much greater interpretive leeway. This is certainly true in the case of "A Very Old Man with Enormous Wings" with its mysterious winged visitor and colorful cast of villagers. If you choose to write this kind of essay, begin by identifying all of the textual references to the character, whether he or she speaks, simply appears in the scene, or is merely referenced by someone else. Is the character dynamic or static? Does the character change from the beginning to the end of the story? What is the nature of the change? Does he or she represent an idea or a particular point of view? Most important, why is the character in the story? How is the narrative altered by the character's inclusion? What makes the character important to the story?

Sample Topics:

1. **The angel:** Analyze the role of one of García Márquez's unique and most enigmatic characters.

   The old man with wings is an absolute mystery. While there is much speculation about his origins and his motives, the text never divulges any definitive answers. His language is incomprehensible, and he remains "alien to the impertinences of the world" (219). Is he an angel? Apart from his wings, are there any other indications that he is a supernatural being? How does the angel affect the life of the village? What effect, if any, do the villagers have on him? Is the angel best understood as the main character in the story or as the pretext to a tale about people whose lives are changed by a supernatural encounter?

2. **Father Gonzaga and the wise neighbor:** Analyze the role of these two self-proclaimed authorities on angels.

   While neither the reader, nor Pelayo and Elisenda, nor the people of the village can explain the origin of the unusual visitor, two characters in the story do offer their "expert" opinions. A neighbor, always identified in the text as "wise," is convinced the creature is one of the "fugitive survivors of a celestial conspiracy" and advocates that Pelayo "club him to death" (218). Father Gonzaga, who interrogates the old man in Latin, concludes that he is not an angel because "he did not understand the language of God or know how to greet His ministers" (219). What role do these two characters play in the story? How do the other members of the community receive their comments? What effect do they have on the reader? Do you see the two more as antagonists, as comic elements, or both? What is the text suggesting about "experts" and society's need for such individuals?

3. **The spider woman:** Write an essay that examines the story's other supernatural visitor.

The impact of the unfortunate girl-turned-tarantula on the town's perception of the old man with wings is made plain by the text: "A spectacle like that, full of so much human truth and with such a fearful lesson, was bound to defeat without even trying that of a haughty angel who scarcely deigned to look at mortals" (222). John Gerlach describes her as the textual "foil" through whose presence "the winged man's humanity is underlined" (84). Do you agree with Gerlach? Reread the passages surrounding the spider woman. Is she truly part human, part tarantula, or is she merely a sideshow deception? How would the reader's perception of her legitimacy affect the interpretation of her character and her role in the story?

History and Context

An interesting interdisciplinary approach to literary analysis is to examine the work with attention to its historical or cultural context. Even works of pure fantasy, as is the case with "A Very Old Man with Enormous Wings," can be studied as cultural artifacts or, in other words, the conscious and unconscious elements of daily life that influence artistic creation. The added challenge of this type of essay is the need to conduct research not related directly to the text. For example, if you want to examine the influence of African myth and folklore on the story, you will have to find sources dealing with the impact of African beliefs on popular culture in Latin America. Similarly, an essay on the relationship between the winged old man and the Judeo-Christian conception of angels will require that you familiarize yourself with both religious doctrines and popular belief. You do not have to be an authority on the historical or cultural context, but your essay should contain documentation from scholarly sources to support your thesis.

Sample Topics:

1. **The influence of African culture in Latin America:** Examine the short story in the context of African mythology and its influence on Latin American literature.

In her essay "Gabriel García Márquez and Afro-American Literature," Vera M. Kutzinski argues that "A Very Old Man with Enormous Wings" should be read in the context of the centuries-old "myth of the flying Africans" (173), which can be traced in Latin America back to Juan Rodríguez Freyle's colonial-era story of the witch Juana García. Begin by reading Kutzinski's essay, as well as the Juana García story (it is included in several anthologies, including Roberto González Echeverría's *The Oxford Book of Latin American Short Stories*). Next, you will want to investigate the influence of African culture on Latin American literature, especially on García Márquez and other magic realists. Do you agree with Kutzinski's thesis? What are the similarities between the García Márquez text and that of Rodríguez Freyle? Is there an argument that these common traits are either coincidental or attributable to other influences? Given the way the town treats the angel, what might the text be suggesting about the history of African people in Latin America?

2. **Judeo-Christian belief in angels:** Explore cultural notions about the existence and the nature of angels through the villager's encounter with the old man.

Regina Janes observes: "The story's splendor is the implicit contrast between what we expect angels to be like and what this one is" (75). What is an angel? How is the creature defined in the Bible? How are angels typically represented in European and Latin American painting? Referencing the latter, Lois Parkinson Zamora comments: "The epic insouciance of García Márquez's very old man with enormous wings, in the story of that title, corresponds to any and all of a vast flock of Baroque angels" (2). What argument can be made that the strange visitor is, in fact, an angel? Beyond religious belief, what cultural, psychological and sociological factors affect people's belief in angels? How does the text represent these factors in the behavior of the villagers? Does their eventual rejection of the old man mean that they do not believe him to be an angel, or is there another reason? What does the text want the reader to conclude about the existence of angels?

Philosophy and Ideas

An essay dealing with philosophy and ideas is one that explores the concepts—ideological, metaphysical, and theoretical—engaged in the text. In "A Very Old Man with Enormous Wings," you might choose to explore the story's epistemological implications. Epistemology is the branch of philosophy that explores the nature of knowledge. When a previously unknown phenomenon is introduced into our world, how do we establish an understanding? The story raises clear implications for our capacity to comprehend the world around us, as well as the problematic status of knowledge. Another possible topic deals with the carnivalesque, a cultural theory involving the use of comedy in a socially subversive manner. Does this fantasy "Tale for Children" (as stated in the story's subtitle) also contain a revolutionary ideological component?

Sample Topics:

1. **Epistemology:** Examine the story in regard to what it is suggesting about the gap between our need to understand the world and our ability to do so.

Mark Millington has studied "A Very Old Man with Enormous Wings" using the linguist Teun van Dijk's theory of "knowledge frames," which Millington explains as the culturally based "organizing principles [that] unify concepts of various types and at various levels of representation under the constraint of typicality and normality" (128). Millington argues that the short story "subverts" our ability to understand because the "physical laws within our knowledge frames are overridden with no attempt at explanation" (129). Read Millington's article (which includes a more detailed description of van Dijk's theory). Do you agree with van Dijk's concept of how we define knowledge? Next, revisit the passages in the story containing statements about the nature of the old man with wings. How does the story define knowledge? What is the basis for the characters' understanding of the creature? How does the text undermine this understanding? What difference is there between the community's understanding of the angel and of the spider woman? Is the text proposing that we cannot be certain of anything, or does it offer another view on the limits of our knowledge?

2. **The carnivalesque:** Analyze the story in light of Mikhail Bakhtin's theory of the carnivalesque.

The carnivalesque is a concept first introduced by the 20th-century Russian linguist Mikhail Bakhtin in his classic study of medieval popular literature, entitled *Rabelais and His World.* Bakhtin identified the subversive power of popular festivals in the Middle Ages, such as the Carnival period preceding Lent, where "open-air amusements, with the participation of giants, dwarfs, monsters, and trained animals" (6) represented a kind of temporary revolt against the rigid social hierarchy of the period: "This is why festive folk laughter presents an element of victory not only over supernatural awe, over the sacred, over death; it also means the defeat of power, of earthly kings, of the earthly upper classes, of all that oppresses and restricts" (92). The term *carnivalesque* has come to describe works of art that use the grotesque and the absurd in a similarly subversive fashion. Reflecting on works including "A Very Old Man with Enormous Wings," Gene H. Bell-Villada comments: "As the great Soviet scholar Bakhtin observed about Rabelais, García Márquez's fiction helps deflate the official truths and reinterpret them from the point of view of people's laughter" (80). Begin by familiarizing yourself with Bakhtin's theory of the carnivalesque (a good general introduction is Pam Morris's *The Bakhtin Reader*). What elements in the story seem to reflect Bakhtin's concept? How are social and cultural hierarchies subverted in the text? Thinking about Pelayo and Elisenda's life at the beginning and at the end of the story, in what way can it be argued that the social order is permanently transformed by the time the angel flies away? Can "A Very Old Man with Enormous Wings" be considered a revolutionary text in a political sense?

Form and Genre

When addressing issues of form and genre, you are studying the overarching structures and artistic concepts around which the text is built. An obvious topic for "A Very Old Man with Enormous Wings" is its relationship to magic realism. Although this topic will require you to begin by answering the question, "What is magic realism?" the topic goes to the heart of García Márquez's importance as a writer. Another genre question deals with the story's subtitle: "A Tale for Children." Should the story be read as a fairy tale? How do you define a fairy tale, and what does "A Very Old Man" have in common with that genre? Is the subtitle meant to be ironic? If so, how can the story be read as a parody? A third possibility is to examine the text within the conventions of the short story genre.

Sample Topics:

1. **Magic realism:** Study the text as an example of magic realism.

   Dana Gioia asserts that "All of the main features of Latin American Magic Realism can be found in García Márquez's story, 'A Very Old Man with Enormous Wings'" (n.p.). You will want to begin by gaining a better understanding of what is meant by the term *magic,* or *magical realism.*" A good starting point is María-Elena Angulo's introductory chapter to her book *Magic Realism: Social Context and Discourse.* Once you have researched the principal elements of the genre—both form and content—return to "A Very Old Man with Enormous Wings" and try to identify which of them are present in the text. Where does the story converge with magic realism and where, if anywhere, do you find inconsistencies with your understanding of the genre? Given that fantasy and tales of the supernatural can be traced back to the origins of literature, what distinguishes "A Very Old Man with Enormous Wings" and magic realism as unique from earlier "magical" texts?

2. **Fairy tales:** Consider "A Very Old Man with Enormous Wings" within the context of the fairy-tale genre.

"A Very Old Man with Enormous Wings" is subtitled "A Tale for Children." For Gene H. Bell-Villada, "what fairy-tale characteristics it has are affectionately parodied throughout" (136). Thinking about traditional fairy tales, such as those of the Brothers Grimm or Hans Christian Andersen, what traits does García Márquez's story have in common with the genre? Do you agree that the story is a parody of the genre, or are there aspects of the text that are consistent with fairy tales? For example, fairy tales are typically didactic in nature: They teach children a lesson or a moral truth. Is there an implicit moral to the story?

3. **Short story:** Examine the way "A Very Old Man with Enormous Wings" functions as a work of short fiction.

Magic realism aside, García Márquez is widely acknowledged as one of the foremost short story writers of the 20th century. Reflect upon the traditionally accepted tenets of the genre as seen in the works of Maupassant, O. Henry, and Hemingway: concise narration, few characters, emphasis on plot over character development, and frequently, an unexpected ending. Rubén Pelayo identifies three "salient characteristics" of García Márquez stories: the "fragmentation of narrative time," the "subjectivity of plot, normally determined by the difference of the character's viewpoint," and plot "ambiguity" resulting from the "main theme [being] left open-ended" (71). To what extent, if any, is "A Very Old Man with Enormous Wings" consistent with traditional short story writing? Do you find Pelayo's observations to be accurate?

Language, Symbols, and Imagery

When studying a literary work's language you are examining how text creates meaning at its most essential level. Perhaps the most compelling issue of language lies in whether the old man should be understood as an allegorical figure. Allegories are works of art that are symbolic rather than literal (for example, George Orwell's *Animal Farm* is an allegory for Russian history from Lenin to Stalin). If the story is allegorical, what is the essence of the allegory? Does a close reading confirm your thesis with specific images and symbols? Another aspect of the story's language that merits closer consideration is the ambiguous ending. The angel suddenly flies away, leaving no apparent clue to his identity. Apart from Elisenda's "sigh of relief" (225), there is no indication of the villagers' reaction to their incredible experience. Return to the end of the story and conduct a close reading of the passage. Does the text offer any clues? How does the language reinforce the ambiguity of the ending?

1. **Allegory:** Argue that there is a symbolic meaning underlying the incredible events in the text.

   Is the old man with wings simply the curious pretext for a fantastic story, or should the character and the events surrounding his visit be understood as allegorical? John Gerlach weighs the possibility that "the wings themselves might be taken as allegorical evidence of the true dignity of man" (87) but ultimately finds the text too inconclusive to ascribe it with such specific symbolic meaning. Do you agree with Gerlach, or does your own reading suggest that the story is, in fact, allegorical? If so, there are many possible allegorical readings. Rather than focusing exclusively on the old man's wings, think about the entire narrative. Allegories are frequently of a political or religious nature. It has been argued that the story of the angel may be an allegory for the biblical account of Jesus. Could it be read as a symbolic treatment of the artist? Whatever case you make for an allegorical reading, your argument will be stronger the more details of the story you can take into account. For example, if you decide the angel is an allegorical representation of Jesus, what does the spider woman represent? Finally, remember that allegories are rarely objective. What is the text saying about the subject it allegorizes?

2. **The end of the story:** Explain the story's ambiguous ending.

Harley D. Oberhelman observes: "There is no moment of closure that identifies the writer's intentions. While it is suggested that the angel's departure is the result of his disillusion with the promotional exploitation surrounding his visit, García Márquez at no time suggests this intent" (39). Do you agree with Oberhelman, or is there, in fact, an explanation to the way the story ends? If there is an underlying explanation, how is it consistent with the logic of the text? If you agree that the ending is intentionally ambiguous, what purpose does the ambiguity serve?

Compare and Contrast Essays

A comparative approach can offer the writer a wide range of interesting topics, as well as a clearly defined essay structure. The challenge of writing a comparative essay lies in choosing a comparison that is not only thought provoking but also appropriate in its critical scope. Ask yourself how the comparison you propose will contribute to your reader's understanding of "A Very Old Man with Enormous Wings." You could compare elements within the text, you could compare it to another work by García Márquez, or you could explore commonalities and differences with the work of another author. An example of the first option would be to contrast Pelayo and Elisenda with the other characters in the story, as well as with each other. Are they the protagonists of the story or merely the most visible members of the ignorant crowd gathered around the angel? Moreover, is there any difference between the spouses? Another possibility would be to compare "A Very Old Man with Enormous Wings" to another of García Márquez's numerous short stories. A good candidate would be "The Handsomest Drowned Man in the World," another children's story from the same collection. Whatever story you choose, be sure to establish the aspects of the texts you plan to compare: themes, characters, language, etc. A third option is to examine the story in relation to the work of another author. This option can be problematic, as you need to be sure that your comparison makes sense. For example, a comparison with a magic realist story by another Latin American writer, such as Carlos Fuentes's "Chac Mool," would allow you to analyze similarities and differences within the same genre.

Sample Topics:

1. **Pelayo and Elisenda:** Write an essay comparing the couple with the other residents of the village and/or with each other.

On the second page of the story, the narrator notes the angel's reluctant hosts: "They looked at him so long and so closely that Pelayo and Elisenda very soon overcame their surprise and in the end found him familiar" (218). Why does the couple not share the rest of the town's initial fascination with the angel? Does their attitude change over the course of the story? How does the couple benefit more than the other villagers from the old man's arrival? Are they actually beneficiaries of a miracle or merely of unusual circumstances? How does the presence of the child affect the reader's attitude toward the couple? Should they be seen as the protagonists of the story? Are they meant to be understood as an Everyman and an Everywoman to whom the reader can relate, or does the text render them unsympathetic, like the other villagers? Is there any difference between Pelayo and Elisenda with regard to their attitude toward their unusual guest?

2. **"A Very Old Man with Enormous Wings" and "The Handsomest Drowned Man in the World":** Compare these two García Márquez stories about the arrival of an unexpected visitor in a small village.

Also subtitled "A Tale for Children" and centered on another magical being, this one discovered awash on the beach, "The Handsomest Drowned Man in the World" invites comparison to "A Very Old Man with Enormous Wings." Begin by reading the other story, paying particular attention to the way the plot, characters, and themes either reflect or differ from "A Very Old Man." In particular, compare the impact of the title character's arrival on the town. Regina Janes sees a clear dichotomy between the two texts: "More than 'A Very Old man with Enormous Wings,' which chronicles the cruelty of simple folk in their treatment of any out-of-the-way creature, 'The Handsomest Drowned Man in the World' is an optimistic tale" (78). Do you concur with Janes's assessment of the difference between the two stories, or do you find they have more in common than might first appear?

3. **García Márquez's "A Very Old Man with Enormous Wings" and Carlos Fuentes's "Chac Mool":** Compare two stories about supernatural beings by two of the leading Latin American magic realists.

Otherworldly entities are common fixtures in Latin American magic realism. One of the best-known examples of this type of writing is "Chac Mool" (1954), a short story by García Márquez's longtime friend Mexican author Carlos Fuentes. The title refers to a type of pre-Columbian statue of a reclining figure. While the figure is common throughout Mexico and Central America, both its function and the identity of its subject remain a mystery. Read Fuentes's story (widely anthologized, it can be found in the collection *Burnt Water*) with special attention to the fantastic elements. Note the similarities and differences between the representation of the winged old man and the statue come-to-life. How do the two texts differ in their treatment of the supernatural? "Chac Mool" is widely seen as one of Fuentes's most Mexican stories, deeply rooted in that country's history and cultural consciousness, whereas Gene H. Bell-Villada sees "A Very Old Man with Enormous Wings" as part of "García Márquez's aim at the time of becoming more broadly a writer of 'the Caribbean'" (133). Can the case be made that the essential difference between these two magic realist texts lies in their regionalism?

Bibliography and Online Resources for "A Very Old Man with Enormous Wings"

Angulo, María-Elena. *Magic Realism: Social Context and Discourse.* New York: Garland, 1995.

Bakhtin, Mikhail. *Rabelais and His World.* Trans. Helene Iswolsky. Bloomington: Indiana UP, 1984.

Bell-Villada, Gene H. *García Márquez: The Man and His Work.* Chapel Hill: U of North Carolina P, 1990.

Fuentes, Carlos. *Burnt Water.* Trans. Margaret Sayers Peden. New York: Farrar, Straus & Giroux, 1986.

García Márquez, Gabriel. "The Handsomest Drowned Man in the World." Trans. Gregory Rabassa. *Collected Short Stories.* New York: Harper-Perennial, 1999. 247–254.

———. "A Very Old Man with Enormous Wings." Trans. Gregory Rabassa. *Collected Stories.* New York: HarperPerennial, 1999. 217–225.

Gerlach, John. "The Logic of Wings: García Márquez, Todorov, and the Endless Resources of Fantasy." *Gabriel García Márquez.* Ed. Harold Bloom. New York: Chelsea House, 1989. 81–89.

Gioia, Dana. "Gabriel García Márquez and Magic Realism." 1998. 18 July 2008. <http://www.danagioia.net/essays/emarquez.htm>.

Gónzalez Echeverría, Roberto, ed. *The Oxford Book of Latin American Short Stories.* New York: Oxford UP, 1999.

Janes, Regina. *Gabriel García Márquez: Revolutions in Wonderland.* Columbia: U of Missouri P, 1981.

Kutzinski, Vera M. "Gabriel García Márquez and Afro-American Literature." *Gabriel García Márquez.* Ed. Harold Bloom. New York: Chelsea House, 1989. 169–182.

Millington, Mark. "Aspects of Narrative Structure in *The Incredible and Sad Story of Innocent Eréndira and Her Heartless Grandmother.*" *García Márquez: New Readings.* Ed. Bernard McGuirk and Richard Cardwell. Cambridge: Cambridge UP, 1987. 117–33.

Morris, Pam. *The Bakhtin Reader: Selected Writings of Bakhtin, Medvedev, Voloshinov.* London: Hodder, 1997.

Oberhelman, Harley D. *Gabriel García Márquez: A Study of the Short Fiction.* Boston: Twayne, 1991.

Pelayo, Rubén. *Gabriel García Márquez: A Critical Companion.* Westport, CT: Greenwood Press, 2001.

Zamora, Lois Parkinson. "Monsters and Martyrs: García Márquez's Baroque Iconography." 21 July 2008. <http://www.uh.edu/~englmi/Monsters AndMartyrs/page2.html>.

THE INCREDIBLE AND SAD TALE OF INNOCENT ERÉNDIRA AND HER HEARTLESS GRANDMOTHER

READING TO WRITE

*T*HE INCREDIBLE *and Sad Tale of Innocent Eréndira and Her Heartless Grandmother* (*La increíble y triste historia de la cándida Eréndira y de su abuela desalmada*) was originally published as a separate novella and later, in 1972, as part of a collection of short fiction, translated into English as *Innocent Eréndira and Other Stories* in 1978. The novella is acknowledged by many critics as "one of García Márquez's most delightful and perfect shorter creations" (Bell-Villada 181). The story of a teenage girl forced into prostitution by her monstrous grandmother, *Innocent Eréndira* is a mixture of fairy-tale fantasy and brutal realism, of wry humor and disturbing cruelty, of innocent love and calculated murder. With so many thematic and stylistic facets, the text poses its readers a wide array of questions and leaves them with an even wider array of possible interpretations. While this intriguing work's popularity means that you should be able to find ample scholarly commentary, before you consider any other opinions you will want to begin by formulating your own ideas. After you have read the novella the first time, your next step should be to select passages that strike you as particularly compelling or that seem especially representative of the story's main characters, themes, or formal elements. For instance, consider the following passage describing the grandmother's scheme to get Eréndira back from the missionaries:

> For several days the grandmother saw the little trucks loaded with pregnant Indian women heading for the mission, but she failed to recognize her opportunity. She recognized it on Pentecost Sunday itself, when she heard the rockets and the ringing of the bells and saw the miserable and merry crowd that was going to the festival, and she saw that among the crowds there were pregnant women with the veil and the crown of a bride holding the arms of their casual mates, whom they would legitimize in the collective wedding. Among the last in the procession a boy passed, innocent of heart, with gourd-cut Indian hair and dressed in rags, carrying an Easter candle with a silk bow in his hand. The grandmother called him over.
>
> "Tell me something, son," she asked with her smoothest voice. "What part do you have in this affair?"
>
> The boy felt intimidated by the candle and it was hard for him to close his mouth because of his donkey teeth.
>
> "The priests are going to give me my first communion," he said.
>
> "How much did they pay you?"
>
> "Five pesos."
>
> The grandmother took a roll of bills from her pouch and the boy looked at them with surprise.
>
> "I'm going to give you twenty," the grandmother said, "Not for you to make your first communion, for you to get married."
>
> "Who to?"
>
> "My granddaughter" (30–31).

The most striking aspect of this passage is its description of the grandmother's predatory instinct. Like a lioness, the sly old woman waits for an opportunity to present itself and, at the right moment, pounces on her prey. She selects the weakest member of the proverbial herd, an "innocent" boy trailing the pack ("among the last in procession"). How does the animal imagery of "donkey teeth" contribute to his metaphorical status? What does the text suggest about her skill as a master manipulator by having her address the young man as "son" and using "her smoothest voice." After engaging him in seemingly banal conversation in order to assess the strength of her opposition—the missionaries—the grandmother finishes of her pursuit of the boy. Not only does she outbid her rivals for the boy's collusion; she also weans a potential member away the missionaries' flock by suggesting he simply forgo one sacrament, his first communion, and proceed directly to the profanation of another in the sham marriage. While this description of the grandmother is negative, in what way does it also elicit the reader's admiration?

As harsh as treatment of the grandmother may be, a second notable element in the passage deals with the use of irony to ridicule organized religion. This humorous form of anticlericalism, found throughout García Márquez's work, is evident even in such subtle details as the choice of Pentecost for the events in question. The feast day marking the descent of the Holy Spirit upon the Apostles finds a decidedly less heavenly entity, in the form of the diabolical grandmother, descending upon the faithful. The hypocrisy of the communal marriage ceremony is made plain by the stark contrast between the pathetic reality of the situation and the missionaries' sacrosanct intent to "legitimize" the literal "truckloads" of rampant promiscuity among the indigenous population. How does the use of the antithetical adjectives ("miserable and merry") to describe the crowd underscore the absurdity of this shotgun wedding en masse? Similarly, how does the image of pregnant women adorned in the traditional veil and headdress of virginal brides clutching their "casual" paramours amid bells and fireworks function to subvert the traditional idea of a wedding procession? What attitude toward the ceremony is connoted later in the passage by the description of the boy as "intimidated" by the Easter candle he holds? The satirical coup de grâce comes with the revelation that these miraculous conversions are economic rather than spiritual in nature. Ultimately, what is the only distinction between the morally corrupt grandmother and the saintly missionaries, given that each is willing to pay for a soul?

A third compelling component of this passage is its representation of those caught between the Mephistophelian old woman and the misguided priests. The "Indians," the Guajiro people who inhabit the region where the events of the story transpire, are portrayed as victims both of socioeconomic marginalization and of indifferent political and civil authorities. The plight of this displaced minority is embodied in the boy, whose own indigenous origins are made clear by his "gourd-cut Indian hair." Why does the text contrast the "silk bow" he carries with the "rags" he wears. How does the description of his "donkey teeth" relate to his status, and that of other indigenous people, in society? What is the reality of his future and that of the generation of unborn children of the impoverished women around him? Given the description of his being "innocent of heart," do you think the passage is drawing a comparison between his decision to sell himself—first to the missionaries and then to the grandmother—and the plight of "innocent" Eréndira?

The elements of *Innocent Eréndira* highlighted in the passage above—the character of the grandmother, García Márquez's anticlerical humor, and the representation of the disenfranchised indigenous minority—are only a few of the many facets of this rich text. The decision as to which aspects of the work make for the most compelling essay ultimately will be determined by your own impressions. Your subsequent close reading of relevant passages will allow you to further refine your ideas and help lead you to the questions from which you will formulate your thesis. As you consider the following potential topics, remember that these are by no means your only options.

TOPICS AND STRATEGIES
Themes

If you decide to write an essay about one of the themes in *Innocent Eréndira* you will be examining what the text has to say about a common human experience, activity, or belief. One obvious theme is prostitution. Prostitution and prostitutes appear frequently in García Márquez's work but not in such a prominent and decidedly disturbing fashion. What is the text saying about the causes and consequences of prostitution? Another possible topic is the theme of romantic love. What is the distinction between love and sex, and are they too frequently confused? You could also choose to write on the theme of freedom. In addition to Eréndira, which other characters are seeking freedom and what kind of freedom do they seek? What does it mean to be free? There are of course a number of other themes that you might decide to explore. As you brainstorm your topic, keep in mind that unlike other types of close reading, such as for characters or symbols, instances of the theme may not always be obvious. In addition, your essay needs to tell your reader what the text is saying about the theme. For example, with the theme of prostitution, you could argue that the text sees it as a social disease that must be eradicated, an unavoidable consequence of human sexuality, or even a form of exploitation of which sex is only the most salient manifestation. Bear in mind that an essay that simply enumerates the instances of the prostitution theme in the text lacks critical insight and is unlikely to either interest or impress your reader.

Sample Topics:

1. **Prostitution:** Write an essay examining the novella's commentary on the universal cultural practice of exchanging sexual intercourse for economic or social gain.

The theme of prostitution can be seen in many of García Márquez's best-known works, including *One Hundred Years of Solitude*, *Chronicle of a Death Foretold*, and *Memories of My Melancholy Whores*. In these three works, prostitution is not treated as a criminal activity or a moral transgression but rather as a commonplace, generally accepted social practice. Is this also the case in *Innocent Eréndira*? What does the novella seem to be suggesting about prostitutes and their activity? Gene H. Bell-Villada argues that the text is not concerned with "the sufferings of real-life Eréndiras [which] admittedly go on by the thousands in our world day after day" (181). Rather, he contends: "The author . . . understands that, in literature, tales of woe make no converts and that social evils are often better lampooned knowledgeably than excoriated morally" (181). Do you concur with this assessment of this theme, or can you make a case that *Innocent Eréndira* is, in reality, a much darker treatment of prostitution than meets the eye? Beyond the physical, what is suggested about the emotional and psychological consequences of prostitution? Moreover, thinking about scenes such as the one in which it is revealed that the missionaries are paying the Guajiro boy to take his first communion, does the prostitution theme extend beyond a sexual connotation?

2. **Romantic love:** What does the relationship between Eréndira and Ulises suggest about the nature of romance and the distinction between love and sexual attraction?

If you choose to write an essay on the theme of romantic love in *Innocent Eréndira,* the first question you might ask is whether the novella is truly a love story? What is the actual nature of the relationship between Eréndira and Ulises? When does Ulises "fall in love" with Eréndira? What is the text suggesting when it describes their reunion in the following manner: "They kissed in the darkness, caressed each other slowly, got undressed wearily, with a silent tenderness and a hidden happiness that was more than ever like love" (50)? What textual evidence exists to indicate that Eréndira is in love with Ulises? Return to the end of the novella, when they plot the grandmother's death. How does Eréndira's tone change from her earlier interaction with Ulises? How do the details of the grandmother's own loves relate to the theme? Shortly before her death, she sings in her sleep:

> *Lord, oh, Lord, give me back the innocence I had*
> *So that I can feel his love all over again from the start* (51).

Can the lyrics to the grandmother's song be read as the novella's message about the reality of romantic love?

3. **Freedom:** What is the story saying about the basic human desire to be free to choose one's own destiny?

The quest of freedom is central to *Innocent Eréndira.* Both Eréndira and Ulises are seeking emancipation from different forms of servitude: the former from a life of prostitution at the hands of her grandmother, the latter from the dreary existence of life tending his father's orange groves. To what extent is each character willing to go to gain her or his liberty? Given the end of the story, how could it be argued that the text shows the desire for freedom to be stronger even than love? Consider the following observation by Martin Kaplan: "As Eréndira serves her monopolistic grandmother, she embodies the frustration of individual and continental freedom. Exemplifying the theme of independence, Eréndira, once released from slavery by Ulises, runs into the desert and is never heard from again" (49). Do you agree with Kaplan's assertion that the struggle for freedom can be understood as a theme with both individual and collective significance? If so, what group in the story has been oppressed in some fashion? Moreover, given that the sea is frequently contrasted with the desert as an escape—Ulises tells Eréndira on the evening of their first attempted escape, "Tomorrow we'll be watching the ships go by" (37)—why do you think Eréndira decides to escape back into the desert when she has finally arrived at the coast? What is the text ultimately saying about the meaning of freedom?

Characters

Innocent Eréndira is structured around three principal characters, any of whom would make for an engaging essay. While each figure seems to have a highly traditional function in the plot—Eréndira as heroine, Ulises as hero, the grandmother as villain—each one is also surrounded by a degree of ambiguity. Why does the title character endure her grandmother's tyranny and then betray the lover who saves her? As "heartless" as the grandmother is, she inspires the reader's admiration and, perhaps, some small degree of pity as her own past is revealed. Ulises, whose valor is more comic than heroic at times, has his own subplot rooted in a father-son conflict. As you read the passages relating to the character about whom you are writing, look for clues as to her or his psychology. In the case of the grandmother and Ulises, what do you know about their respective pasts that might explain their behavior? With regard to Eréndira, what happens to her during the course of the story that alters her "innocence"?

Sample Topics:

1. **Eréndira:** Analyze this character of few words.

One of the challenges in writing about the novella's title character lies in trying to understand her motives when she almost never articulates them. Her responses to her grandmother are typically limited to little more than "yes" and "no." Much of her conversation with Ulises suggests not only moral innocence but also naiveté (it might be noted that in the original Spanish title she is *cándida Eréndira,* which could be translated as either "innocent" or "simple-minded" Eréndira). Which translation do you find to be a better reflection of the character? What do you make of Eréndira's behavior? Why does she not resist her grandmother or attempt to escape before Ulises's arrival? In what ways does Eréndira change as the story progresses? What is the nature of her relationship with Ulises? How does her role in his sexual initiation define their future relationship? Is she truly in love with Ulises? If so, why does she abandon him at the end of the story after he has committed murder to free her? There is only one moment in which Eréndira makes her sentiments plain. Sitting in the mission "alone, with no one to hear her . . . 'I'm happy,' she said" (29). How might this scene explain Eréndira's actions at the end of the novella?

2. **The grandmother:** Write an essay on this morally and physically monstrous antagonist.

Eréndira's grandmother is one of García Márquez's most memorable villains. Described at the outset of the story as a "white whale" (1), she indeed embodies the resilient malice of the iconic antagonist to which her description refers: Herman Melville's leviathan, Moby Dick. Seemingly ageless and magically indestructible, she is also a master manipulator and hard-nosed businesswoman for whom the reader cannot avoid a certain horrified admiration. Which scenes in the novella serve to create this paradoxical view of the grandmother? How does grandmother's manner of speaking to Eréndira reinforce the reader's ambivalent perception? For example, on the morning after the fire, she "sighs," "My poor child. . . . Life won't be long enough for you to pay me back for this mishap" (7). What other instances can you find of this combination of maternal concern and heartlessness? What is known of the grandmother's life prior to the events of the story? How do her memories and dreams and details that are revealed about her youth function to humanize her? Do you agree with Regina Janes's assessment of the grandmother that "she too is a victim" (86)?

3. Ulises: What role does Ulises play in the text? Is he better seen as a hero or as a fool?

Ulises is a difficult character to categorize. At times, he seems to fill the role of a modern-day knight in shining armor trying to rescue his damsel in distress. How does the text subvert the reader's desire to understand the character in this way? Is there any significance to his name, the Spanish version of *Ulysses,* also the name of the hero of Homer's *Odyssey*? What do you make of his relationship with his Dutch father and his Guajiro mother? Does his family life help to illuminate any aspect of his character or help to explain the motives behind his later actions? At the end of the story, Ulises has been repudiated by his family in the form of his "father's curse" (49) and betrayed by his love after committing murder to gain her freedom. He is last seen "lying face down on the beach, weeping from solitude and fear" (59). Why does García Márquez employ these two nouns (*solitude, fear*) to describe Ulises's pain? Is he meant to be seen as the true "innocent" victim in the story or as a pathetic love-sick boy who should have known better than to fall in love with a prostitute?

History and Context

Essays on history and context offer you the possibility of exploring the fictional world of the text as it relates to the real world in which it was created. Although these essays usually ask the writer to conduct further outside research into the historical or cultural context of the text, they can also offer tremendous, otherwise unappreciated insight into the work. While the setting of *Innocent Eréndira* is, at first glance, a rather magical world, it has clear resonance in the social, political, and economic realities of Latin America. One potential topic is to analyze the indigenous characters in the story in light of the status of the people on which they are modeled, the Guajiro of Colombia. A second topic you might choose to write about is how the novella reflects the broader problem of social and economic injustice in Latin America. No less engaging a topic would be a study of Eréndira's horrible existence in the context of the exploitation of women throughout the developing world. Whichever topic you choose—and these are by no means your only options—always keep in mind that the text may not only be reacting to the cultural and historical context; it may also be pointing to its cause, as well as its potential solution.

Sample Topics:

1. **Indigenous peoples in Latin America:** Examine the text's representation of indigenous people through the Guajiro "Indians" who come in contact with Eréndira and her grandmother.

One of the interesting elements of *Innocent Eréndira* is its setting in La Guajira, an inhospitable peninsula of Colombia near the Venezuelan border that is home to the Wayuú, or Guajiro in Spanish. Gene H. Bell-Villada offers the following description of the Guajiro and their existence:

> A traveler in the Guajira wilderness sees taciturn indigenous families housed in the clusters of wooden sheds that dot a desolate landscape. They eke out their living from a few goats, the salt works, the crafts and *mantas* sold in the tourist trade, and the odd jobs they perform as the subproletariat of a frontier economy (20–21).

How is this description reflected in the depiction of the Guajiro characters in the novella? Investigate the Guajiro so that you have a more complete idea about their culture and their status in modern Colombia. Then, return to the text and study the passages in which "Indians" appear or are mentioned. Is García Márquez's portrait of the Guajiro accurate? Does the text offer a sympathetic or an indifferent view of their plight? Consider Ulises's mother. How is she different from the other characters in the story? How does her bond with her son contrast with other familial relationships in the novella? What do you make of the grandmother's treatment of the Guajiro who work for her? Could it be argued that she is symbolic of European attitudes toward indigenous people in Latin America?

2. **Economic exploitation in Latin America:** How can the work be read as commentary on the ongoing cycle of economic exploitation in Latin America?

While the grandmother's mistreatment of Eréndira is a story of an abused individual, it may also be read as a social critique. Rafael C. Castillo believes that "the story is metaphorical with symbols to suggest political allegory. And a case can be made that García Márquez is arguing against exploitation" (77). Where in the text can you find reference to social and economic injustice? Who are its victims? Who are its perpetrators? How is Eréndira's story analogous to the condition in the world around her? What about the impact of colonialism? There are numerous references to Europeans and European culture in the novella: Francis Drake, the so-called privateer, who led Britain's campaign of terror in the Spanish Caribbean; Amadís, the fictional archetype of European chivalric romances; Ulises (Ulysses), the mariner hero of Homer's *Odyssey* and the chief architect of the Greek conquest of Troy in the *Iliad*; Ulises's Dutch father, who literally does not understand his Guajiro wife; and even the décor of the grandmother's house. Consider the following passage from one of the grandmother's dreams:

> "That was during the time the Greek ship arrived," she said. "It was a crew of madmen who made the women happy and didn't pay them with money but with sponges, living sponges that later on walked about the houses moaning like patients in a hospital and making the children cry so they could drink the tears" (50).

Is this curious dream more than just an example of magic realism? Might it also be understood as a description of the impact of colonialism and neocolonialism on Latin American society?

3. **Exploitation of women in the developing world:** Discuss the way the text deals with the exploitation of women in Latin America.

Beyond its parodic humor and the magical world it creates, *Innocent Eréndira* raises the disturbing issue of the exploitation of women both in Latin America and throughout the developing world. Calling attention to the social consciousness lost in the text's formal strategies, Diane E. Marting states:

> My contention is that Eréndira's prostitution is comparable to the massacre of the banana workers in *Cien años de soledad* in that they are narrathemes based on real events which are treated by the fictions as unreal. . . . Hyperbole and incredulity have led the reader. Yet Eréndira's barbaric treatment by her grandmother and by the huge number of men who have paid-sex with her in fact could happen and does happen in reality (176).

Return to the text and consider Eréndira's plight, not as fiction, but as a reflection of the oppression of women throughout the Southern Hemisphere. Which scenes seem to evoke a realistic portrayal of forced prostitution? Which elements of the fictional society might reflect the corrupt world that permits this kind of exploitation? What does the grandmother's own past as a prostitute imply about the cycle of abuse that exists in places where women are regarded as second-class citizens?

Philosophy and Ideas

Essays dealing with philosophy and ideas examine the way the text responds to ethical, moral, ontological (existence), and epistemological (knowledge) problem. Unlike essays on themes, this kind of topic implies a position on the question or an affirmation of a particular worldview. *Innocent Eréndira* raises a number of interesting questions that might lead to an excellent essay. One possible topic deals with the moral dilemma of whether it is right or wrong to put one's own personal happiness before one's obligation to family. A second essay that you might want to write explores the situational ethics of crime. What do the many transgressions committed in the story suggest about when, if ever, one can say that crime is justified?

Sample Topics:

1. **Duty to family versus duty to self:** How do Eréndira's terrible servitude to her grandmother, Ulises's abandonment of his family,

and the grandmother's own obsessive loyalty to the memory of the Amadíses frame this problem?

One of the profound questions raised in *Innocent Eréndira* is whether an individual's first allegiance lies with family or self. This moral quandary, which can be traced in literature back to Sophocles' *Antigone*, finds a three-fold presence in García Márquez's novella. The clearest example is Eréndira's almost ridiculous subservience to her grandmother. Even in plotting the old woman's death, she explains that Ulises must strike the fatal blow because, "I can't. . . . She's my grandmother" (52). A definite case can be made, however, that both of the other principal characters are confronted by the same moral problem. What is the nature of Ulises's relationship to his father? How does the relationship come to an apparent end? Why does the grandmother insist on carrying the heavy bones of the Amadíses across the desert with her? Can it be argued that the grandmother's demands of Eréndira reflect the sacrifices she herself has made in life? Considering the ways each of these three characters deal with the conflict between familial obligation and personal choice, what solution, if any, does the text propose?

2. **When is crime justified?** The novella is filled with characters who turn to crime for different reasons. Does the story offer an answer to this ethical dilemma?

Prostitution is not the only illegal act committed in *Innocent Eréndira*. Many other crimes are perpetrated over the course of the story, including rape, robbery, smuggling, and murder. Other moral transgressions could be added to this list. Each of these offenses has its rationale: For example, the grandmother prostitutes Eréndira because the girl must "pay . . . back for the mishap" (7) that destroyed the family home; Ulises murders the grandmother because he is in love with Eréndira and wants to set her free; the smugglers, including Ulises's father, transport contraband as a means to survive in the impoverished land they inhabit. Can all these crimes be divided into

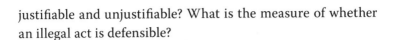

justifiable and unjustifiable? What is the measure of whether an illegal act is defensible?

Form and Genre

Essays on form and genre look at the text as a whole and how it conforms to or breaks with traditional literary models. For this reason, when you are reading a text with an eye to writing this kind of essay, you will want to think about how it resembles or differs from other work you have read within that genre. With *Innocent Eréndira,* one of the most notable elements is the length of the text. You might want to explore the question of whether it is better understood as a long short story or whether it conforms to the generally defined characteristics of the short novel, or novella. Perhaps an even more intriguing essay deals with reading the story as a parody. How does *Innocent Eréndira*'s humor derive from its comic subversion of traditional genres, and what might be the possible purpose of this subversive mode of writing?

Sample Topics:

1. **Novella or short story:** Consider the differences between the two literary genres. Which one better characterizes *Innocent Eréndira*?

   A number of García Márquez's most celebrated works, including *No One Writes to the Colonel, Chronicle of a Death Foretold,* and *Memories of My Melancholy Whores,* have been alternately characterized as short novels or long short stories. Such is also the case with *Innocent Eréndira,* which, at about 60 pages in length, might be classified under either genre. Research definitions of both the short story and the novella. What are the distinguishing features of each? Which one seems to better reflect your reading of *Innocent Eréndira*? For example, it is frequently asserted that a novella bears greater resemblance to a novel in its more thorough development of characters. If this is so, to what extent does the reader come to know Eréndira, her grandmother, and Ulises? What other distinctions can you find between short story and novella that will help you classify *Innocent Eréndira*? If you are so inclined, you might read one or two of the other texts mentioned above and speculate on whether there seem to be similar character-istics in all of García Márquez's long short fiction.

2. **Parody:** In what way can the text be read as a parody of other genres?

In literary parody, a text imitates another text or genre in a humorous manner. Harley D. Oberhelman observes the text's parodic intention even in its long-winded "mock-epic title" (48). Howard Fraser elaborates on the nature of the parody:

> It is a combination of fairy tale, odyssey, novel of chivalry, and historical allegory. As a *cuento de hadas* [fairy tale], it portrays an imprisoned damsel who awaits deliverance by her lover. In a curious, modern way, however, García Márquez reverses the ending in the stereotyped model and thus puts to rest the myth of the heroic male and the passive, mindless heroine (48).

Consider the traditional elements of the chivalric romance or of the fairy tale as a genre. Do you agree with Fraser that *Innocent Eréndira* is consciously imitating the fairy-tale paradigm of the damsel in distress and her knight in shining armor? What case can be made for the grandmother as the mythical monster—the dragon or the ogre—in this story? How might other aspects of the story be understood as components of the parody? Perhaps most important, are there other possible motives behind the parody besides the feminist objective identified by Fraser?

Language, Symbols, and Imagery

Innocent Eréndira is a text filled with symbolism and evocative imag-ery. If you choose to write an essay on language, symbols, and imagery, you will want to seek out every textual mention of the symbol or image. While you will ultimately want to consider scholarly perspectives on the meaning of the symbol or image you choose, you should begin by first making your own interpretation based on your close reading. One of the many possible symbols you might choose is the bones of the two Amadíses. Why does Eréndira's grandmother insist on carrying the remains of her husband and son wherever she travels? Nature also offers several compelling symbols for you to consider. You might want to explain the function of the "wind of misfortune" that blows from the beginning of Eréndira's servitude to her final escape. Another possibility is an analysis of the antithetical images of the desert and the sea. Whichever aspect of language you choose to explore, always keep in mind that your goal is not simply the identification of images or symbols; you also need to propose a coherent explanation of their function that is consistent with the plot, characters, and themes in the text.

Sample Topics:

1. **The bones of the two Amadíses:** Why are the remains of the grandmother's husband and son mentioned so frequently in the story?

   Although both Eréndira's father and grandfather died long before the story begins, their presence is notable. Dead and buried near the grandmother's house, their physical remains travel with her as she travels across the desert, and their memory haunts her dreams. What is the symbolism of the bones of the two Amadíses? Reflect on the complaint by the truck loader about the weight of the truck containing the bones. Jokingly, he implies that the grandmother is probably attempting to smuggle "marble statues" in the guise of human remains (11). Why does the grandmother insist on bringing the bones with her? How does their memory "weigh" on her psyche? What does this suggest about the power of the past, both individual and collective, to alter the present and the future? It has been further noted that the name *Amadís* harkens back to the hero of the chivalric romance *Amadís of Gaul* (1508), caricatured in Cervantes's *Don Quixote* (Bell-Villada 178). Why is it meaningful that García Márquez chooses a name inseparably connected to one of the most famous instances of a brave knight in prose romance and parodied hero in all the history of literature?

2. **The wind:** Write an essay analyzing the function of the wind as a symbol.

The wind is an image repeated throughout the text. Harley D. Oberhelman observes: "From the beginning it is Eréndira's 'wind of misfortune' that causes the conflagration. During a fierce wind she is captured by the nuns and taken to the convent, and in the end she runs 'beyond the arid winds' into the desert" (51). Return to the passages mentioned by Oberhelman and others you may find in your reading. What is the physical description of the wind? What do these descriptions suggest about the wind? For example, is it always associated with "misfortune" (7), or does it have other connotations as well? Thinking about the presence of the wind in other works of literature or cinema with which you are familiar, does García Márquez's use of this imagery reflect or differ from these other works? Should the wind be seen as a magical force, a metaphor for an idea such as fate, or a symbol of Eréndira's struggle for freedom?

3. **Sea and desert:** Examine the interplay between these two antithetical images.

While almost the entire story takes place in the desert, there are constant references to the sea. For example, Ulises recounts to Eréndira his mother's enigmatic assertion that "people who die in the desert don't go to heaven but to the sea" (20). Later, the text reveals that both Ulises and the grandmother have made plans to take Eréndira to the sea. Consider the archetypal significance of desert and sea. Does the story remain consistent with traditional symbolism associated with the desert and the sea? What symbolic associations are created within the text itself? For example, is it significant that the grandmother originally came from an island and is attempting to return to "the Caribbean after half a lifetime of exile" (47)? What about the obvious mythical maritime association of Ulises's "sailor name" (21)? Finally, what might be the meaning of Ulises's description of the sea as being "like the desert but with water" (21)? What might the text be implying here, and how might it be related to Eréndira's decision at the end of the novella to flee, not toward the sea, but rather back into the desert?

Compare and Contrast Essays

Compare and contrast essays offer most intriguing possibilities in that they allow the writer to go beyond the text itself to draw on other literary experiences. The challenge is to select texts that offer additional insight into the primary work being studied. A comparison for its own sake will not make for a very good essay. While you certainly could compare some salient aspect of *Innocent Eréndira* with a work with similar elements by another author, there are also several good points of comparison with other texts by García Márquez. One potential essay is to compare the character of the grandmother with another of García Márquez's most horrendous maternal figures, Sierva María's mother in *Of Love and Other Demons*. A very different kind of comparison involves reading the novella, not as an individual work, but within the context of the collection in which it was published.

Sample Topics:

1. **Eréndira's grandmother and Sierva María's mother:** Write an essay comparing the antagonist of *Innocent Eréndira* with the heroine's reprehensible mother in *Of Love and Other Demons*.

   If there is a García Márquez character that rivals Eréndira's grandmother as a heartless parental figure, it is Bernarda Cabrera, a slave trader addicted to both the laxative qualities of cacao and unbridled promiscuity with her servants. The text notes of Bernarda's daughter, Sierva María, that, "Her mother hated her from the moment she nursed her for the first and only time, and then refused to keep the baby for fear she would kill her" (42). After reading *Of Love and Other Demons*, return to the passages in both that text and *Innocent Eréndira* where the respective characters appear or are discussed. What parallels do you see between the two? What are the similarities and differences between the Bernarda–Sierva María and the grandmother-Eréndira relationships? Thinking about similar figures from other works with which you are familiar (Medea from Greek tragedy or even Cinderella's stepmother), why does the idea of a mother or grandmother hating and or mistreating her own flesh and blood strike such a powerful chord in readers?

2. *Innocent Eréndira* and the short stories from the collection: Analyze the connections between *Innocent Eréndira* and the short stories from the same collection with regard to plot, characters, and themes.

Referring to *Innocent Eréndira,* Raymond Williams asserts: "[I]f one reads it as the last story of the total volume, it contains elements of play which are lost in an isolated reading" (103). Read the other texts that make up the original collection: "A Very Old Man with Enormous Wings," "The Handsomest Drowned Man in the World," "The Sea of Lost Time," "Blacamán the Good, Vendor of Miracles," "The Last Voyage of the Ghost Ship," and "Death Constant Beyond Love." (All of the texts can be found in the HarperPerennial anthology of *Collected Stories*). As you read, note passages that reference *Innocent Eréndira,* and look for characters, themes, or narrative elements common to both texts. For example, as with Eréndira's "wind of misfortune" (1), Mark Millington notes that "every story . . . begins with an arrival—a space or a consciousness is invaded by an unknown presence" (117). What other types of similarities can you identify? After you have completed your reading and have identified as many common traits as possible, make an argument for reading, not *Innocent Eréndira* the novella, but *Innocent Eréndira* the collection as a single, integrated work of fiction.

Bibliography for *The Incredible and Sad Tale of Innocent Eréndira and Her Heartless Grandmother*

Bell-Villada, Gene H. *García Márquez: The Man and His Work.* Chapel Hill: U of North Carolina P, 1990.

Castillo, Rafael C. "Recommended: Gabriel García Márquez." *The English Journal* 77.6 (1984): 77–78.

Fraser, Howard. "Review of *La increíble y triste historia de la cándida Eréndira y de su abuela desalmada." Critical Essays on Gabriel García Márquez.* Ed. George R. McMurray. New York: Frederick Ungar, 1977. 47–49.

García Márquez, Gabriel. *Collected Stories.* New York: HarperPerennial, 1999.

———. *Innocent Eréndira and Other Stories.* Trans. Gregory Rabassa. New York: HarperPerennial, 2005.

———. *Of Love and Other Demons.* Trans. Edith Grossman. New York: Penguin, 1995.

Janes, Regina. *Gabriel García Márquez: Revolutions in Wonderland.* Columbia: U of Missouri P, 1981.

Kaplan, Martin. "Review of *Innocent Eréndira and Other Stories.*" *Critical Essays on Gabriel García Márquez.* Ed. George R. McMurray. New York: Frederick Ungar, 1977. 49–52.

Marting, Diane E. "The End of Eréndira's Prostitution." *Hispanic Review* 69.2 (2001): 175–90.

Millington, Mark. "Aspects of Narrative Structure in *The Incredible and Sad Tale of Innocent Eréndira and Her Heartless Grandmother.*" *García Márquez: New Readings.* Ed. Bernard McGuirk and Richard Cardwell. Cambridge: Cambridge UP, 1987. 117–33.

Oberhelman, Harley. D. *García Márquez: A Study of the Short Fiction.* Boston: Twayne, 1991.

Williams, Raymond. *Gabriel García Márquez.* Boston: Twayne, 1984.

THE AUTUMN OF
THE PATRIARCH

READING TO WRITE

WHILE *The Autumn of the Patriarch* (1976; first published in Spanish as *El otoño del patriarca*, 1975) may not enjoy the popularity of *One Hundred Years of Solitude* or *Love in the Time of Cholera*, it is frequently ranked among Gabriel García Márquez's greatest achievements. Among those who hold the novel in such high esteem is the author himself, who believes that its level of artistic innovation far exceeds even his acknowledged masterpiece: "I've often read reviews that said that *One Hundred Years* was the definitive Latin-American novel. That's ridiculous! If it were the definitive book, I wouldn't have gone on writing. Frankly, I think *The Autumn of the Patriarch* is, as a literary work, much more important as an experimental book" (Dreifus 123–24). The product of nearly seven years of painstaking work in Mexico, Spain, and Colombia and at least three abortive drafts, *The Autumn of the Patriarch* is certainly García Márquez's most stylistically complex novel, arguably his most politically engaged piece of fiction, and perhaps his most astonishing mixture of humor and horror. Recounting the century-long rule of a Caribbean despot known only as "the general," *The Autumn of the Patriarch* represents the Colombian writer's contribution to the Latin American subgenre known as the dictator novel. This fascinating and frightening character study is accomplished through a series of highly sophisticated narrative techniques reminiscent of James Joyce and William Faulkner: a shifting narrative point of view, a nonlinear chronology structured around a dreamlike stream of consciousness, and serpentine sentences often more than a page in length. While this complex structure has led at least one critic to describe the novel as "almost unread-

able" (Strathern 102), it also provides an intricate labyrinth of potential topics for you to explore, first as a reader and then as a writer.

Given that perhaps no other work by García Márquez demands more
critical attention to detail than *The Autumn of the Patriarch*, it behooves
you to be especially focused during the all-important process of close
reading. Consider, for example, the following passage describing the general's resolution of a scandal involving 2,000 children abducted by the
government to cover up fraudulent lottery drawings:

> . . . God damn it, he shouted, either them or me, he shouted, and it was
> them, because before dawn he ordered them to put the children in a
> barge loaded with cement, take them singing to the limits of the territo-
> rial waters, blow them up with a dynamite charge without giving them
> time to suffer as they kept singing, and when the three officers who car-
> ried out the crime came to attention before him with news general sir
> that his order had been carried out, he promoted them two grades and
> decorated them with the medal of loyalty, but then he had them shot
> as common criminals because there were orders that can be given but
> which can not be carried out, God damn it, poor children (106).

This horrifying description of an unspeakable atrocity, which brings an end
to one of the most disturbing subplots of the general's brutal rule, serves as
an excellent example of not only the novel's fictional assault on all-too-real
tyrants but also the arsenal of stylistic techniques at the writer's disposal.
With regard to content, perhaps the first aspect of the passage that the
reader notices is the dictator's modus operandi. Determined to rid himself
of his innocent hostages before they are discovered by an increasingly sus-
picious outside world, he is equally unwilling to assume the blame for his
horrific crime. What effect is created by the inclusion of the detail of having the children sing? What about the general's stated concern that they be
blown up immediately, while still singing, so that there will be no "time to
suffer"? Why does the general promote the two officers and decorate them
if he subsequently has them executed?

Beyond the very nature of the gruesome events described in the passage,
its shocking impact on the reader is heightened by García Márquez's narrative technique. How does the text shift its narrative point of view from the
general, to a third-person narrator, to the officers, and back to the general?
How does this use of shifting voices work to compact narrative time? How

is this telescoping effect reinforced by recounting the entire episode in a single sentence? Consider the general's repeated blasphemy, first followed by the desperate declaration that it's either them or him, and then, later, by his lament for the "poor children." In what way do these curses function as bookends to the incident? How does the contrast between the two assertions linked by the repetition of "God damn it" reinforce the reader's perception not merely of the general's cruelty but also of his hypocritical self-delusion?

As you can see from the portion of the text you have just read, *The Autumn of the Patriarch* is a work that requires you to give equal attention to both content and form—both the message and the manner in which it is relayed. With each of the essay topics that follow here, as well as the many other possibilities you may arrive at from your own careful reading, consider the way the novel's unique use of language functions to inform the meaning of its themes, the perception of its characters, and the power of its ideological positions. Although the text's formal artistry may complicate your task, the resulting essay will be all the richer for your efforts.

TOPICS AND STRATEGIES
Themes

The Autumn of the Patriarch's formal complexity should not be an impediment to your exploration of its content. One area with numerous possibilities for an engaging essay is that of the novel's themes. Consider the author's decision to create a nameless country and a nameless dictator and how this anonymity contributes to the kind of universal meaning typically associated with literary themes. Perhaps the most obvious of these is the theme of power. What does the story of this ageless tyrant imply with regard to political ambition and the consequences of authority? A second theme, found in so many of García Márquez's works, is that of solitude. What does isolation stem from in the text, and what does it suggest about the relationship between power and solitude? Old age is yet another theme addressed in this as well as in other García Márquez texts. How does the patriarch's impossible age figure into the story? How does this meditation on physical decline and inevitable mortality transcend the novel's political ideology? Which other themes might you explore? What kinds of questions are raised for the reader by a book about dictatorship and its terrible effect on the human spirit?

Sample Topics:

1. **Power:** Write an essay exploring what the novel has to say about the troubling human impulse to control and dominate others.

   The patriarch's rise to power and his all-encompassing determination to maintain control seem to dominate the text. Return to the text and reconstruct the patriarch's political career. Why is he able to ascend to a position of absolute authority? How does the text reveal his gradual decline into irrelevance? For Raymond Williams, it is this latter facade of authority, "the illusion of reality and power" that is the "principle [*sic*] theme" in the novel (*García Márquez* 133). What evidence can you find to support Williams's thesis that the general's power, like so much of his legend, is merely an illusion? On the penultimate page of the novel, the general seems to have an epiphany: "[H]e became convinced in the trail of yellow leaves of his autumn that he had never been master of all his power" (254). What does this passage and others seem to suggest about the nature of power and the centuries of human efforts to possess it?

2. **Solitude:** Explore this overarching theme in García Márquez's work as it is manifested both in the title character's isolation and in that of his people.

   While solitude is perhaps the most prevalent theme in García Márquez's writing, Ronald De Feo argues that *The Autumn of the Patriarch* is his "most intense and extreme vision of isolation" (58). De Feo goes on to explain his rationale:

   > In this fabulous, dream-like account of the reign of a nameless dictator of a fantastic Caribbean realm, solitude is linked with the possession of absolute power. The author has worked with this theme before—notably when tracing the career and increasing loneliness of Colonel Aureliano Buendía—but here it receives the grand treatment (58).

   Do you agree with De Feo's characterization of the theme? What evidence can you find in the text to support this assertion?

Besides power, what other factors contribute to his solitude? Is the patriarch the only isolated character? Is it possible to speak of the collective solitude of the citizens living under more than a century of oppression?

3. **Old age:** How does the novel represent the effects of old age through the characters of the general, his mother, and the exiled despots?

As you consider the title of the novel, it becomes apparent that old age is one of its principal themes. What does the season autumn connote with regard to age? What is the archetypal image of a patriarch? Why does the text assign the character an impossible age of "somewhere between 107 and 232 years" (79). How do the general's advanced years affect not only his political power but also his relationships with those around him? Does this aspect of the patriarch lend him a degree of humanity, or does it render his character even more opaque? What other images of old age are represented in the text in characters such as Bendición Alvarado or the other "retired" dictators? What is the novel suggesting about the effects of growing older? Ignacio López-Calvo comments on the presence of the *ubi sunt* theme, a nostalgic meditation on lost youth:

> The title of the novel indicates the moment of the dictator's life that is most meaningful for the author. In chapter 6 a decrepit dictator reaches the autumn of his life persecuted by his victims' ghosts and the memories of his own glorious (in his own view) past. Along with his physical deterioration, the Patriarch grows increasingly nostalgic and pessimistic. The *ubi sunt* theme dominates his last days, once he realizes that his entire life has been a disappointment (30–31).

What do you make of this reading of the text? Does the general's awareness of his own mortality, brought about by advanced age, bring about a final epiphany? What alternative interpretation might you offer, considering the patriarch's desire to remain in control well beyond his natural lifespan?

Characters

With a novel like *The Autumn of the Patriarch*, there is a temptation to explore the criminal psyche of the title character. This is an excellent example of the need to narrow the focus of your topic. Writing on why the character of a ruthless dictator is evil does not make for a very compelling essay. When you want to analyze a monumental figure like the patriarch, you will be better served by choosing a less evident aspect of the character. Another strategy would be to select one of the minor characters. Which of these secondary figures seem to have the most depth and the greatest impact on the novel? Three interesting choices are the female characters that dominate the general's life: Manuela Sánchez, Leticia Nazareno, and Bendición Alvarado. Whether you select one of these figures or a different one altogether, be certain to ask yourself not only why the character is interesting but also why his or her presence bears on the rest of novel. How would the plot, themes, and other characters be affected if your character did not exist?

Sample Topics:

1. **The patriarch:** Write an essay that examines some less obvious aspect of this monstrous, yet extremely complex figure.

   It could be argued that the general's presence dominates *The Autumn of the Patriarch* more so than any other fictional character in any other García Márquez novel. Given both the complexity of the character and the sheer volume of references to him in the novel, it might behoove you to focus on one single aspect of his persona. As you revisit the portrait of the general created by the text, consider those elements not necessarily related to his villainy. For example, what might you say about humor in the depiction of the patriarch? Raymond Williams notes the comic subversion of the character's omnipotence: "The inside view of the General and his power supports this God-like characterization, and it also creates humor by showing the pettiness of his conception of power (in contrast with the grandiosity of the god figure), and his paranoia and puerility" (*García Márquez* 126). What other aspects of his character could make for a compelling essay? In what way can the general also be seen as a tragic figure? How could you explore his relationships with women or with the soldiers and politicians who surround him?

2. **Manuela Sánchez:** Analyze the working-class beauty who becomes the general's obsession.

Manuela Sánchez is distinct from the other characters in the novel. Unlike the many soldiers and civilians who fall victim to the patriarch's bloody reign; unlike his mother, Bendición Alvarado, and his wife, Leticia Nazareno; unlike the ruler himself, Manuela escapes death and, in a sense, achieves a kind of retribution. Kessel Schwartz notes her uniqueness: "Manuela Sánchez, beauty queen winner, disappears during an eclipse and reappears in his nightmares as the only one to escape his power" (557). Reread chapter 2, which deals with the relationship between the dictator and Manuela. How does her character further the reader's understanding of the general and his world? Why does this character, unlike all the others, escape and endure? Should Manuela Sánchez and the subplot surrounding her be read metaphorically, perhaps as a hopeful symbol of survival for those living under oppression?

3. **Leticia Nazareno:** Write an essay about the general's wife and her function in the novel.

Leticia Nazareno is one of the most dynamic figures in the novel. First an innocent of the general's vindictiveness, then his only true love, and finally an extension of his corrupt rule through her own excess, Leticia Nazareno offers the opportunity for an intriguing character study. If you choose to write an essay on this character, begin by returning to the parts of the text where she figures most prominently. What do you know about her biography? How does she go from a kidnapped nun, "petrified with terror" (152), to an all-powerful consort who has "come far with her airs of a queen" (175)? Why does Leticia hold such a lofty position when so many of her predecessors and successors are used by the general and cast aside? Ignacio López-Calvo contends that Leticia fulfills "the protagonist's unattainable quest to return to the safe times of his childhood . . . [in] his mother's double or for a new mother" (30). What evidence can you find in the text for what López-Calvo describes as the way the patriarch is "infantilized" (30) by Leticia Nazareno? Is her own eventual corruption the result of the evil influences around her, or is she herself immoral?

4. **Bendición Alvarado:** Explore the role of the general's mother in both life and death.

The general's mother is certainly one of the most memorable characters in the novel. Her naiveté and working-class mindset stand in stark contrast to the political intrigue and decadence that surround her and are one of the most notable sources of humor in the novel. Consider the following passage where she scolds her son about his economic extravagance:

> It's fine for you to enjoy it, she said, but think about the future, I don't want to see you begging hat in hand at the door of some church if tomorrow or later God forbid they take away the chair you're sitting in, if you knew how to sing at least, or were an archbishop or a navigator, but you're only a general, so you're not good for anything except command (58).

What is basic for the comedy in this scene? What does it reveal about the character and her relationship with the fearful dictator? Revisit the other parts of the novel dealing with Bendición Alvarado, and gather as many details as you can about her life. How would you characterize her role in the story? Pay special attention to the events following her death. Why is it so important to the general that she be canonized?

History and Context

Even though *The Autumn of the Patriarch* is set in a fictitious country with a mythical despot, the novel has numerous connections to the culture and history of Latin America. Perhaps the most obvious topic for this kind of essay would be for you to trace the character of the patriarch back to the actual historical dictators from whom he seems to have been drawn. You might choose one particular historical figure identified by critics, or you might attempt to examine the patriarch as a composite of several contemporary tyrants. A different historical context for you to explore would be the repeated allusions to colonialism and neocolonialism in the novel. What is the consequence of foreign intervention, and how is it, in some ways, as nefarious as the dictatorship? A third topic deals, not with politics, but with poetry. You could write an essay analyzing the significance of the real-life Nicaraguan poet Rubén Darío, who appears in chapter 5 of the novel. Why does García Márquez include an artist in the story, and why does he choose Darío in particular? Beyond these three topics, there are many more possibilities for an essay on history and context. Just remember that while you need to have a solid grasp of the historical context you study, you also need to be sure that you always relate it back to your principal subject, the text itself.

Sample Topics:

1. **Dictatorships:** Write an essay on the actual regimes that may have been the inspiration behind the novel.

Neither the protagonist nor the events recounted in *The Autumn of the Patriarch* were drawn from the experience of any single country. Observers cite the names of numerous despots whose criminal regimes may have inspired García Márquez, from Venezuela's Marco Pérez Jiménez and Haiti's François "Papa Doc" Duvalier (Williams, *García Márquez* 110–11) to Chile's Augusto Pinochet and Spain's Francisco Franco (Yardley C103). You might choose one or more of these dictators and trace the similarities between his rule and that of the patriarch. A second option would be to select specific events in the story and look for historical parallels in the amalgam of dictatorships upon which García Márquez has drawn. An example of this kind of analysis can be seen in Marjorie Agosín and Barbara E. Pierce's work, as they note the similarity between the crowd's discovery of the patriarch's body and "the same image upon encountering [Nicaraguan dictator Anastasio] Somoza's body" (329) after the triumph of the Sandinista revolution. No matter the direction you choose to take your essay, keep in mind that you are writing a literary essay and that, while you will need to familiarize yourself with the underlying history, your analysis must ultimately lead back to the fictional text. How does the fictionalization of history render it more powerful than fact?

2. **Colonialism and neocolonialism in Latin America:** How does the history of European and U.S. hegemony in Latin America figure into the novel?

While *The Autumn of the Patriarch* is clearly an indictment of the dictatorial regimes that plagued much of Latin America from the 1950s through the 1970s, the novel also takes clear aim at the wealthy nations—namely the United States and the imperial powers of Europe—that had been exploiting the region for centuries. Consider the many references to the "ambassadors" and what they ask—and sometimes demand—of the patriarch? Think about the repeated attempts by the U.S. government to buy the sea and reflect on the following passage:

> . . . Ambassador MacQueen answered him that conditions don't warrant any more discussion . . . either the marines land or we take the sea, there's no way, your excellency, there was no other way, mother, so they took the Caribbean in April, Ambassador Ewing's nautical engineers carried it off in numbered pieces to plant it far from the hurricanes in the blood-red dawns of Arizona, they took it with everything it had inside general sir . . . (232).

What is the symbolic value of this surreal transaction? How does the ambassador's use of extortion—either economic exploitation or military intervention—reflect the historical experience of Latin America with regard to the United States? In what way does the patriarch's staunch resistance to the Americans (prior to this ultimatum) ennoble an otherwise reprehensible character? How does this aspect of the novel speak to Latin American nationalism in the face of U.S. imperialism?

3. **The poetry of Rubén Darío:** Explain the inclusion in the novel of this celebrated Latin American poet and his work.

Rubén Darío (1867–1916) is widely held to be one of the greatest and most influential Spanish-language poets of the modern period. Both the poet and his work figure prominently in the section of the novel dealing with Leticia Nazareno. Return to chapter 5 and conduct a close reading of the passages mentioning Darío, especially the night of his poetry recital at the National Theater (182–83). You will also want to familiarize yourself with the poet and his work ("Triumphal March," which is specifically referenced in the passage, is included in the anthology *Selected Writings*). How does Darío's poetry affect the general? In what way does it reflect the dynamics of his relationship with Leticia Nazareno? How does the theme of military glory and self-sacrifice in "Triumphal March," as well as the themes common to many other Darío poems—aesthetic beauty, decadence, fatality—reverberate in the novel? With regard to the significance of the poetic act itself, Jo Labanyi asserts:

> What attracts the patriarch in Darío's poetry is his attempt to create an eternal, universal poetic language that transcends the limitations of human existence. For the patriarch, writing has the value of memory; it is an attempt to perpetuate through repetition that which otherwise is condemned to oblivion (138).

What do you make of Labanyi's interpretation? The dictator is never named, whereas Darío, described as "well-known" (173) and "famous" (181), is also deeply admired by Leticia Nazareno. Could the text be making a statement about the proverbial superiority of the pen to the sword?

Form and Genre

Given that *The Autumn of the Patriarch* is generally recognized as García Márquez's most stylistically ambitious novel, you should have no trouble formulating a good topic for your essay. It may seem paradoxical, but those aspects of the text that make it the most difficult to read might also afford you some of your most intriguing potential subjects. While a more straightforward topic is the text's relationship to the subgenre of the dictator novel, consider the possibilities within the narrative structure. For example, you could examine the use of narrative point of view. Why does the novel shift so frequently between first-, second-, and third-person subjects? Another somewhat confusing narrative technique that would make for an excellent essay is the text's rejection of a traditional linear chronology. How does time "flow" in *The Autumn of the Patriarch*? Whether you choose one of these topics or another one dealing with form and genre, remember that your essay should not limit itself to simply identifying the book's formal structures. It should also offer an explanation as to how those structures affect the reader's understanding of the novel's characters, plot, and themes.

Sample Topics:

1. **The dictator novel:** Study García Márquez's novel within the context of this Latin American literary subgenre.

The dictator novel is a subgenre that can be traced to the 19th century. Research the evolution of this almost uniquely Spanish-American narrative form, and identify its principal elements (a good starting point is Raymond Williams's *The Twentieth-Century Spanish American Novel*). How does *The Autumn of the Patriarch* reflect or differ from the traditional tenets of the subgenre? Roberto González Echeverría contends the essential innovation by García Márquez lies in transforming the dictator motif into "a mock foundation myth whose ultimate model is Christianity itself" (213). He elaborates: "The dictator with his 'holy family,' his providential advent (from utterly obscure origins—he is fatherless but for more worldly reasons than Christ) to 'save' the Republic, and his 'resurrection' at the beginning of the book make him a farcical *figura Christi*" (213). Does your own reading of the text support this thesis? If so, what further textual evidence can you find to confirm it? If not, what is the fundamental element of the text's assault on totalitarianism?

2. **Point of view:** How does the text use shifting narrative point of view?

One of the most salient formal aspects of *The Autumn of the Patriarch* is its constant shifting between narrators, often within the same sentence. Consider, for example, the following shift in a passage describing the power struggle between the title character and the other members of the military junta:

> I had more power than any of one of them but much less than two of them plotting together, still unaware that he saw the others just as they were while the others were never able to glimpse the thoughts of the granite old man whose serenity was matched only by his smooth-sailing prudence and his immense disposition for waiting, we saw only his lugubrious eyes, his thin lips, his chaste maidens hand which did not even tremble on the hilt of his saber that noon of horror when they came to him with the news general sir (52).

The narration moves from the first person singular (*I*) to the third person plural (*they*), to the first person plural (*we*) (the rival generals), to a different third person plural (other government officials), to another first person plural addressing the "general sir." Gene H. Bell-Villada contends that the "psychological shock of these displacements . . . manages to convey the full sense of despotism and its both systematic and arbitrary network of relationships" (464–65). Do you agree with this interpretation? Beyond re-creating the "linguistics . . . of dictatorship" (465), as Bell-Villada puts it, what other effects does constant narrative transition have on the reader's experience?

3. **Narrative time:** Analyze the novel's nonlinear chronology and how it functions to re-create the process of memory.

One of the most noticeable aspects of the novel is its repetition of events. For example, almost every chapter returns to the discovery of the dictator's body. What other events in the story are repeated? Which ones recur in the general's mind, and which ones form part of the collective memory of the nation? Thinking about the organization of these recollections, what is the novel suggesting about the nature of memory and its relationship to reality (that is, history)? Lois Parkinson Zamora contends that the text "cycles and recycles a character, a nameless dictator who dies and returns from death to impose an endlessly repeating series of political abuses. His status as an archetype depends on this sense of repetition and return . . ." (82). Do you agree with this assessment? What other functions might be served by the novel's nonlinear chronology?

Language, Symbols, and Imagery

Essays on language, symbols, and imagery allow you to think about how a text creates meaning from within. Given the cyclical representation of the plot, you will notice the repetition of certain images and objects. You can write a very engaging essay on how these images function to convey an idea, create a mood, or raise a question in the reader's mind. One of the first images you encounter in the novel is that of the cows who have taken over the presidential palace. A second image appearing from the outset and, like the cows, reappearing throughout the story is the body of the patriarch itself. What other images seem to have some kind of symbolic or metaphorical value? Remember that merely identifying a symbol does not constitute a good essay. You also need to explain what it means and perhaps how its meaning changes over the course of the novel.

Sample Topics:

1. **Cows:** What is the symbolism of the cows that populate the presidential palace?

In the opening scene of the novel, the crowd entering the presidential palace discovers that another invader has already overrun the building:

> We saw the ruined offices and the protocol salons through which the brazen cows wandered, eating the velvet curtains and nibbling at the trim on the chairs, we saw heroic portraits of saints and soldiers thrown to the floor among broken furniture and fresh cow flops, we saw a dining room that had been eaten up by the cows, the music room profaned by the cows breakage, the domino tables destroyed and the felt billiard tables cropped by the cows . . . (3).

The image of the cows in the palace is one that returns again and again during the course of the story. If you decide to write this essay, begin by reflecting on the broader symbolism of this particular animal. Why does García Márquez choose cows rather than, for instance, dogs or pigs? Then, return to the text and identify all of the passages relating to the animals. How do they first get into the palace? Why does the patriarch want them there, and what does this reveal about his character? How might the cows be symbolic of the people of the country over whom the patriarch has ruled for so long?

2. **The general's corpse:** Why is the image of the general's decaying corpse repeated so many times in the novel?

Every chapter of the book but one begins with a similar description of the general's body (or that of his double) as it is found in the palace by a group of onlookers who are, presumably, members of the populace. Returning to these passages, what is the attitude of the spectators? Are they convinced that the body is indeed that of the general? Why are they not more enthusiastic, given the nature of the general's long, heinous rule? Adelaida López Mejía provides two potential explanations, both of which interpret the corpse as symbolic of the citizenry. First, she sees one of the on-lookers' motives as "the possible satisfaction they derive from gloating over the body of the man who formerly ruled them" (306), but she also raises the possibility of the people's "complicit dependence upon him," arguing that "in their fascination with the dictator's body they remain under its sway" (307). Which of these two interpretations do you find more convincing? Could they both be accurate? Are there other explanations of the body's symbolic value? What else might it represent besides the people's view of their leader?

Compare and Contrast Essays

When you think about writing a compare and contrast essay on *The Autumn of the Patriarch*, reflect on the elements of the novel you found most compelling in your reading. Now consider whether you have seen similar elements in other literature you have read—both by García Márquez and other writers. The most striking aspect of the text is almost certainly its style. Knowing that García Márquez's principal inspiration in this area was William

Faulkner, you could compare the formal innovation in *The Autumn of the Patriarch* with one of Faulkner's major works, such as *Absalom, Absalom!* or *The Sound and the Fury.* If you want to explore the way García Márquez treats an element common to two of his own works, you might write on the solitude of power by comparing the patriarch with Colonel Aureliano Buendía in *One Hundred Years of Solitude* or Simón Bolívar in *The General in His Labyrinth.* Keep in mind that this type of essay offers almost endless possibilities; it is as broad as your own background as a reader and your ability to find commonalities between texts.

Sample Topics:

1. ***The Autumn of the Patriarch* and Faulkner's *Absalom, Absalom!*:** Compare one of William Faulkner's masterpieces to one of García Márquez's most Faulknerian works.

It is widely acknowledged that the author of *The Autumn of the Patriarch* was "deeply influenced by the work of Faulkner" (Kennedy 64). As Harley D. Oberhelman observes, there are numerous stylistic similarities between García Márquez's dictator novel and Faulkner's fictionalized accounts of the American South:

> In many of Faulkner's writings and in *El otoño del patriarca,* the work begins at or near the end of the action, and flashbacks related by different narrators fill out the picture. Each point of view is incomplete; often it is the memory of the past as recalled by the nebulous present. Often there is an incompleteness at the end of the work, and the reader is called upon to "finish" the novel (77).

Oberhelman further notes that the Colombian writer was "especially interested" in Faulkner's *Absalom, Absalom!* (1936), and that its "structure and technique are evident . . . models" for *The Autumn of the Patriarch* (76). Working from *Absalom, Absalom!* (you could also use another Faulkner novel that you have already read), search for specific examples of the stylistic elements identified by Oberhelman that are common to both novels. Are all of these Faulknerian narrative strategies also present in García Márquez's book? Which ones are the most prevalent? Are any absent or less frequent in the latter text? Is García Márquez merely imitating Faulkner, or can it be argued that *The Autumn of the Patriarch* represents a new trajectory?

2. **The general in his palace and *The General in His Labyrinth*:** Examine the ironic similarities between García Márquez's portraits of a fictional tyrant and a fictionalized hero.

The protagonists of these two texts—the general, an amalgam of so many petty tyrants, and Simón Bolívar, the Liberator of Latin America—would seem to have little in common. While one novel is the portrait of a monster and the other of a hero, both works examine the paradoxical solitude of those who lead nations and the inevitable victory of time over even the mightiest rulers. Consider the dying Bolívar's lament: "I've become lost in a dream, searching for something that doesn't exist" (*The General in His Labyrinth* 221). How does this compare to the patriarch's own decline into a meaningless existence in the final years of his rule? What other quotations can you identify that reveal Bolívar's situation to be much like that of the dictator? How does this similarity between two such antithetical characters lend even greater veracity to the themes shared by the two novels?

Bibliography and Online Resources for *The Autumn of the Patriarch*

Agosín, Marjorie, and Barbara E. Pierce. "Inhabitants of Decayed Palaces: The Dictator in the Latin American Novel." *Human Rights Quarterly* 12.2 (1990): 328–35.

Bell-Villada, Gene H. "Pronoun Shifters, Virginia Woolf, Béla Bartók, Plebian Forms, Real-Life Tyrants, and the Shaping of García Márquez's 'Patriarch.'" *Contemporary Literature* 28.4 (1987): 460–82.

Darío, Rubén. *Selected Writings.* Ed. Ilan Stavans. New York: Penguin Viking, 2005.

De Feo, Ronald. "The Solitude of Power." *Critical Essays on Gabriel García Márquez.* Ed. George R. McMurray. Boston: G. K. Hall, 1987. 58–60.

Dreifus, Claudia. "*Playboy* Interview: Gabriel García Márquez." *Conversations with Gabriel García Márquez*. Ed. Gene H. Bell-Villada. Jackson: U of Mississippi P, 2006. 93–132.

García Márquez, Gabriel. *The Autumn of the Patriarch*. Trans. Gregory Rabassa. New York: HarperPerennial, 2006.

———. *The General in His Labyrinth*. Trans. Edith Grossman. New York: Vintage, 1990.

González Echeverría, Roberto. "The Dictatorship of Rhetoric/The Rhetoric of Dictatorship: Carpentier, García Márquez, and Roa Bastos." *Latin American Research Review* 15.3 (1980): 205–28.

Kennedy, William. "The Yellow Trolley Car in Barcelona: An Interview." *Conversations with Gabriel García Márquez*. Ed. Gene H. Bell-Villada. Jackson: U of Mississippi P, 2006. 59–78.

Labanyi, Jo. "Language and Power in *The Autumn of the Patriarch*." *Gabriel García Márquez: New Readings*. Ed. Bernard McGuirk and Richard Cardwell. Cambridge: Cambridge UP, 1987. 135–49.

López-Calvo, Ignacio. *"God and Trujillo": Literary and Cultural Representations of the Dominican Dictator*. Gainesville: UP of Florida, 2005.

López Mejía, Adelaida. "Burying the Dead: Repetition in *El otoño del patriarca*." *MLN* 107.2 (1992): 298–320.

Oberhelman, Harley D. "William Faulkner and Gabriel García Márquez: Two Nobel Laureates." *Critical Essays on Gabriel García Márquez*. Ed. George R. McMurray. Boston: G. K. Hall, 1987. 67–79.

Schwartz, Kessel. "Review of *El otoño del patriarca*." *Hispania* 59.3 (1976): 557.

Strathern, Paul. *García Márquez in 90 Minutes*. Chicago: Ivan R. Dee, 2004.

Williams, Raymond L. *Gabriel García Márquez*. Boston, Twayne, 1984.

———. *The Twentieth-Century Spanish American Novel*. Austin: U of Texas P, 2003.

Yardley, Jonathon. "When a Great Novelist Turned His Pen on Tyranny." *Washington Post* 26 May 2003: C103. 27 September 2008. <http://www.washingtonpost.com/ac2/wp-dyn/A39273-2003May25>.

Zamora, Lois Parkinson. *The Usable Past: The Imagination of History in Recent Fictions of the Americas*. Cambridge: Cambridge UP, 1997.

CHRONICLE OF A
DEATH FORETOLD

READING TO WRITE

*C*HRONICLE OF *a Death Foretold* (*Crónica de una muerte anuciada*, 1981),
translated into English in 1983, is one of Gabriel García Márquez's
most popular and most original works. A departure from the magic realism of *One Hundred Years of Solitude* and the short stories of the *Innocent
Erénrida* collection, as well as from the baroque narrative technique of
The Autumn of the Patriarch, this 120-page novella raises a broad range of
fascinating issues within an engaging and enigmatic tale of sex, betrayal,
and murder. Based on the actual honor killing of one of García Márquez's
friends some 25 years earlier, *Chronicle of a Death Foretold* finds the author
applying the journalistic technique of his early years as a reporter to a fictionalized search to learn why a man is murdered during broad daylight in
a small town despite the fact that virtually every member of the community has foreknowledge of both the crime and its perpetrators. Characterized as everything from "a mystery turned inside out" (Grossman 61) to "a
parody of Greek tragedy" (King 305), this multifaceted text should provide
you with ample material to write an engaging essay. And, as you begin to
search for a topic for your paper, your first step should be to return to the
passages that struck you as most compelling and undertake a close reading. You might, for example, choose the description of Bayardo San Román
at the beginning of chapter 2:

> Bayardo San Román, the man who had given back his bride, had turned
> up for the first time in August of the year before: six months before the

wedding. He arrived on the weekly boat with some saddlebags decorated with silver that matched the buckle of his belt and the rings on his boots. He was around thirty years old, but they were well-concealed, because he had the waist of a novice bullfighter, golden eyes, and a skin slowly roasted by saltpeter. He arrived wearing a short jacket and very tight trousers, both of natural calfskin, and kid gloves of the same color. Magdalena Oliver had been with him on the boat and couldn't take her eyes off him during the whole trip. "He looked like a fairy," she told me. "And it was a pity, because I could have buttered him and eaten him alive." She wasn't the only one who thought so, nor was she the last to realize that Bayardo San Román was not a man to be known at first sight (25–26).

One of the most noticeable elements of this passage is its feigned objectivity in describing the character. A combination of chronological events, realist details, and eyewitness commentary worthy of García Márquez's journalistic background, the third-person narrator never offers a subjective opinion on the enigmatic Bayardo San Román. For example, how does the first "fact" concerning San Román's initial appearance, "six months before the wedding," contribute to the reader's suspicions? What is the connotation of stating that the character "had turned up" rather than simply "had arrived"? The passage also projects an image of sexual ambiguity. How do his thin waist, his clothes, and the elaborate silver decoration on his leatherwork suggest not only his patrician status but also a decidedly feminine aspect to San Román's personality? How does the description of his age as "well-concealed" allude both to his unmanly vanity and a secret he might be hiding from the world? Thinking about the traditional costume of a bullfighter, what do you make of his characterization as looking like a "novice" in the sport? How does the reference to San Román's "golden eyes" simultaneously connote both his wealth and his striking, yet disturbingly unnatural appearance? Consider Magdalena Oliver's comment. In what way do the decidedly vulgar conclusions she draws about Bayardo San Román's sexuality punctuate the suspicions already planted by the prior "objective" details? How do all of these insinuations, which lead to the conclusion that the character "was not a man to be known at first sight," affect the reader's understanding of the events surrounding the murder of Santiago Nasar?

As is made plain by the description of Bayardo San Román, another aspect of the novella that is present in this passage is the rigid concept of gender roles in traditional Latin American society. Magdalena Oliver's assertion that San Román is a homosexual seems to flow as a logical conclusion based on the character's appearance. While this seems to be a logical assumption within the context of the passage, it also reminds the reader that *Chronicle of a Death Foretold* reflects the *machista* prejudice of the culture in which it is set. For example, think about the observation that "he had a waist like a novice bullfighter." Beyond the suggestion of a feminine body type, what is the significance of bullfighting within Hispanic culture, and what might thus be implied by a man being a "novice" in the ultimate ritual of machismo? In what way does Magdalena Oliver's gastronomic expression of lust also serve to emasculate San Román in light of prevailing attitudes about the respective roles of sexual predator and prey?

The passage that introduces Bayardo San Román is an excellent example of how an apparently simple character description can lead to any number of essays—ranging from the text's feigned objectivity to the cultural context underlying gender roles. As you consider the potential topics that are discussed in the following pages, keep in mind that they represent only a handful of the many different directions your essay can take. If you allow your decision to be guided not by the most obvious, or the seemingly easiest option, but rather the one that stands out most based on your own reading of the text, you can be confident that you will find more than ample material for an engaging essay.

TOPICS AND STRATEGIES
Themes

For a relatively short novel, *Chronicle of a Death Foretold* touches on a wide range of those essential aspects and ideas of the human experience that we commonly label as literary themes. One such theme you may wish to explore is love. There seems to be a paradox that a story involving a wedding and an alleged love affair makes little reference to genuine sentiment. How can this be, and what does it suggest about the nature of romantic love? Honor is another major theme that merits further investigation. It is the stated reason for Santiago Nasar's murder, but it is never clearly defined by any of the parties involved. Your essay could explore not only the meaning of honor to the characters in the story but also the statement the novella is making about the concept of honor and its consequences. A third topic that would make for a good essay on theme is fate. Given the case of Santiago Nasar, is the text arguing that human fate is predestined?

Sample Topics:

1. **Love:** What is this violent and disturbing story saying about love?

   Gene H. Bell-Villada argues that "at the core of *Chronicle* is a love story, a narrative about the customs, clashes, illusions, and emotions of love" (187). If this is so, then who is in love? Angela Vicario expresses "fear" toward Bayardo San Román and tells the narrator, "He reminded me of the devil" (28). Bayardo, for his part, seems to marry Angela on a whim: "When I wake up . . . remind me I'm going to marry her" (29). Santiago Nasar, ironically, is shown to have no relationship whatsoever with the woman he has allegedly seduced. You might also discuss other relationships, such as that between Santiago Nasar and his fiancée, Flora Miguel, or the role of "the most tender woman" (64) in the town, the prostitute María Alejandrina Cervantes. What, then, is the novella suggesting about love? How much of this powerful emotion is actually rooted in sex, ego, and economics? After you have reread the passages dealing with love, offer your own explanation of its paradoxical role in the novella. Be sure to include in your explanation the only apparent manifestation of genuine sentiment: the rapprochement between Angela and Bayardo and her curious epiphany "that hate and love are reciprocal passions" (93).

2. **Honor:** How is honor defined in the novella, and what statement is being made about its consequences?

   Chronicle of a Death Foretold is replete with references to honor. But, how does the text define the concept? For example, consider the following reflection on the aftermath of the murder: "Santiago Nasar had expiated the insult, the brothers Vicario had proved their status as men, and the seduced sister was in possession of her honor once more" (83–84). To what "insult" does the quotation refer? Why was the murderers' "manhood" dependent on killing Santiago Nasar? In what sense did Angela Vicario lose "her honor"? What connection does the text create between honor, violence, and female sexuality? Revisit other passages that mention or refer to honor. Do they reflect the same relationship? Once you have determined the way the text defines honor, reflect on what it is saying about this attitude. Is honor, as represented in the novella, a virtue or a scourge on society?

3. **Fate:** Explore the theme of destiny as it relates to Santiago Nasar's "death foretold."

The second sentence in the novella relates a dream that Santiago Nasar had the night before his murder. The text notes that the victim fails to "recognize the omen" and that his mother, despite her "well-earned reputation as an accurate interpreter of other people's dreams" also misrecognizes "any ominous augury" (4). Given the title of the novel and the lengthy discussion of clairvoyance at its outset, the thematic importance of fate is rather evident. Reread passages in the novella that either discuss or allude to Santiago Nasar's death in terms of fate or destiny. Beyond the supernatural conception of fate represented by the passage cited above, how does the text conceive of a different kind of predestination related to the progress of the actual events in the story? In what way can it be said that Santiago Nasar is doomed by completely unforeseen, socially determined circumstances?

Characters

Essays on characters may be the simplest with regard to identifying a topic, but they also offer a number of challenges. While you will want to begin by constructing the character's "biography," such an activity, in itself, does not constitute an analysis. When you write about a specific character, you need to offer an original argument as to what its function is in the text and why such said role is important to the text's broader themes, symbolism, or philosophy. The obvious first choice for a character essay on *Chronicle of a Death Foretold* is Santiago Nasar. Less evident is which aspect of his character to explore. You might choose to investigate the question of whether he is completely innocent or partially the cause of his own death? Perhaps the most truly tragic figure in the novella is Angela Vicario. What might you say about her? Is she the true victim in the story? What direction could you take in an essay about the murderers, the Vicario brothers? Are they willing, cold-blooded assassins or pathetic products—victims in their own right—of an antiquated honor code? Finally, you might choose to write on the ambiguous figure of Bayardo San Román. Who is he? Why does he marry Angela Vicario? What does he symbolize in the novella? Beyond these principal characters, what might you say about the many other minor personages who all seem to have a part in the death being chronicled?

Sample Topics:

1. **Santiago Nasar:** Is Santiago Nasar an innocent victim, or is he responsible, albeit partially, for his own death?

   If you choose to write an essay on Santiago Nasar, your principal task will be to reconstruct the events surrounding his murder. While the ultimate question—whether or not he was the seducer of Angela Vicario—remains an enigma, the text invites the reader to speculate on how the character's behavior contributes to his demise. Michael Bell describes Santiago Nasar in the following way:

   > At an immediate dramatic level it is necessary to see Santiago as innocent, for all we know, of the offence for which he is killed, although at the same time he must not become merely an object of sentimentally innocent pathos. His treatment of women . . . gives him a significant personal failing while enabling us to understand this in terms of his own anachronistic code (90).

   Do you agree with Bell's assessment? What is the "anachronistic code" to which he refers? Is he ultimately no different from the other males in the novel, or does his difference—his class and ethnicity—make him an easy target for a moral transgression he has not committed?

2. **Angela Vicario:** Analyze Angela Vicario's role in the murder of Santiago Nasar and her behavior subsequent to the crime. Is she the true victim in the story?

In many ways, it is not Santiago Nasar but Angela Vicario who should be seen as the novella's central character. She is the common link between the victim, the murderers, and the aggrieved Bayardo San Román. Given that she is forced into a marriage to a man she does not love, beaten into a seemingly false accusation, and resigned to a life of repentance, is hers the actual tragedy? What might you write about her life after the murder? Consider this passage regarding her newfound love for the husband she once loathed: "She became a virgin again just for him, and she recognized no other authority than her own nor any other service than her obsession" (93). Why does Angela change so dramatically, and what does it suggest about her character?

3. **The Vicario brothers:** Analyze the behavior of Santiago Nasar's killers. Do they truly want to carry out the killing? Are both equally responsible for the crime?

If you choose to write an essay on Pedro and Pablo Vicario, the first step you will want to take is to reconstruct their biographies. What are the differences between the twins? Given their biological relationship and their consistent decisions to act in tandem, can it be argued that they are essentially one character? Why are there two murderers in the story if they are so similar? A second point you will want to consider is whether they truly want to kill Santiago Nasar. Critics such as Michael Bell frequently contend that they "are living up to a principle which they do not wish, and partly know they do not wish to carry out" (87).

4. **Bayardo San Román:** Write an essay on the character identified as "the victim" in the novella.

The text leaves no doubt as to the status of Angela Vicario's unhappy groom: "For the immense majority of people there was only one victim: Bayardo San Román" (83). At the same time, perhaps no character in the novel is as mysterious and as morally ambiguous as he. Return to the passages, such as the one at the beginning of this chapter, where the text seems to allude to his underlying motivations. For example, what do you make of

Bayardo San Román's cavalier attitude toward buying the widower Xius's house? Reflecting on that scene, Rubén Pelayo asserts that "Bayardo, as character, shows no value system greater than his own monetary system" (126). Is Bayardo San Román actually the antagonist of the novel? If so, how do you interpret his decision, years after the murder, to return to Angela Vicario? Is he in any way redeemed by this reconciliation?

History and Context

Essays on history and context represent a unique opportunity and a unique challenge. While they allow you to approach the work of literature in relation to the social, political, and cultural environment in which it was created, such essays often require additional research to achieve a better understanding of that context. One potential topic for a history and context essay on *Chronicle of a Death Foretold* is the novel's treatment of the multiethnic society so typical of Latin American countries in the Caribbean. Another, quite distinct, cultural topic would be to examine the way the text reflects gender roles in Latin American society.

Sample Topics:

1. **The Caribbean as a multiethnic society:** Write an essay focusing on the representation of relations between different ethnic groups in the novel as a reflection of the cultural and ethnic diversity of the Caribbean.

One of the distinguishing features of the nameless town in *Chronicle of a Death Foretold* is its ethnic diversity. Three distinct ethnic groups are identified in the novella: characters of African descent (Victoria Guzmán and her daughter), characters of European descent (the San Román and Vicario families), and characters of Middle Eastern descent (the Nasars and the "Arab" community). The origins of the first two groups are plainly traceable to the Spanish conquest of the Caribbean and the subsequent slave trade. The so-called Arab population reflects the massive immigration of Lebanese, Syrian, and Palestinian Christians who fled the Ottoman Empire (for this reason they are sometimes referred to as "Turks" in the novel) in the late 19th and early 20th centuries (Holland 7). How does the text represent the relations between these three ethnic groups? Returning to the relevant passages, such as Victoria Guzman's confrontation in the kitchen with Santiago Nasar (9) and the scene describing the Vicarios' fear of "revenge by the Arabs" (81), explain how ethnicity seems to play a role in the story. Pay particular attention to the instance when Santiago Nasar is described in terms of his Middle Eastern heritage. Can it be argued that ethnic divisions in the community play as important a role as honor in the murder?

2. **Gender roles in Latin America:** How does machismo function as a subtext to the events in the novella?

While sexism and patriarchy are forms of gender-based oppression found in almost all societies, one of the most pernicious manifestations of this type of prejudice is the distinctly Latin social code known as machismo. Begin by reflecting on Evelyn P. Stevens oft-quoted definition of machismo as "a cult of virility, the chief characteristics of which are exaggerated aggressiveness and intransigence in male-to-male interpersonal relationships and arrogance and sexual aggression in male-to-female relationships" (315). Such behavior has clear implications for understanding the cultural context of *Chronicle of a Death Foretold*. Reread the passages dealing with the principal male characters' attitudes and actions toward women. Working from Stevens's definition, what difference, if any, do you find between Santiago Nasar, Bayardo San Román, and the Vicario brothers? Do other members of the community (including female characters) resist or reinforce their *machista* tendencies? Can you make an argument that it is machismo, as much as any other factor, that is responsible for the murder?

Philosophy and Ideas

When writing an essay dealing with philosophy and ideas, you are examining the way a work supports, refutes, or reflects a particular worldview. Such topics can often be stated in the form of a question. In *Chronicle of a Death Foretold*, one such topic deals with the possibility of knowing the truth—the underlying significance of words and actions—embodied in the question "Can the truth ever be known?" A different kind of essay dealing with philosophy and ideas is one that explores the presence of specific ideological positions or theories within the text. This might relate to a particular "-ism," such as anticlericalism, the opposition to institutional religion. While this latter type of essay may oblige you to do some additional outside reading on the history of the idea you plan to study, it also permits you to draw connections between the literary text and the broader intellectual currents it engages.

Sample Topics:

1. **Can the truth ever be known?** How can the novella be read as a commentary on our desire as human beings to give rational meaning to the often irrational world around us?

   Asserting that the subject of the novella is "the problem of knowing and narrating the past," Lois Parkinson Zamora asks, "Can one really know what really happened, or why? If so, can one's knowledge ever be satisfactorily told, or shown?" (59–60). Reflect on the narrator's stated mission, the statements of witnesses, and the comments of those responsible for "solving" the crime. Are their explanations consistent? What does the narrator actually learn after all of his work? What does the enigma surrounding Santiago Nasar's murder imply about the work of reconstructing the past and of separating truth from fiction and myth? How do these implications challenge our rationalist worldview and the validity of such disciplines as law, history, and even science?

2. **Anticlericalism:** Analyze the novella's critique of institutional religion.

   Anticlericalism, the criticism of religious institutions rather than religious faith itself, is an idea that can be traced back to medieval literature, and it permeates García Márquez works, from *In Evil Hour* to *Of Love and Other Demons*. Arnold M. Penuel asserts that "*Crónica* contains a subtle and indirect yet strong and persistent attack on the Catholic Church" (192), adding, "The Church's role in the novel places it in clear contradiction to its original mission of promoting faith, hope, and charity" (194). Revisit the passages dealing with the church, in particular, the bishop's visit and Father Amador's role in the inquest. How does the text represent their respective attitudes toward their pastoral duties? What blame does the church share in the town's twisted sense of honor and justice? What does this reveal about the negative role of institutional religion in this or any society?

Form and Genre

Chronicle of a Death Foretold offers an especially interesting range of topics in the area of form and genre. Raymond Williams comments that the novella "is the product of a writer with the ability to successfully manipulate several genres: the novel, journalism, and detective fiction" (139–40). As you reflect on your reading, which discursive forms do you find most present in the text? Given García Márquez's background as a reporter, one of the obvious answers is journalism. How does this very particular approach to writing affect the narrative? Another topic related to genre draws attention to the novella's title. Why does García Márquez call the story a "chronicle," and what are the implications for such a mode of writing? Yet a third option is the book's affinity with the detective story. You might explore the connection between *Chronicle of a Death Foretold* and this popular genre. What other questions of form and genre can you identify in the novella? Considering Williams's observation, how might you explore the intersection between two or more genres?

Sample Topics:

1. **Journalism:** How does García Márquez's background as a journalist manifest itself in the text, and what impact does it have on the reader's experience?

   García Márquez says of *Chronicle of a Death Foretold*: "For the first time I have managed a perfect integration of journalism and literature . . . journalism helps maintain contact with reality, which is essential to literature" (Grossman 62). What distinguishes journalism from other forms of writing? For example, one concept typically associated with journalistic writing is "objectivity." Is the narrator truly objective, or is there a subjective subtext to the "facts" he reports? Examine passages where the narrator functions as a seemingly objective reporter, and analyze the "perfect integration" described by the author. Consider, for instance, the detailed description of the autopsy performed by Father Amador:

> He had a deep stab in the right hand. The report says: "It looked like a stigma of the crucified Christ." The encephalic mass weighed sixty grams more than that of a normal Englishman, and Father Amador noted in the report that Santiago Nasar had a superior intelligence and a brilliant future. Nevertheless, in the final note he pointed out a hypertrophy of the liver that he attributed to a poorly cured case of hepatitis. "That is to say," he told me, "he had only a few years of life left in any case" (75–76).

What devices does the text employ to maintain the facade of impartiality? How does it reveal the priest's ingenuousness, as well as his desire to bring the matter to a close as quickly as possible? Look for similar passages. What conclusions can you draw about the function of this fictionalized journalistic technique?

2. **Chronicle:** Is the novella a true chronicle or a parody of that genre?

Why is the novella presented as a "chronicle"? What is the nature of that genre? What are its origins and its traditional elements? Based on your definition, do you consider the novella to be a chronicle? Jorge Olivares contends: "Even through *Crónica* claims it is a chronicle, that is, a historical record of facts or events arranged chronologically, it subverts its apparent intention" (483). Do you agree with Olivares's interpretation? In light of Olivares's definition of a chronicle, the title of the novella seems to constitute a paradox: An event "foretold" cannot, by necessity, occur in chronological order. How do you explain this apparent contradiction, and what does it suggest about discursive modes such as chronicle, history, or journalism that claim to be factual depictions of the past?

3. **Detective story:** Write an essay analyzing *Chronicle of a Death Foretold* in relation to this popular literary genre.

Is *Chronicle of a Death Foretold* a detective story? Noting that, "*Chronicle* manifests many traits of the detective genre," Bernard McGuirk raises the following dilemma:

> Given the traditional elements of victim, motive, weapon, criminal(s), and the refinements of legal trappings, policeman, autopsy, prosecution and judge, the sign, read as crime-novel, is virtually transparent. But the element "missing" from the whodunit model is mystery. The fact that the text reveals victim, criminals and motive so early has a concomitant effect on narrative sequence (174).

Although the victim, killers, and motive are indeed made known from the outset, are there still mysteries for the narrator to solve? What might these be? Might it be argued that the "crime" being solved is not the murder of Santiago Nasar by the Vicario brothers but the criminal negligence, or perhaps even complicity, of the community at large?

Language, Symbols, and Imagery

An essay on language, symbols, and imagery for *Chronicle of a Death Foretold* is made all the more interesting by the very ambiguity of the text. One of the most compelling topics for this kind of analysis is the choice of character names. Yet another is to explore the numerous bloody images found throughout the text. What other symbols does your reading reveal? What objects or imagery are repeated on numerous occasions? What is the context of their usage? Are they associated with a particular character or theme? Can you build an argument about the meaning of the symbol or image that is consistent for all of the references in the novella?

Sample Topics:

1. **Character names:** Analyze the possibly symbolic meanings of character names and how they relate to their respective roles in the story.

Arnold M. Penuel notes that *Chronicle of a Death Foretold* is a "novel [that] abounds with evocative names" (188). With the aid of a good Spanish-English dictionary, begin by searching for the literal meanings of the characters' names. Also look for their cultural and/or religious significance. For example, what might the text be implying by the name *Angela* (from the word *ángel*, or "angel") and *Vicario* (the word for "vicarious")? How is she a "vicarious angel"? Is Santiago Nasar's name meant to be an allusion to Jesus (Santiago is the patron saint of Spain, and Nasar seems to reference *Nazarín*, or "Nazarene") or to his outsider status in the community (*Nasar* is a common Arab name)? Once you have put together a list of character names and their possible meanings, try to formulate a thesis that contextualizes them within a unified interpretation.

2. **Blood and gore:** Examine the graphic depiction of violence in the text, specifically the images of blood and viscera.

Leonard Michaels believes Santiago Nasar's horrific death scene stands out "among the innumerable murders of modern literature as one of the best and most powerfully rendered" (n.p.). In fact, it is only one of many bloody moments in the novella. Return to these scenes and examine the way in which they depict such gruesome details. Consider what purpose such depictions serve. For example, the morning of the murder, the reader finds the Nasars' cook, Victoria Guzmán, preparing that evening's dinner as a hungover Santiago attempts to drink his coffee. The text notes "Santiago Nasar's horror when she pulled out the insides of a rabbit by the roots and threw the steaming guts to the dogs" (10). Return to this passage and examine it in the larger context of Santiago's sexual advances toward Victoria's daughter, Divina Flor. What is the relationship between the cook's violent handling of the rabbit she is dressing and her attitude toward Santiago? What does this reveal about the function of violence in this fictional world? How does this scene prefigure the murder, as well as the autopsy? Why do you think García Márquez resorts to such gory images? How might it relate to topics such as the honor code, sexuality, and Santiago's symbolic status as a martyr?

Compare and Contrast Essays

Compare and contrast essays offer a greater variety of potential topics than almost any other kind of literary analysis. You might choose to explore similar elements between works by two different authors. With *Chronicle of a Death Foretold,* for instance, you might look at it in relation to a work that may have in part inspired it, Sophocles' tragedy *Oedipus Rex.* Given the text's affinity with the detective, or crime, genre, what other novels might offer you an interesting compare and contrast essay topic? You might also wish to explore the way García Márquez treats similar elements in *Chronicle of a Death Foretold* and another one of his own works. One possibility would be to compare social and political commentary between this novella and another, perhaps more overtly ideological work, such as *No One Writes to the Colonel* or *In Evil Hour.* What other comparisons might you make between characters, themes, or formal devices?

Sample Topics:

1. ***Chronicle of a Death Foretold* and Sophocles' *Oedipus Rex*:**
   Compare these two texts with regard to their common themes of fate and plots driven by unfortunate coincidence.

   Katherine Callen King remarks on the fundamental similarities between García Márquez's novella and his "favorite work of literature." She states: ". . . like *Crónica, Oedipus* presents every human attempt to forestall catastrophe as something that only brings it closer" (312). Read Sophocles' play (also called *Oedipus Tyrannus*) and consider King's observation. Do you agree with King's assessment of the two works? At what points in the play and in the novella does the reader see the tragic paradox she describes? Given García Márquez's affinity for *Oedipus Rex,* which he sees as "the apotheosis of technical perfection" (Guibert 50), can it be argued that the novella is a conscious attempt to write a modern version of Greek tragedy? If so, how does he reproduce traditional elements of the genre, such as the concept of hubris or the presence of the chorus? Is

Santiago Nasar a tragic hero in the classical sense? How might it be contended that the novella is not so much an imitation of *Oedipus Rex* as it is a parody?

2. **Political and social criticism in** *Chronicle of a Death Foretold* **and** *In Evil Hour:* Compare the way these two novellas function as commentaries on government and society.

Social and political criticism is a frequent element in the writing of García Márquez. Some texts, such as *In Evil Hour* and *The Autumn of the Patriarch,* horrify the reader with their representation of brutal and corrupt government. Others, including *Chronicle of a Death Foretold* or "A Very Old Man with Enormous Wings," seem to take a subtler but no less effective approach to the subject. Raymond Williams, for example, writes of "the confluence of economic, personal, and possibly even political interests . . . underlying Santiago Nasar's death" (138). Examine the representation of political or social authority in the novella. Which characters play this role in the story? How do similar characters in *In Evil Hour* and *Chronicle of Death Foretold*—the military governors (the lieutenant and Colonel Lázaro Aponte), the judges (Judge Arcadio and *Chronicle*'s nameless judge), and the priests (Father Angel and Father Carmen Amador)—compare? What other characters might you include to represent socioeconomic elites in the two works? Are these two groups essentially the same? If not, what is the basis of the difference? Based on the two texts, what can you infer about García Márquez's view of rural Latin American society?

Bibliography and Online Resources for *Chronicle of a Death Foretold*

Alonso, Carlos. "Writing and Ritual in *Chronicle of a Death Foretold.*" *Gabriel García Márquez: New Readings.* Ed. Bernard McGuirk and Richard Cardwell. Cambridge: Cambridge UP, 1987. 151–63.

Bell, Michael. *Gabriel García Márquez: Solitude and Solidarity.* New York: St. Martin's Press, 1993.

Bell-Villada, Gene H. *García Márquez: The Man and His Work.* Chapel Hill: U of North Carolina P, 1990.

García Márquez, Gabriel. *Chronicle of a Death Foretold.* Trans. Gregory Rabassa. New York: Vintage, 2003.

Grossman, Edith. "Truth Is Stranger Than Fact." *Critical Essays on Gabriel García Márquez.* Ed. George R. McMurray. New York: Frederick Ungar, 1977. 60–65.

Guibert, Rita. "Gabriel García Márquez." *Conversations with Gabriel García Márquez.* Ed. Gene H. Bell-Villada. Jackson: U of Mississippi P, 2006. 31–58.

Holland, Clifford. "Ethnic and Religious Diversity in Central America: An Historical Perspective." 2005. 9 October 2008. <http://www.prolades.com/Ethnic_Religious_Diversity_CAM-Holland.pdf>.

King, Katherine Callen. "Santiago Tyrannos: Dialogic Voices in García Márquez's *Crónica de una muerte anunciada.*" *Comparative Literature* 43.4 (1991): 305–25.

McGuirk, Bernard. "Free-play of Fore-play: The Fiction of Non-consummation: Speculations on *Chronicle of a Death Foretold.*" *Gabriel García Márquez: New Readings.* Ed. Bernard McGuirk and Richard Cardwell. Cambridge: Cambridge UP, 1987. 169–89.

Michaels, Leonard. "Murder Most Foul and Comic." *New York Times* 27 March 1983. 10 October 2008. <http://www.nytimes.com/books/97/06/15/reviews/marquez-chronicle.html>.

Olivares, Jorge. "García Márquez's *Crónica de una muerte anunciada* as Metafiction." *Contemporary Literature* 28.4 (1987): 483–92.

Pelayo, Rubén. *Gabriel García Márquez: A Critical Companion.* Westport, CT: Greenwood Press, 2001.

Penuel, Arnold M. "The Sleep of Vital Reason in Gabriel García Márquez's *Crónica de una muerte anunciada.*" *Critical Essays on Gabriel García Márquez.* Ed. George R. McMurray. New York: Frederick Ungar, 1977. 188–209.

Stevens, Evelyn P. "The Prospects for a Women's Liberation Movement in Latin America." *Journal of Marriage and the Family* 35.2 (1973): 313–21.

Williams, Raymond. *Gabriel García Márquez.* Boston: Twayne, 1984.

Zamora, Lois Parkinson. *The Usable Past: The Imagination of History in Recent Fictions of the Americas.* Cambridge: Cambridge UP, 1997.

LOVE IN THE TIME
OF CHOLERA

READING TO WRITE

A MONG GARCÍA Márquez's most critically acclaimed works, *Love in the Time of Cholera* (published in 1985 as *El amor en los tiempos del cólera* and translated into English in 1988) stands second in status only to *One Hundred Years of Solitude*. The writer's longest book, this "good old-fashioned love story" with its "intentional return to nineteenth-century realism" (Bell-Villada 191) is often also cited as his most accessible work. Its somewhat more traditional narrative structure and relative absence of magic realist elements have prompted the noted American author Thomas Pynchon to declare, "In this novel we have come a meaningful distance from Macondo" (n.p.). A highly original rendition of the classic love triangle, it tells the story of a youthful romance that, cut short first by social pressures and then the young woman's sudden change of heart, is finally renewed and consummated more than half a century later. Spanning so many years in the existence of both the protagonists and their world, the novel explores the effects of time on both individuals and societies. Above all, it traces, with a combination of psychological insight and narrative eloquence, the evolution of romantic love from adolescence to the twilight of life. Should you decide to write an essay on this profound and magnificently written book, you will find no shortage of potential topics. Your challenge will be to penetrate the facade of what may seem, at first glance, to be a rather conventional romance. As you proceed with the close reading of the passages relating to your potential topic, pay particularly close attention to the way the characters perceive actions and situations. How is their vision, and thus their understanding, filtered through the lens of their cultural values, prejudices, and, especially, their emotions? Reflect, for example, on the following passage in which Florentino Ariza sees Fermina Daza and her husband one evening at a restaurant:

> One night he went to Don Sancho's Inn, an elegant colonial restaurant, and sat in the most remote corner, as was his custom when he ate his frugal meals alone. All at once, in the large mirror on the back wall, he caught a glimpse of Fermina Daza sitting at a table with her husband and two other couples, at an angle that allowed him to see her reflected in all her splendor. She was unguarded, she engaged in conversation with grace and laughter that exploded like fireworks, and her beauty was more radiant under the enormous teardrop chandeliers: once again, Alice had gone through the looking glass.
>
> Holding his breath, Florentino Ariza observed her at his pleasure: he saw her eat, he saw her hardly touch her wine, he saw her joke with the fourth in the line of Don Sanchos; from his solitary table he shared a moment of her life, and for more than an hour he lingered, unseen, in the forbidden places of her intimacy. Then he drank four more cups of coffee to pass the time until he saw her leave with the rest of the group. They passed so close to him that he could distinguish her scent among the clouds of other perfumes worn by her companions (228).

At first glance, the text evokes a rather stereotypical scene from a romance novel: the lonely hero pining for his beloved who is proverbially "so close, and yet so far." The key to understanding the underlying significance of this passage lies in the way Florentino Ariza literally views the evening. First, what do the references to the "remote corner" and the habit of eating "frugal meals alone" at "his solitary table" connote with regard to the character's mindset? How does he feel vis-à-vis the world around him? Florentino can see Fermina only through her reflection in the mirror: "reflected in all her splendor." Given that a mirror is only a representation of reality, a kind of mirage, what is being implied about his perception? In what sense does use of hyperbole—"laughter that exploded like fireworks"; "her beauty was more radiant"—underscore Florentino's romanticized vision of the woman who, sitting in the same dining room, fails to even notice him? Why is the reference to Lewis Carroll's *Alice's Adventures in Wonderland* sequel, thus, so appropriate to the moment? A second aspect of this passage related to the protagonist's perception deals with the eroticism of the passage. Consider the initial description of Fermina from Florentino's perspective: "She was unguarded." How does this connote an element of voyeurism? Why is he "holding his breath" as he "observe[s] her at his pleasure," and what is intimated sexually by the way he watches "unseen, in the forbidden places of her intimacy"? What is communicated about Florentino's desire by his consumption of so many cups of coffee? Finally, how does the olfactory image at the end of the passage both heighten the sensuality of the scene and underscore Florentino's obsession with Fermina?

This passage illustrates not only the value of close reading but also several of the numerous potential topics you might want to pursue in your essay. As you read over the other topics discussed in this chapter, keep in mind that this is not a definitive list but rather an initial guide to help you formulate your own ideas about the text. While selecting a good topic is certainly one of the most important steps to writing a good essay, the best topic is not always the most obvious one. If you choose a subject for your analysis that interests you, one that seems to resonate in the text, you will find the writing process to be more enjoyable, more productive, and in all likelihood, more successful as well.

TOPICS AND STRATEGIES
Themes

An essay on the themes in a work of literature looks to explore the feelings, values, and ideals that are common to the human experience. While the title of the novel makes "love" an obvious thematic topic, there are many different variations to choose from on the love theme. One such alternative to writing simply about romantic love would be to analyze what the text is saying about the relationship between love and aging. Does romance change with age and, if so, in what way? A very different take on love would be for you to write about the connection between love and one of García Márquez's other major themes, solitude. You could investigate the fascinating paradox of isolation resulting from the desire for intimacy with another human being. Of course, you need not write about love. There are many other themes in *Love in the Time of Cholera*, such as the very different but no less powerful sentiment of nostalgia. What does the text have to tell the reader about the longing for the past that all people seem to sense as they grow older?

Sample Topics:

1. **Love and aging:** How does the text portray romance in the face of the inexorable process of growing old and confronting one's own mortality?

The novel's exploration of love between two people of an advanced age is, unquestionably, one of its most notable attributes. Should you choose to explore this very original intersection of two rarely associated themes, you need to start by examining the distinction the text makes between the two protagonists' romance at its abortive inception and at its final realization. García Márquez has stated: "I think aging has made me realize that feelings and sentiments, what happens in the heart, are ultimately the most important" (Simons 155). How is this assertion reflected in the novel? Consider the following passage:

> They were together in silence like an old married couple wary of life, beyond the pitfalls of passion, beyond the brutal mockery of hope and the phantoms of disillusion: beyond love. For they had lived together long enough to know that love was always love, anytime and anyplace, but it was more solid the closer it came to death (345).

What distinction is the text making between youthful love and love between an older couple? What is meant by the "pitfalls of passion" and "mockery of hope," and how is this paradox reflected in the novel? Why does the presence of death strengthen the love between Florentino and Fermina?

2. **Love and solitude:** Write an essay that examines the isolation brought on by feelings of unrequited or unfulfilled love.

Rubén Pelayo states: "*Love in the Time of Cholera,* like all of Gabriel García Márquez's works, explores the solitude of the individual and of humankind. In this novel, the existential anguish of feeling alone is portrayed through the solitude of love and being in love" (136). Identify the scenes in the novel where Florentino Ariza, Fermina Daza, or other characters either sense or express a feeling of loneliness because of their romantic circumstances. For example, reflect on the following sentence in which Florentino resists the temptation to confess his feelings for Fermina to his longtime confidante, Leona Cassiani: "No: he would not reveal it, not even to Leona Cassiani, not because he did not want to open the chest where he kept it so carefully hidden for half his life, but because he realized only then that he had lost the key" (192). If the locked chest is symbolic of Florentino Ariza's heart, how does it reflect his solitude? What is the significance of the lost key, and how does it increase the hopelessness of the character's quest for love? While Florentino's plight is clearly the principal example of the love and solitude theme, where else is it manifested? Can you make the argument that the "solitude of love and being in love" is, for García Márquez, a universal theme?

3. **Nostalgia:** What does the novel say about the human impulses to regret and often romanticize the past?

Nostalgia, the longing for an idealized past, is a central theme in *Love in the Time of Cholera*. It is articulated in both the characters' reflection on their own youth and on a society, a way of life, that lives only in memory. Commenting on the latter manifestation of the theme, Jason Wilson contends that the novel "is an elegy to a lifestyle that is over; nostalgia is the dominant mood" (281). Think about the two principal characters, Florentino and Fermina. How does each express this sense of loss? How does the narrator's description of their world mirror the characters' regret?

Characters

Given the love triangle that dominates most of the novel, there are three obvious choices for an essay on characters in *Love in the Time of Cholera*. One interpretation of the book is to see it as Florentino Ariza's story. But, if you view him as the main protagonist, you must ask whether he is heroic, tragic, pathetic, or even comic? Fermina Daza would also make for a good character study. It she a feminist heroine or a sad bourgeois housewife who is saved from an empty existence by the love of Florentino Ariza? The third figure in the text, Dr. Juvenal Urbino, also allows for decidedly disparate interpretations. Is he essentially a foil to Florentino, or does his worldview make him the embodiment of one of the novel's central themes? Lastly, there are many minor characters—from Fermina's cousin to one of Florentino's numerous lovers—about whom you could write a very thought-provoking essay. One of the most interesting of these possibilities is Jeremiah de Saint-Amour, the character whose suicide at the beginning of the novel can be read as a symbolic key to the story that follows. No matter which character or characters you choose, keep in mind that you are not merely reconstructing a fictional biography but must analyze and explain his or her function in the text.

Sample Topics:

1. **Florentino Ariza:** Write an essay exploring the novel's male protagonist. In what way is he a genuine romantic hero? How can he also be understood as something of a parody of that character?

   García Márquez has remarked of Florentino Ariza, "I don't really like him. I think he is very selfish, as all men are" (Simons 165). Do you agree with this opinion, or is the author being too critical of his creation? Reconstruct Florentino Ariza's biography and the motivations underlying the decisions that most affect his life. Are his initial feelings for Fermina Daza truly a case of "love at first sight" or merely a manifestation of his naive romanticism? How do you interpret the character's extreme promiscuity? Is he searching for emotional fulfillment or merely justifying his desire for self-gratification? Is this period of his life better understood as tragic, comic, or pathetic? What does he mean when he laments, "My heart has more rooms than a whorehouse" (270)? Does Florentino change over the course of the novel? If so, in what ways is he transformed? How do you interpret his reunion with Fermina at the end of the story: redemption, revindication, reward, or resignation?

2. **Fermina Daza:** Is the female character in the novel's love triangle best understood as the object of male desire, one of two protagonists, or the sole protagonist in the novel?

Fermina Daza presents a particularly interesting opportunity for a character essay in that her status in the novel can be seen from many perspectives. The first question you may want to ask yourself is whether she can be understood as the main character. What about the novel's essential structure could allow for this interpretation? How is she different from either Juvenal Urbino or Florentino Ariza? For example, Thomas Fahy remarks: "Fermina comes to terms with her anxieties about aging in ways that the men in the novel never do" (58). Is her character more insightful or more realistic than the two male principals? With regard to her husband, the text notes that, "She knew that he loved her above all else, more than anyone else in the world, but only for his own sake: she was in his holy service" (221). What does this quotation reveal about Fermina's insight? Why does it also expose the tragic aspect of her existence? Find other passages in the novel that describe Fermina's feelings about her life and the two men with whom she shares it. Is she ultimately a feminist heroine, a sad figure who compromises a lifetime of happiness until she is redeemed by Florentino Ariza, or someone else?

3. **Dr. Juvenal Urbino:** Analyze the function of this antipode to Florentino Ariza.

As is the case with other García Márquez characters—for example, Santiago Nasar in *Chronicle of a Death Foretold* or Big Mama in "Big Mama's Funeral"—Juvenal Urbino's death serves as the pretext to the story. But, is the character's function in the novel more than simply as an obstacle to the ultimate reunion of Florentino Ariza and Fermina Daza? The narrator notes Juvenal's reflection on his wedding night: "He was aware that he did not love her. He had married her because he liked her haughtiness, her seriousness, her strength, and also because of some vanity on his part, but as he kissed her for the first time he was sure there would be no obstacle to their inventing true love" (159).

This passage calls attention to two of the character's principal traits. First, while in no way an antagonist, how is he shown to be unworthy of Fermina's love? Second, how does the peculiar expression "inventing true love" allude to Juvenal Urbino's exaggerated scientific worldview and rather naive belief in progress? How are these two aspects of the character manifested elsewhere in the text? Is Juvenal Urbino meant to function only as a foil to Florentino Ariza, or does his character also embody other traits central to the novel's central themes?

4. **Jeremiah de Saint-Amour:** Write an essay on Juvenal Urbino's mysterious friend, whose suicide seems to lay the foundation for many of the novel's essential themes.

Jeremiah Saint-Amour dies before the novel even begins, but his suicide, which opens the text, suggests the importance of this seemingly minor character. Rubén Pelayo comments: "The reader feels the curiosity of a private detective in trying to figure out who Jeremiah de Saint-Amour is [and] why he committed suicide . . ." (136). Reconstruct the character's life and the motives behind his suicide. What do you make of his assertion, "I will never be old" (15), and the narrator's observation that "Jeremiah de Saint-Amour loved life with a senseless passion" (15)? How does the meaning of his name—*Jeremiah* is the name of a prophet and Hebrew for "the Lord exhalts"; *Saint-Amour* is French for "Holy Love"—reveal the character's function in the novel? How do the major characters react to his death, and what does that reveal about their respective attitudes?

History and Context

Essays on history and context allow you to take an interdisciplinary approach to a literary work. In the case of *Love in the Time of Cholera,* an obvious topic is the one suggested by the title itself. How does the text reflect the impact of an epidemic on a population, either one specific to Colombia's experience or any of the many plagues that have affected human beings throughout the course of history? Given that this is a novel set in Colombia's late 19th and early 20th centuries, social and political history constitutes another fertile ground for mining potential topics. You might even explore the way the text's representation of the nation's past can also be read as a commentary on its situation over recent decades.

Sample Topics:

1. **Epidemics:** After researching the history of diseases such as cholera in the late 19th and early 20th centuries, analyze the role of the cholera epidemic as an element in the novel.

While cholera clearly functions as a metaphor in the novel, it also reflects the historical reality of devastating disease pandemics in the modern era. Colombia's own wave of cholera outbreaks, beginning in 1850 (Hays 229), serves as the backdrop for the epidemic in the story, but the depiction of the disease, its effects, and treatment efforts by the nascent science of epidemiology, all have much broader implications for an essay. Begin by researching the history of cholera epidemics in Colombia and elsewhere at the turn of the 19th century (Manuel Martínez-Maldonado's essay "Numbers, Death, and Time in García Márquez's *Love in the Time of Cholera*" is an excellent resource; J. N. Hays's *Epidemics and Pandemics: Their Impacts on Human History* offers a more global perspective). Based on your research, how faithful is the text's re-creation of the disease's impact on the world of Florentino Ariza and Fermina Daza? How does Dr. Juvenal Urbino reflect the work of medical science at that time? Although Martínez-Maldonado notes that "the fictional Urbino is pioneering sanitary efforts" (131) similar to those of actual physicians of the day, how does he also betray the social and racial prejudices of the period?

2. **Colombian politics and society in the 19th century:** How does Colombia's turbulent political history serve as a backdrop to the events in the novel?

Love in the Time of Cholera is not as overtly political as other García Márquez works such as *In Evil Hour* or *The Autumn of the Patriarch*, but there is no question that Colombia's history resonates strongly in the novel. Michael Wood observes: "The country is not named . . . but it has Colombia's Liberals and Conservatives . . . its War of a Thousand Days. . . . It even anticipates the terrible peacetime violence for which Colombia has become notorious since 1947" (143). If you want to write this kind of essay, a necessary first step will be for you to research the historical period in question (you might begin with Marco Palacios's *Between Legitimacy and Violence: A History of Colombia, 1875–2002*). Then, return to the text and identify passages that seem to reference either specific events, such as the Thousand Days War, or broader sociopolitical realities underlying the events in the story. For example, consider the "preoccupation" expressed by Florentino's uncle Leo XII over European economic hegemony in the country: "I am almost one hundred years old, and I have seen everything change, even the position of the stars in the universe, but I have not seen anything change yet in this country. . . . Here they make new constitutions, new laws, new wars every three months, but we are still in colonial times" (266). How does the character's concern reflect the actual status of early 20th-century Colombia (perhaps Latin America as a whole) vis-à-vis the neocolonialist practices of Europe and the United States? Is his critique of the country's political turmoil and intermittent warfare meant to reflect only the temporal setting of the novel, or is it also a commentary on Colombia in García Márquez's own time?

PHILOSOPHY AND IDEAS

Essays on philosophy and ideas allow you to examine the text's relationship to intellectual currents. This may come in the form of a critique, an affirmation, or a metaphorical representation of the belief or metaphysical system in question. As with essays of history and context, writing on this topic may oblige you to do some outside research on the philosophical concept in question. For instance, like other García Márquez texts, *Love in the Time of Cholera* is sometimes read as a commentary on—even a repudiation of—modernity. Once you are familiar with the idea of modernity, you could begin to explore its manifestations in the novel. Similarly, you might analyze the feminist implications of the novel, provided you either possess or acquire a grasp of feminism's basic tenets. Ask yourself whether García Márquez should be considered a feminist writer. If not, might you even find misogynist overtones in the novel?

Sample Topics:

1. Modernity: How does the novel critique the post-Enlightenment fascination with modernity and the myth of progress?

The works of García Márquez, like those of many other modernist writers, reveal a preoccupation with the social and political changes brought about by the so-called scientific and technological progress of the 19th and 20th centuries. *Love in the Time of Cholera* is certainly no exception. Thomas Fahy argues: "Throughout *Love in the Time of Cholera*, García Márquez suggests that modernization is often at odds with both love (or at least the romantic idealizations of love) and culture" (32). If you want to examine the novel's critique of modernity, you should begin by formulating a definition of the concept itself (you might begin with the first chapter, "Modernity and Modernism," in Art Berman's *Preface to Modernism*). Once you are confident about your understanding of modernity, return to the text and analyze the passages relating to the role played by science and technology in the gradual transformation of the city and its people. How is progress shown in the novel? What technological innovations represent this progress? Mabel Moraña comments: "The ideas of reason, progress, social prestige and integration and public duty come together in the character of Juvenal Urbino" (89). What role is played by Urbino in the modernization of the town? How does the text subvert the myth of progress through the disparity between Urbino's beliefs and the reality of his world? How does his battle against the cholera epidemic epitomize the fallacy underlying the concept of modernity?

2. Feminism: Discuss García Márquez's feminism on the basis of his treatment of female characters, especially Fermina Daza.

While he has numerous strong and interesting female characters—from *One Hundred Years of Solitude*'s Úrsula Buendía to *The General in His Labyrinth*'s Manuela Sáenz—García Márquez has not always been seen as a feminist. *Love in the Time of Cholera* is no exception to the controversy. Anny Brooksbank

Jones observes that a "tension arises between García Márquez's increasingly detailed and complex female characters and his continuing use from time to time of clichéd encounters between men and women which seem to have very little to redeem them in feminist—and arguably human—terms" (637). Revisit the descriptions both of Fermina Daza and of the many secondary female characters that populate the novel. How are they represented in comparison to their male counterparts? What does the novel have to say about female sexuality? Are women exclusively the object of male desire, or is their libido also acknowledged? Is *Love in the Time of Cholera* as much Fermina Daza's story as it is Florentino Ariza's?

Form and Genre

Essays on form and genre explore a text as it relates to established literary movements or aesthetic paradigms. While *Love in the Time of Cholera* represents something of a departure from García Márquez's more noticeably ambitious narratives, such as *The Autumn of the Patriarch* or *Chronicle of a Death Foretold,* it has a number of interesting formal elements that would make for an engaging essay. You might analyze the novel as a work of satire. How does the humor in the text constitute a rather mordant critique of the society in which it is set? Another, perhaps even more intriguing, topic is the text's relationship to the realist tradition of the 19th century. Why does one of the 20th century's great formal innovators return to such an outdated genre for his inspiration?

Sample Topics:

1. *Love in the Time of Cholera* as social satire: Analyze the novel as a critique of human sentimentality in the face of social and political reality.

   Claudette Kemper Columbus rejects the common reading of the novel as a "love story." She contends that, "Many readers read *Love* with the comfortable conviction that García Márquez is a 'magical realist' and forget that he is an open partisan of the far left." She adds:

> He is writing about the vast majority of us entering the twenty-first century supposedly enlightened on psychological, social, and environmental issues, but actually substituting our own narcissistically sentimental selves. . . . So it is that, by keeping ourselves the objects of our sentimental gaze, we remain out of time and out of touch, like the characters in *Love*, distanced from the historical events of which they are components (91).

If you decide to write on the novel as social satire, your first step will be to be sure you have a firm grasp of satire as a literary form (you might start with Alvin B. Kernan's essay "Satire"). Next, you should focus your close reading on parts of the text that reference characters' attitudes about the world around them. Do their views consistently reflect Columbus's interpretation, or are certain characters more reflective of the "narcissism" of which the critic speaks?

2. **Realism:** Explore the novel's affinity with the 19th-century realist novel.

The affinity between *Love in the Time of Cholera* and the realist novels of the 19th century has been noted by numerous commentators. Rubén Pelayo argues, however, that the novel undercuts its own realist tendencies when it romanticizes the central love story:

> The detailed representation of both people and nature in *Love in the Time of Cholera* seems to come up short when it comes to the idealization of Fermina by Florentino. This concept of love itself loses its entire realist meaning and changes the novel into a *romantic realist* novel, which is a combination of the two. Unlike the objectivity of realism, the love of Florentino for Fermina is totally subjective (139).

Study the basic principles of realist narrative in the works of 19th-century writers such as France's Honoré de Balzac,

England's Charles Dickens, and Spain's Benito Pérez Galdós (you may also want to consult Erich Auerbach's classic study of the genre, *Mimesis*). Where do you find elements of realism in *Love in the Time of Cholera*? Do you agree with Pelayo's thesis, or can you offer an alternative explanation of García Márquez's choice of this genre for his novel?

Language, Symbols, and Imagery

Essays on language, symbols, and imagery allow you to examine the way a text creates meaning at the most essential level through the relationships between words and ideas. You will find numerous potential topics for this kind of essay in *Love in the Time of Cholera*. One such topic is the novel's use of erotic imagery. How does the text use language to separate the sexual from the sensual, to distinguish lust from love? Another significant image is the recurrent cholera epidemic that threatens the town and its inhabitants. How does the plague function as a metaphor? A different but no less important instance of symbolic meaning is the river. A common metaphorical device in literature, what is the significance of the ever-flowing body of water that plays a pivotal role in both the physical and emotion journey of the protagonists?

Sample Topics:

1. **Eroticism:** Explore the erotic imagery in the text. How does it defy traditional representations of human sexuality and literary notions of the sensual?

Eroticism can be defined as the artistic representation of sexual desire. While depictions of sexual intercourse and physical desire can be found throughout the novel, not all of them are erotic in nature. For example, consider the scene of Fermina Daza's wedding night with Juvenal Urbino, which is presented as a dispassionate anatomy lesson. The groom explains the mechanics of sex "with authoritative methodology," while the bride follows at first "with the obedience of an exemplary pupil" (158) but eventually declares in exasperation, "'Let's not go on with the medical lesson'" (159). Now read the following passage that transpires between Fermina and Florentino Ariza on their first night together: ". . . he dared to explore her withered neck with his fingertips, her bosom armored in metal stays, her hips with their decaying bones, her thighs with their aging veins. She accepted with pleasure, her eyes closed, but she did not tremble, and she smoked and drank at regular intervals" (338). How does this passage convey the passion between the two characters that is lacking in the other scene? Why is Fermina's physical condition emphasized in the description, and how is the erotic nature of the scene heightened by the discrepancy between her aged body and Florentino's desire? How do the phrases "dared to explore," "accepted with pleasure," and "did not tremble" evoke both a youthfulness and a communion between the two lovers? Finally, what connection exists between Fermina's indulgence with alcohol and tobacco, and how does it reinforce the sensuality of the scene? Find other scenes in the text that capture this kind of eroticism. How does the novel use eroticism to differentiate between sex and the physical expression of romantic love?

2. **Cholera:** Analyze the metaphorical value of cholera in the novel.

The association between the dread disease and romance is explicitly stated on several occasions. One such instance occurs when Florentino Ariza's godfather, a homeopath, examines his godson, who has the symptoms of "a dying man." After questioning Florentino and his mother, the doctor "conclude[s] once again that the symptoms of love were the same as those of cholera" (62). Return to the novel and identify all of the passages that reference the disease. In addition to its metaphorical relationship to love, what other symbolic meaning can you find? García Márquez has said of epidemics such as the one depicted in *Love in the Time of Cholera*, "They make people want to live more. It's that almost metaphysical dimension that interests me" (Simons 156). How does this resonate in the novel?

3. **The river:** Explore the function of the river as a symbol of time in the novel.

Rivers are frequently used as symbolic devices in literature. The Mississippi, for instance, is often seen as a symbol of freedom in

Mark Twain's *Adventures of Huckleberry Finn,* while the Congo has been interpreted as a metaphor for the human psyche in Joseph Conrad's *Heart of Darkness.* Colombia's Magdalena River is the setting for two important sections in *Love in the Time of Cholera.* Jean Franco interprets the symbolic meaning of the river in this way:

> In the course of Florentino's lifetime, the boat's passengers have killed off the wildlife and the boats engines have consumed the forest. Whereas the dissolution of the colonial city had been slow and entropic, the death of the river is swift and irreparable. It is in this terminal scenery that love triumphs. Nevertheless, as in his other novels, García Márquez's deeply pessimistic outlook has been cleverly camouflaged by the rapid surface motion of the narrative which forestalls but cannot overcome death (103).

Return to the two sections in question, and read them closely. Do you agree with Franco, or do you find another possible interpretation of the river? How does Florentino's first voyage on the Magdalena relate to the final trip he takes with Fermina at the end of the story? On the final page of the book, what is the thematic significance of Florentino's description of the Magdalena as "the waters that could be navigated forever" (348)?

Compare and Contrast Essays

Compare and contrast essays afford you the opportunity to explore intertextual similarities and differences between *Love in the Time of Cholera* and other literary texts. The key to selecting a good topic for this kind of essay is to find another work that has a logical connection to the novel. The most obvious relationship is that of common authorship. For example, you might want to examine the shared societal values in *Love in the Time of Cholera* and *Of Love and Other Demons.* Another direction frequently taken in comparative literature analyses is to study a text's relationship to a work of another author who seems to have influenced it in some way. One such instance is the affinity between García Márquez's novel and 19th-century French realist Gustave Flaubert's masterpieces *Madame Bovary* and *Sentimental Education.* Of course, these are far from your only two possibilities. As long as you can justify the value of the comparison as a means to achieving a better understanding of the original text (and not a comparison for its own sake), you probably have the makings of a solid essay.

Sample Topics:

1. **Class and race in** *Love in the Time of Cholera* **and** *Of Love and Other Demons*: Compare the two societies set in the same place but separated by a century in time.

The worlds of *Love in the Time of Cholera* and *Of Love and Other Demons* are far more similar than they might seem at first glance. While the events of the latter novel transpire when Colombia is still part of the Spanish colony of New Granada, a comparison of the two works seems to suggest that many aspects of Colombian society changed (and perhaps have changed) very little over the centuries. With both novels set in the coastal city of Cartagena, García Márquez seems to establish a subtle link between the two worlds by using the fictional "palace of the Marquis de Casalduero, whose existence and coat of arms had never been documented," (*Love in the Time of Cholera* 220) as the Urbino family home and as the initial setting for *Of Love and Other Demons*. Perhaps the most compelling commonality between the two novels is their treatment of ethnicity and class relations. Read the short novel *Of Love and Other Demons*, making note of these and other aspects of the society that seem to reflect those you found in *Love in the Time of Cholera*. How are the attitudes of Europeans toward Africans and of the aristocracy toward the lower classes mirrored in the two texts? Can it be argued that Dr. Juvenal Urbino is a figurative descendant of the 18th-century family in whose former home he lives? By demonstrating the persistence of racial and class prejudices from the 18th to the 19th and early 20th centuries, what might García Márquez be implying about the nature of these prejudices in contemporary Colombia, Latin America, or even the world?

2. *Love in the Time of Cholera* **and** *Sentimental Education:* Analyze García Márquez's novel as a meditation on the central theme of Gustave Flaubert's masterpiece.

Commenting on the texts that seem to have inspired García Márquez to write *Love in the Time of Cholera*, Gene H. Bell-Villada contends that "an even more important influence is Flaubert's *Sentimental Education*" (196). *Love in the Time of Cholera* seems to make an intentional allusion to Flaubert's 1869 novel when an older Florentino Ariza reflects back on his own "sentimental education" (63). There are striking similarities between the two novels. Both works relate the story of an ambitious but hopelessly romantic young man who falls in love "at first sight" with a woman of a higher social rank. Both male protagonists spend years in pursuit of this woman, who seems trapped in a loveless marriage but bound by social convention. Like Flaubert's antihero, Frédéric Moreau, Florentino Ariza seeks consolation in a series of self-indulgent, empty love affairs. Finally, both texts can be read as subversions of the traditional realist bildungsroman. While Bell-Villada notes many of these common elements, he argues that there is an essential difference between the two texts: "Whereas Flaubert's novel ends in bleak desolation, Florentino, throughout all his affairs will sustain his romantic dream and succeed in making it reality" (197). Read (or reread) *Sentimental Education*, taking care to note the similarities and differences between the two works.

Bibliography and Online Resources for *Love in the Time of Cholera*

Auerbach, Erich. *Mimesis: Representation of Reality in Western Literature.* Trans. Willard R. Trask. Princeton, NJ: Princeton UP, 1991.

Bell-Villada, Gene H. *García Márquez: The Man and His Work.* Chapel Hill: U of North Carolina P, 1990.

Berman, Art. *Preface to Modernism.* Urbana: U of Illinois P, 1994.

Columbus, Claudette Kemper. "Faint Echoes and Faded Reflections: Love and Justice in the Time of Cholera." *Twentieth Century Literature* 38.1 (1992): 89–101.

Fahy, Thomas. *Gabriel García Márquez's* Love in the Time of Cholera. New York: Continuum, 2003.

Franco, Jean. "Dr. Urbino's Parrot." *Gabriel García Márquez's* Love in the Time of Cholera. Ed. Harold Bloom. Philadelphia: Chelsea House, 2005. 99–112.

García Márquez, Gabriel. *Love in the Time of Cholera*. Trans. Edith Grossman. New York: Vintage, 2003.

Hays, J. N. *Epidemics and Pandemics: Their Impacts on Human History*. Oxford: ABC-CLIO, 2005.

Jones, Anny Brooksbank. "Utopia and Other Commonplaces in García Márquez's *El amor en los tiempos del cólera*." *Modern Language Review* 89.3 (1994): 635–44.

Kernan, Alvin B. "Satire." *Dictionary of the History of Ideas*. 2003. 27 October 2008. <http://etext.virginia.edu/cgi-local/DHI/dhi.cgi?id=dv4-29>.

Martínez-Maldonado, Manuel. "Numbers, Death, and Time in García Márquez's *Love in the Time of Cholera*." *The Body and the Text: Comparative Essays in Literature and Medicine*. Ed. Bruce Clarke and Wendell Aycock. Lubbock: Texas Tech UP, 1990. 127–37.

Moraña, Mabel. "Modernity and Marginality in *Love in the Time of Cholera*." *Gabriel García Márquez's* Love in the Time of Cholera. Ed. Harold Bloom. Philadelphia: Chelsea House, 2005. 83–97.

Palacios, Marco. *Between Legitimacy and Violence: A History of Colombia, 1875–2002*. Trans. Richard Stoller. Durham, NC: Duke UP, 2006.

Pelayo, Rubén. *Gabriel García Márquez*. Westport, CT: Greenwood Press, 2001.

Pynchon, Thomas. "The Heart's Eternal Vow." *New York Times*. 18 May 1997. 24 October 2008. <http://www.nytimes.com/books/97/05/18/reviews/pynchon-cholera.html>.

Simons, Marlise. "The Best Years of His Life: An Interview with Gabriel García Márquez." *Conversations with García Márquez*. Ed. Gene H. Bell-Villada. Jackson: U of Mississippi P, 2006: 163–67.

Wilson, Jason. "Happy Endings." *Third World Quarterly* 11.4 (1989): 279–82.

Wood, Michael. "Reading Dazzle." *Gabriel García Márquez's* Love in the Time of Cholera. Ed. Harold Bloom. Philadelphia: Chelsea House, 2005. 141–52.

THE GENERAL IN
HIS LABYRINTH

READING TO WRITE

*T*HE *GENERAL in His Labyrinth* (1990; published first in Spanish, *El general en su laberinto*, 1989) is Gabriel García Márquez's portrait of South America's legendary "Liberator," Simón Bolívar (1783–1830), as he makes the final journey of his life from Bogotá to the Colombian coast. Part history, part biography, part fiction, it is described by Michiko Kakutani as "an improvisation on the life and times of the Latin American revolutionary ... that turns a mythic hero into a fallible human being" (n.p.). This iconoclastic treatment of such a lionized figure has been alternately praised for its realism and criticized—especially by Latin Americans—for its denigration of the visionary who brought independence to half a continent (Borland 439–40). Weighing in on the debate, Selden Rodman ultimately concludes: "García Márquez's scenario does not show his hero in the best light, but doubtless it was not intended to. As a way of unfolding Bolívar's whole life, however, it is brilliant" (n.p.). Indeed, the brilliance of the novel extends far beyond its biographical implications. As with such masterworks as *One Hundred Years of Solitude* and *Love in the Time of Cholera*, *The General in His Labyrinth* is a penetrating inquiry into such essential human themes as love, death, heroism, nostalgia, and, of course, solitude. While not heavily influenced by magic realism, the interplay between journalistic objectivity, wry humor, and dramatic irony also clearly marks the text as García Márquez's own unique and significant contribution to the genre of historical fiction. With what is obviously a broad spectrum of potential topics, your first step before beginning to write should be a close reading of those passages that seem to reflect the aspect or aspects of the novel you find most compelling. Consider, for instance, the following scene in which Bolívar's trusted valet, José Palacios, packs the general's bags for the journey from which he will never return:

> On the morning of their departure, in the bags that José Palacios packed without haste while the General finished dressing, there were only two well-worn sets of underclothing, two changes of shirt, the battle tunic with a double row of buttons that were supposed to have been made from the gold of Atahualpa, the silk cap for sleeping, and a red hood that Field Marshal Sucre had brought him from Bolivia.
>
> His footwear consisted of his house slippers and the patent-leather boots he would be wearing. In his personal trunks José Palacios was carrying, along with the chest of medicines and a few other articles of value, Rousseau's *Social Contract* and *The Art of War* by the Italian general Raimundo Montecuccoli, two bibliographical treasures that had belonged to Napoleon Bonaparte and had been given to him by Sir Robert Wilson, the father of his aide-de-camp. There was so little that it all fit into a soldier's knapsack. When [the general] saw it as he was about to go to the room where the official delegation was waiting, he said:
>
> "We never would have believed, my dear José, that so much glory could fit into a shoe" (30–31).

The passage begins as an inventory of the essential items the general will require for his trip: undergarments, shirts, and shoes. The description of each garment, however, imbues it with a meaning beyond its mundane function. For example, what is revealed by the use of the modifiers "only two" and "well-worn" to describe the underwear? What is the effect of contrasting this privation with the elaborate gold-buttoned uniform jacket? Moreover, how do the legendary origin of the gold (Who was Atahualpa and what was his symbolic significance to the Latin American resistance to imperial Spain?) and the historical significance of red hood (Mentioned frequently in the novel, who was Antonio José de Sucre, and what role did he play in the struggle for independence?) accentuate the gulf between the protagonist's glorious past and his current condition? In what way do the items mentioned in the passage also underscore the novel's goal of revealing the more intimate side of this illustrious figure: "cap for sleeping" and "hood," "boots" and "slippers," and especially the transition from the chests of clothing to "his personal trunks"? What is the significance of placing the medicines in Bolívar's personal baggage? How does this fore-shadow later events in the novel? What does it reveal about the general's concern for maintaining a public image in the face of his rapidly declin-ing health? References to specific works of literature often have a symbolic meaning. Who was Jean-Jacques Rousseau and what was the significance of his treatise? How does it reflect Bolívar's political beliefs? Montecuccoli was a relatively obscure 17th-century general, but what meaning might be inferred from the title of his book? How does this second work not only contrast with the first but also embody the duality of Bolívar's career? Why is the reference to Napoleon Bonaparte as the books' original owner thus so appropriate? Given Napoleon's ambivalent historical status as both the leader who spread the social ideals of the French Revolution as well as a megalomaniacal tyrant, what is being implied about the protagonist? Finally, what is the purpose of the consecutive references to the paucity of the general's possessions? In particular, what is the meaning of the mixed metaphor that ends the passage, and how does it encapsulate the novel's central theme?

This passage offers a good example of how a close reading can help you to identify elements that you may not have considered the first time you read the text—which, in turn, will help you to select a topic for your essay. As you read over the additional topics discussed in this chapter, keep in mind that this is not intended to be an exhaustive list but rather an initial guide to help you brainstorm your own ideas about the text. If you derive a topic from your reading, instead of choosing an arbitrary topic and then attempting to search the novel for textual documentation, you will find your writing process to be a much more productive one.

TOPICS AND STRATEGIES
Themes

Writing on themes in a work of historical fiction is particularly interest-ing, as it often sets the idea or value in question against the backdrop of events that have shaped human destiny. In the case of *The General in His Labyrinth,* many of the topics offer you the opportunity to explore the theme, not in the life of an Everyman, but rather in that of one who altered the future of an entire continent. Consider the theme of solitude, which, while encountered throughout García Márquez's work, here takes on an added dimension: the sense of isolation suffered by those who have achieved greatness. Similarly, while death may come to all people, how might its approach be different for those whose accomplishments confer upon them a kind of cultural immortality? A related theme is nostalgia in that another consequence of leading an illustrious life would seem to be the increased poignancy connected with memories of the past. Essays on nostalgia, death, or solitude, as those themes relate to the life of one of the world's most legendary leaders, are only some of the numerous possibilities for thematic topics. What other themes take on a new significance when seen in the light of a figure such as Bolívar?

Sample Topics:

1. **Solitude:** Examine what the novel has to say about solitude— especially as a consequence of fame and power—through the character of Bolívar.

While solitude is a constant in the writing of García Márquez, *The General in His Labyrinth* surely constitutes one of his most notable treatments of the theme. Through what might be termed the solitude of great men and women, it explores the isolation confronted by those whose lives are conducted in the public eye, whose existence becomes the subject of history. Michael Bell comments: "Bolívar's solitude is a conscious necessity on his part but it is no less of a personal burden for that" (135). Return to the text and search for the passages that describe the protagonist's sense of loneliness or separation from the world around him. You might, for example, consider the scene of a mass in Bolívar's honor in the Mompox church during which he complains to the mayor of the sweltering heat:

> "Believe me, I don't deserve this punishment."
> "The love of the people has its price, Excellency," said the mayor.
> "Sad to say, this isn't love, it's curiosity," he said (107).

What is Bolívar implying about the people who have come to pay him tribute? How does his comment betray his sense of isolation? Where do you find other incidents of the protagonist either feeling isolated or consciously isolating himself from others because of his status? What is the novel saying about the relationship between solitude and fame? Is solitude a necessary, albeit tragic consequence of greatness?

2. **Death and dying:** Write an essay exploring the novel's treatment of the way human beings—even great heroes—must ultimately confront their own mortality.

Observing that "Death and the past are present and alive . . . throughout García Márquez's fiction," Lois Parkinson Zamora calls particular attention to "the mythic almost corpse in *El general en su laberinto*" (82). Indeed, this vision of a moribund Bolívar that predominates in the novel is in stark contrast to the character's apparent imperviousness to the many mortal dangers he has confronted in life, never "suffering a scratch" in battle and "emerg[ing] unharmed from every assassination attempt" (8). The text goes on to explain that "his disinterest was not a lack of awareness or fatalism, but rather a melancholy certainty that he would die in his bed, poor and naked and without the consolation of public gratitude" (8). Explain the paradox of the protagonist's "melancholy certainty" of surviving so many confrontations with death. What can be gleaned from this attitude with regard to the choice between a longer life and a more meaningful, but shorter life?

3. **Nostalgia:** Analyze what the novel has to say about the sense of loss associated with the memory of an often idealized past.

Reflecting on *The General in His Labyrinth*, Jean Franco notes: "'Nostalgia,' a familiar word in García Márquez's vocabulary, marks a history that is distorted in memory, is unrepeatable and therefore associated with mourning for something that is forever lost" (103). This sense of a lost past is pervasive throughout the general's voyage. Reflect on the following scene in which Bolívar goes to see his old friend, the gravely ill general Lorenzo Cárcamo. Having "lamented their misfortunes" and "mourned the frivolity of nations and the ingratitude of victory" (116–17), their visit comes to an end: "Lorenzo Cárcamo watched him stand up, sad and stripped of everything, and he realized that for both the General and himself, memories were more of a burden than the years" (117–18). How does the text convey the nostalgia of the two old soldiers? In what way is paradox ("ingratitude of victory"; "memories . . . years") employed to heighten the melancholic tone? Find other passages in the novel that capture this nostalgic sense of loss. Are they all related to the protagonist's past glory, or are there other causes underlying his nostalgia? Is the text showing nostalgia to be a condition common to all human beings, or is it more of a psychological state that afflicts some individuals more than others?

Characters

With regard to character, *The General in His Labyrinth* is something of a paradox. While the complicated political background intersects with the protagonist's journey to infuse the text with dozens of minor personages (many of whom are only referenced and never actually appear), the narrative is dominated to a great extent by the title character. An essay on Bolívar is an obvious choice. You will want, however, to be sure that you focus on the fictional character, rather than treating the general as an extension of the real-life person on whom he is based. If you want to write on a minor character, your selection is rather limited. There are, nevertheless, two intriguing possibilities. Manuela Sáenz, the general's mistress, is one of the most striking female characters in all of García Márquez's work. Another engaging topic might be to analyze the role of José Palacios, the former slave who becomes a kind of Sancho Panza to the general's Don Quixote. Are there other minor characters whose presence in the text, separate from their respective historical roles, merit further analysis?

Sample Topics:

1. **Simón Bolívar:** Write an essay that assesses Bolívar, not as a historical legend, but rather as a very real, flawed literary character.

   García Márquez has been both praised and criticized for creating a character who transcends the heroic myth. In his review of the novel, David Bushnell comments that "here is a Liberator who wanders naked through the house, suffers constipation, uses foul language, and much more besides" ("El general ensulaborinbo"

200). In addition to his obvious health problems, what other aspects of the general's character contribute to the text's iconoclastic treatment of the hero? While visiting the town of Mompox, for instance, the general inquires with the local priest as to the whereabouts of his former lover and benefactor, the wealthy Josefa Sagrario, so that he might return to her a chest of gold she had given him in a time of great need during the war:

> But the priest . . . astounded him with the news that Josefa Sagrario and her family were living in exile in Italy for conspiring against the security to the state.
>   "More of Santander's shit, of course," said the General.
>   "No, General," said the priest. "You exiled them yourself without realizing it after the troubles in '28.
>   He left the chest of gold where it was while he clarified the matter, and then he did not concern himself anymore about her exile (115).

What negative character traits are revealed in this short conversation? How does the scene capture both Bolívar's magnanimity and his pettiness? Why does he assume that General Francisco de Santander is to blame, and why does he react to the truth in such a cavalier fashion? How is the effect of the scene heightened by the knowledge that the general once believed that he and Josefa "loved each other more than anyone in this world ever had before" (115)? Find other instances in the text where Bolívar's human weaknesses are weighed against his greatness. Do you find this portrait lends the character greater humanity, or is it suggesting that this celebrated hero—perhaps all heroes—are ultimately much more deeply flawed than their legends would have us believe?

2. **Manuela Sáenz:** Write an essay on the woman who transcends the mere role of Bolívar's mistress to emerge as a heroic figure in her own right.

Neither the character of Manuela Sáenz, nor her relationship with the protagonist can be considered typical for a historical novel set in the 19th century. When she first appears, the novel describes her "dressed in a cavalry uniform," "smok[ing] a sailor's pipe," smelling of "the verbena water favored by the military as her perfume," and with a "husky voice still suited for the penumbra of love" (6–7). What image of the character does this representation connote? Why is the last phrase especially important? Given that Manuela spends very little time with Bolívar during the course of the novel, how does the text establish the nature of their relationship and the depth of her commitment? How does it portray Manuela Sáenz's historical role in preventing an assassination attempt by Bolívar's political enemies? Can it be argued that her heroism is equal to that of the Liberator? Is it accurate to view her as a feminist, a champion of women's equality, or does her behavior suggest that she seeks acceptance by assuming the role of a man in all realms beyond the bedroom?

3. **José Palacios:** Explore the character of Bolívar's lifelong servant, companion, and confidant.

While it is not uncommon for protagonists to have an aide, companion, or underling, the function of these typically minor roles may vary from merely a stereotypical stock character such as the *servus stultus* (low comic, bumbling valet) to that of a fully formed, psychologically complex character, such as Sancho Panza in Miguel de Cervantes's *Don Quixote* or Berenice Sadie Brown in Carson McCullers's *The Member of the Wedding*. Where does José Palacios belong on this continuum? What is the nature of the relationship between this former slave (the text provides a short biography on page 266) and his celebrated master? Why do you think he tells Bolívar, "The fitting thing is for us to die together" (266)? Should José Palacios be understood as an eminently noble figure who stands by a great man in his darkest hour, or is there a tragedy in the character's complete sacrifice of self? How might the sociohistorical reality of persons of color, especially former slaves, play a part in García Márquez's fictional depiction?

History and Context

By its very nature, *The General in His Labyrinth* should afford you no shortage of potential topics for an essay on history and context. Many of these will relate to the historical Simón Bolívar and his pivotal role in reshaping Latin America in the 19th century. Rather than trying to attempt a broad comparison between the real Liberator and his fictional counterpart, you might want to choose a specific aspect of his life on which to focus. On such angle could be the way the text reflects and comments upon the political ideals that inspired Bolívar's struggle for Latin American independence. Or, you could analyze the power struggle in the fictional narrative in the context of the actual political events in Colombia at the time of Bolívar's death. With either of these topics or any other related to history and context, you will need to keep in mind that extra research will be necessary: You cannot comment on how "fiction" relates to "fact" until you have a solid grasp of the latter.

Sample Topics:

1. **The foundation of Bolívar's political beliefs:** How faithful is García Márquez's protagonist to the real Simón Bolívar with regard to his political beliefs?

   If you choose to write an essay on this topic, it will behoove you to begin by researching Simón Bolívar's political beliefs (among the many biographies of Bolívar, you might start with David Bushnell's *Simón Bolívar: Liberation and Disappointment*). What was the basis of his thought, and where is this foundation reflected in the novel? Who were Jean-Jacques Rousseau and Alexander von Humboldt? Are the references to these men in the text and, in the case of Rousseau, his writings (*Émile, Nouvelle Héloise, Social Contract*) reflected the real Bolívar's intellectual formation? The text also references what is probably Bolívar's best-known political treatise, the "Jamaica Letter" (77). Read the Jamaica Letter (Bolívar's "A Reply of a South American Gentleman to a Gentleman of This Island" is available online), and then reread the passage in question. Does the fictional Bolívar of 1830 embody the principles put forth by the young exiled patriot in 1815?

2. **Bolívar and Colombian politics:** Write an essay exploring the relationship between the events in the novel and the power struggle that took place at the end of Bolívar's life.

The General in His Labyrinth is filled with references to the political and military struggle that plagued Bolívar's attempts to govern in his final years. Before you turn to the events in the novel, you will need to understand the history itself (you might begin with Vinicio Romero Martínez's chronology included at the end of the novel, and then read the pertinent chapters of Richard W. Slatta's *Simón Bolívar's Quest for Glory*). How do the historical "facts" corroborate or contradict the protagonist's perception? Slatta states:

> Unlike George Washington, his North American counterpart, Bolívar could not make the transition from soldier to statesman. Bolívar could be charming, charismatic, and convincing, but unfortunately, his gigantic ego and almost fanatical quest for glory clouded his judgment and made him appear a megalomaniac. No longer needing his military leadership and finding his dictatorship odious, even one-time friends turned against him (289).

In his review of the novel, however, David Bushnell points out that the text depicts an altruistic leader: "In this account, Bolívar was obsessed with Latin American unity above all, dreaming of a single great nation from Mexico to Argentina, and was saddened and embittered when selfish local oligarchies continually frustrated his dream" (*"El general"* 201). What do you make of this contradiction? Does the novel reveal Bolívar to be culpable in the conflict with his political enemies? More important, is he aware of his own political failure, or does he engage in a perpetual process of rewriting history?

Form and Genre

Given that the work of García Márquez is typically associated with magic realist narratives structured around nonlinear plots and told by unreliable narrators, The *General in His Labyrinth* might seem somewhat pedestrian in the area of form and genre.

Your only initial impulse might be to examine the way it intersects with the historical novel (or perhaps biography). While García Márquez's unique approach to the genre makes this an interesting topic, to be sure, it is far from your only option for this kind of essay. You might choose to examine the novel's epigraph and its relationship to the rest of the text. Still, a very distinct essay could be written on the way García Márquez applies Ernest Hemingway's theory of omission, or the "iceberg principle," to the telling of the story. As you conduct your close reading exercise and brainstorm topics, consider the other formal elements of the novel that you may have overlooked in this very atypical García Márquez text.

Sample Topics:

1. **Historical novel:** Analyze the novel's affinity with the genre of the historical novel.

Margaret Atwood has written of *The General in His Labyrinth*: "It is set in the past, but to call it a historical novel would be to do it an injustice" (n.p.). What do you think the celebrated Canadian writer means by this comment? Familiarize yourself with the essential tenets of the historical novel (a good reference is Georg Lukács's appropriately titled classic, *The Historical Novel*). How does García Márquez's book conform to the traditional concept of the genre? In what ways is it distinct? For example, very few historical novelists use a famous figure as their main protagonist, preferring to assign such characters to a minor role (for example, while both Czar Alexander and Napoléon appear in Leo Tolstoy's *War and Peace*, both are secondary characters). What is the purpose of focusing on someone as well known as Bolívar? García Márquez has admitted that his motive for writing about the final weeks of Bolívar's life—a period on which there exists almost no documentation—"was that it allowed me to write without any major limitations to my imagination" (Samper 171). Given this information, should *The General in His Labyrinth* be considered a historical novel, a fictionalized biography, both, or neither?

2. **The novel's epigraph:** Explain the relationship between the quotation preceding the novel's text and the text.

Merriam-Webster's Collegiate Dictionary defines *epigraph* as "a quotation set at the beginning of a literary work or one of its divisions to suggest its theme." The epigraph to *The General in His Labyrinth,* taken from an actual letter written by Bolívar in 1823 to his then vice president, Francisco de Santander, declares: "It seems that the devil controls the business of my life" (1). Why do you think García Márquez chose this quotation? To which aspect(s) of the novel does it apply: themes, character, or context? How does the epigraph influence the reader's understanding of the text? In what way, if any, might the reader understand the book differently without first reading the epigraph?

3. **Hemingway's "iceberg principle":** Write an essay exploring the way García Márquez employs Hemingway's theory in *The General in His Labyrinth.*

Interviewer María Elvira Samper asked García Márquez about the influence of American novelist Ernest Hemingway's celebrated iceberg metaphor for writing, in which, "The gigantic mass of ice we see floating turns out to be invulnerable, because underneath the water, it's sustained by seven-eighths of its volume" (Samper 171). The author's reply was affirmative: "What can be noted in *The General* is the enormous amount of information that is submerged" (171). Find specific instances in the novel where the iceberg principle is applied. First, speculate as to which "information . . . is submerged." Then, explain how these missing details affect the reader's understanding of the passages in question. Given that the iceberg principle is almost exclusively associated with the depiction of purely fictional characters and events, use the example of *The General in His Labyrinth* to speculate on the possible implications for applying Hemingway's idea to the representation of history. How might it be argued that it constitutes a more truthful approach to historical fiction?

Language, Symbols, and Imagery

Essays on language, symbol, and imagery allow you to study a specific element within the text, typically for its metaphorical value. The most prevalent symbol in the novel is the labyrinth from which the protagonist cannot escape. Another image that is repeated on numerous occasions is that of writing, and in particular the general's aversion to it. With either of these two symbols or any others you might choose to explore, remember that it is not sufficient simply to identify their presence; you need to offer a coherent explanation of how they are used to create or change the meaning of the text. Rather than write on a specific symbol or image, you could also investigate the use of language to convey meaning. A common exercise is to examine a particular character's way of speaking. In this case, you might analyze the very obscure speech often used by the general, which seems to suggest much more than is actually said. Once again, with this or any other topic you choose in this area, you will need to go beyond the mere recognition of the character's distinct way of expressing himself or herself to offer an explanation of how it affects the reader's understanding of the novel.

1. **Labyrinth:** Write an essay on the maze symbolism in the novel.

   In addition to its inclusion in the title, the image of the labyrinth is repeated in the dying Bolívar's last words: "'Damn it. . . . How will I ever get out of this labyrinth!'" (267). Return to the text and identify images or language that seem to evoke this idea. Keep in mind that the reference may connote the essence of a labyrinth without specifically naming it as such. For example, Bolívar tells his doctor, "I've become lost in a dream, searching for something that doesn't exist" (221). To what do you think is he referring in these comments? What is the nature of a labyrinth, and what affinities does it have with the protagonist's situation? Is he speaking of his political dilemma, his health, his entire life, or something else altogether?

2. **Writing:** Examine the references to writing in the novel, and explain their metaphorical meaning.

   The text references a number of memoirs, letters, histories, and official documents that serve as part of the basis for García

Márquez's portrait of Bolívar. Commenting on one such text, the diary of Irish general Daniel Florence O'Leary, Bolívar states, "'O'Leary is a great man, a great soldier, and a faithful friend, but he takes notes on everything. . . . And there's nothing more dangerous than a written memoir'" (155). Isabel Alvarez Borland observes, "Throughout the narrative, Bolívar's voice is explicit regarding his disdain for written history and cautious against the trap that is the illusion of capturing facts with words" (443). Identify the passages in the novel that mention writing. Is Borland correct in her assessment? How might the general's aversion to having his life documented be read as a reflexive commentary on the act of writing about history?

3. **The general's speech:** Write an essay that analyzes Bolívar's opaque language.

As opposed to what might be expected with a figure of Bolívar's stature, the character gives no sweeping speeches nor reveals any profound beliefs to those around him. Commenting on this "special case of Bolívar," Michael Bell argues that the text "constantly withholds omniscience to preserve the mystery of the character" (140). The critic goes on to explain, "His speech repeatedly takes on the quality of pronouncements or aphorisms emerging in a highly self-conscious way from a constant, private process of reflection whose mystery is only partly illuminated by the utterances themselves" (141). One such example is when Bolívar's barge arrives in Mompox and an officer demands to see each passenger's passport. The general replies, "Although you may not believe it, Captain, I have no passport" (102). Why does Bolívar not identify himself? Given that a passport is a document that proves an individual's citizenship, how does the general's response imply the kind of "process of reflection" described by Bell? Return to the text and search for other instances of the general's opaque language. What is the effect of this kind of speech on the reader's understanding of the character? Why might it be argued that this type of discourse is perhaps even more appropriate with an individual of such immense historical stature?

Compare and Contrast Essays

Compare and contrast essays allow you to explore connections between the text you are studying and others that seem to evidence similar themes, characters, or stylistic elements. *The General in His Labyrinth* is especially interesting in its affinities with other García Márquez novels. For instance, you might decide to compare it with one of the author's earliest works, *No One Writes to the Colonel,* whose central theme and main character seem to mirror those of the later work. Yet another possible intertextual study is the striking parallel between García Márquez's Bolívar and his best-known hero, Colonel Aureliano Buendía in *One Hundred Years of Solitude.* Of course, you need not limit yourself to other works by García Márquez. You might explore the similarities between this work and historical novels or fictional biographies by other writers. The more you are able to offer a good rationale for your comparison— why it will shed light on the reader's understanding of *The General in His Labyrinth*—the stronger your essay is likely to be.

Sample Topics:

1. *The General in His Labyrinth* **and** *No One Writes to the Colonel:* Compare the thematic similarities and differences between *The General in His Labyrinth* and *No One Writes to the Colonel.*

   García Márquez has acknowledged the affinity between the two works, noting of *The General in His Labyrinth,* "It's like *No One Writes to the Colonel* again, but now historically based. Ultimately I've written a single book, the same one that goes round and round, and continues" (Samper 170). Read the novella, noting the elements that seem to anticipate *The General in His Labyrinth.* What similarities do you find between the two texts? What does the story of the colonel suggest about the status of forgotten heroes like Bolívar? In what way is the solitude of both characters similar? Do they both confront their plight in the same way, or can it be said that the colonel ultimately breaks free from his labyrinth? What is the significance of the nostalgia theme in the two texts? How does the use of flashback as a narrative device function to heighten the melancholy tone of both works? Finally, how does each work function as a commentary on not only Colombia's past but also on its social and political reality in the latter part of the 20th century?

2. Simón Bolívar and Aureliano Buendía: Explore the affinities between García Márquez's most celebrated fictional hero and the celebrated hero he fictionalizes.

It can be argued that Colonel Aureliano Buendía, the war hero and champion of the Liberal cause in *One Hundred Years of Solitude*, is a character both inspired by the historical Simón Bolívar and the inspiration of the fictional Liberator of *The General in His Labyrinth*. Michael Bell, for example, ponders the similarities between the two protagonists:

> What was revealed as a personal and family trait of Col. Aureliano is seen to be the necessary condition of Bolívar's historical role. Hence if we sense in him any actual echo of Aureliano it adds an ambivalence to each of them, and gives further pathos and mystery to Bolívar. Is it only a similarity of circumstance or is there, of necessity, an Aureliano in Bolívar? (137).

Do you believe that Aureliano Buendía is the fictional embodiment of the historical Simón Bolívar? Is García Márquez's fictional Bolívar drawn, at least in part, from the hero of the earlier novel? What traits do the two characters share? How are their journeys similar? Unlike Bolívar's indisputable military success, it is noted in *One Hundred Years of Solitude* that, "Colonel Aureliano Buendía organized 32 armed uprisings and lost them all" (103). Can it be argued that Aureliano Buendía represents the quixotic aspect of the real Bolívar's heroism? Do you find this trait manifested in the protagonist of *The General in His Labyrinth*? Given that the name of Colonel Aureliano Buendía appears in many of García Márquez's novels as a footnote in his fictional universe, how do both characters constitute a commentary on society's attitudes about history and historical figures?

Bibliography and Online Resources for *The General in His Labyrinth*

Atwood, Margaret. "A Slave to His Own Liberation." *New York Times* 15 June 1997. 5 December 2008. <http://www.nytimes.com/books/97/06/15/reviews/marquez- general.html>.

Bell, Michael. *Gabriel García Márquez: Solitude and Solidarity.* New York: St. Martin's Press, 1993.

Bolívar, Simón. "A Reply of a South American Gentleman to a Gentleman of This Island." *Selected Writings of Bolívar.* Trans. Lewis Bertrand. New York: Colonial Press, 1951. 8 November 2008. <http://faculty.smu.edu/bakewell/BAKEWELL/texts/jamaica-letter.html>.

Borland, Isabel Alvarez. "The Task of the Historian in *El general en su laberinto.*" *Hispania* 76.3 (1993): 439–45.

Bushnell, David. *"El general en su laberinto."* *Hispanic American Historical Review* 70.1 (1990): 200–01.

———. *Simón Bolívar: Liberation and Disappointment.* New York: Pearson, 2004.

Franco, Jean. "Dr. Urbino's Parrot." *Gabriel García Márquez's* Love in the Time of Cholera. Ed. Harold Bloom. Philadelphia: Chelsea House, 2005. 99–112.

García Márquez, Gabriel. *The General in His Labyrinth.* Trans. Edith Grossman. New York: Vintage, 1990.

———. *One Hundred Years of Solitude.* Trans. Gregory Rabassa. New York: HarperPerrenial, 2006.

Kakutani, Michiko. "Books of the Times: The Human Behind the Heroic Pose." *New York Times* 11 September 1990. 3 November 2008. <http://query.nytimes.com/gst/fullpage.html?res=9C0CE2DA143AF932A2575AC0A966 9582 60&sec=&spon= &pagewanted=1>.

Lukács, Georg. *The Historical Novel.* Trans. Hannah Mitchell and Stanley Mitchell. Lincoln: U of Nebraska P, 1983.

Rodman, Selden. *"The General in His Labyrinth*—Book Review." *National Review* 15 October 1990. 2 November 2008. <http://findarticles.com/p/articles/mi_m1282/is_n20_v42/ai_9016904>.

Samper, María Elvira. *"The General in His Labyrinth* Is a 'Vengeful' Book." *Conversations with García Márquez.* Ed. Gene H. Bell-Villada. Jackson: U of Mississippi P, 2006. 168–80.

Zamora, Lois Parkinson. *The Usable Past: The Imagination of History in Recent Fiction in the Americas.* Cambridge: Cambridge UP, 1997.

OF LOVE AND
OTHER DEMONS

READING TO WRITE

*O*F *LOVE and Other Demons* (1995; in Spanish, *Del amor y otros demonios*, 1994) may not be one of Gabriel García Márquez's best-known works; however, it certainly is one of his most notable. Set in the 18th-century city of Cartagena in the viceroyalty of New Granada (modern-day Colombia), it relates the story of a girl who, stricken with rabies, is accused of demonic possession and the priest who, sent to perform an exorcism, falls in love with her.

Inspired by an event that García Márquez witnessed in 1949, when the colonial-era crypt of a young woman, identified only as Sierva María de Todos los Angeles, was opened to reveal a supernatural "stream of living hair the intense color of copper" (4), *Of Love and Other Demons* is a fantastic speculation on the mysterious Sierva María's life set against a vivid portrait of Colombian life in the 1700s. With its complex characters, powerful themes, and rich historical setting, the novel presents a broad range of potential essay topics. As you consider your many options, your first step should be to conduct a close reading of those passages that seem most closely related to the topic that you are considering. For example, look at the following passage dealing with the rearing of Sierva María by Dominga de Adviento and the other servants in the marquis de Casalduero's household.

The girl, daughter of an aristocrat and a commoner, had the childhood of a foundling. Her mother hated her from the moment she nursed her for the first and only time, and then refused to keep the baby with her for fear she would kill her. Dominga de Adviento suckled her, baptized her in Christ, and consecrated her to Olokun, a Yoruban deity of indeterminate sex whose face is presumed to be so dreadful it is seen only in dreams, and always hidden by a mask. Transplanted to the courtyard of the slaves, Sierva María learned to dance before she could speak, learned three African languages at the same time, learned to drink rooster's blood before breakfast and to glide past Christians unseen and unheard, like an incorporeal being (42).

The beginning of the passage focuses on Sierva María's biological parents. How does the initial, antithetical description of an aristocrat-commoner relationship suggest the tumultuous foundation into which the girl is born? What is a "foundling," and why is this term's connotation so powerful with regard to the mother-child relationship? What is the visceral impact on the reader of Bernarda Cabrera's reason for refusing to nurse her baby? Given the previous sentence, how does the first phrase related to Dominga de Adviento work to shift the maternal status from the mistress of the house to her servant? How does the remainder of this sentence reveal Dominga's influence on the child she virtually comes to adopt? What do you make of her paradoxical decision to have the infant "baptized in Christ" and "consecrated . . . to Olokun," and why is it so significant in shaping the reader's understanding of Sierva María's character? How does the description of the Olokun compare with the traditional Christian idea of God, and why do you think it is included in the text? Why is it significant that the African deity is such a contrast to its European counterpart, and how does it reinforce the protagonist's duality. Finally, what is the significance of Sierva María's experiences in the "courtyard of the slaves"? How do the details concerning "dance" and "African languages" underscore her transformation? By noting that Sierva María learns how to "glide past Christians," what is the text implying about her worldview by the end of her upbringing? As you consider these questions, give thought as well to the different essay topics all suggested in the same passage. How might you use it to develop an essay about the character of Sierva María? By the same token, why might it also form the basis of an analysis of Dominga de Adviento? How could you draw on this close reading to explore the presence of African culture in the novel? What other topics does the passage suggest to you?

TOPICS AND STRATEGIES
Themes

Do not be misled by the 18th-century setting in *Of Love and Other Demons*. Many authors of great works of literature have set events in the historical past precisely in order to underscore the universality of their themes. García Márquez seems to be implying the timeless nature of certain "truths" in the tragic story of Sierva María. One such theme is that of forbidden love. Why do individuals pursue romance with those whose love is most proscribed by society? Why does society proscribe certain relationships? Should we condemn the transgressors or those who condemn their transgression? Another timeless theme explored in the text is that of the outsider, or the Other. Why do communities reject, even persecute those who are different? Yet another theme you could explore is the age-old struggle for freedom by human beings in bondage. Is subjugation always physical? Does every person face some form of tyranny—either physical or psychological? What other universal themes can you identify in the novel?

Sample Topics:

1. **Forbidden love:** Write an essay that examines the novel's treatment of the double taboo of love both between an adult man and a 12-year-old girl and between a priest and his parishioner?

   Forbidden love is a theme seen in literary works from William Shakespeare's *Romeo and Juliet* (1597) to Vladimir Nabokov's *Lolita* (1955). García Márquez explores this theme from two perspectives: that between an adult male and an adolescent girl, as well as between a priest and a member of his congregation. Begin by identifying all of the references in the text to the relationship between Cayetano Delaura and Sierva María. In what ways, if at all, does the text represent it as taboo? What causes Cayetano to fall in love with Sierva María? Does the novel portray him as a predator, a rescuer, as neither, or as both? Is it significant that their love is never consummated sexually? What other romantic or marital relationships appear in the novel, and how do they compare to that of the protagonists? How do you interpret the couple's tragic fate? What is the novel ultimately suggesting about both the nature of love and about society's attempts to codify it?

2. **The Other:** Analyze what the novel is saying about difference and how society judges those who are different.

Many characters in the novel can be understood as manifestations of the Other: Dominga de Adviento (a woman of color in a Caucasian household), Bernarda de Cabrera (a commoner in an aristocratic family), Abrenuncio de Sa Pereira Cao (a Jew, a non-Spaniard, and a humanist in a Spanish-speaking society rooted in fervent Catholicism), to name but a few of the most obvious examples. What other instances of the Other can you identify? What are the consequences of "otherness" for each of these figures? Reflect on the young marquis's response to his father's objection that Bernarda was an unfit bride because she is insane: "'Crazy people are not crazy if one accepts their reasoning'" (35). How might this quotation be applicable to the novel's message on society's attitude toward those who are different?

3. **Bondage versus freedom:** Explore what the novel has to say about the subjugation of human beings and their struggle to be free.

Many of the characters in *Of Love and Other Demons* confront some kind of limitation on their freedom. For some, it is slavery; for others, incarceration; and still for others, this bondage is emotional. Return to the text and consider how each of the characters confronts a limitation to his or her personal liberty. Ask yourself in what way each of them is restrained from exercising his or her free will. Who or what restricts his or her freedom? In what way does each one suffer from a lack of freedom? How does the reader see the character's struggle? Do any of these figures achieve independence, and if so, at what cost? Does the text suggest that all humans face some form of bondage? Do they always fight for emancipation, or do some individuals accept their fate?

Characters

Essays on character(s) can be deceptively easy, especially with a work like *Of Love and Other Demons*. While it certainly is not difficult to identify your subject, it is never enough simply to retell a particular character's story. Instead, you need to explain his or her particular function in the text. You must ask yourself, Why does this particular personage exist? In the case of Sierva María, for example, it is even difficult to determine what her true nature is. Ethnically European, is she actually more culturally African? Should she even be seen as the protagonist of the novel? Another intriguing but problematic character is Sierva María's father, the marquis de Casalduero. He first ignores his daughter, then desperately attempts to save her life, and ultimately condemns her to death in the hands of the Inquisition. Similarly, his wife, the debauched Bernarda Cabrera, is the antithesis of motherhood but, at the same time, strangely tragic in her own way. Attempting to "define" any of these three characters will challenge your critical acumen. The novel has numerous other fascinating and complex figures such as Cayetano Delaura, Abrenuncio, and Dominga de Adviento. What might you say about their roles?

Sample Topics:

1. **Sierva María:** Write an essay exploring this ethereal character. What makes her such a problematic protagonist?

   Sierva María is one of García Márquez's most enigmatic protagonists. From her conflicting social origins (an aristocratic father and a middle-class mother) to her estrangement from her parents and her dual Euro-African cultural identity, Sierva María seems to embody the idea of paradox. Indeed, as A. S. Byatt points out, "'Sierva,' [meaning] servant of God, is also the Spanish word for slave" (n.p.). What purpose does it serve to have such a composite of contradictions in a single character? How might it be said that her antithetical nature is symbolic of Latin America's historical experience? On another note, what does the reader actually know about Sierva María from a psychological perspective? Is she magical? Is she possessed by demons? Given that she is so ethereal in nature compared to her father, her mother, Cayetano Delaura, or even many of the secondary characters, is it accurate to see her as the main protagonist? Return to the novel and reconstruct Sierva María's biography, as well as her role in the story. In what way might you argue that she is more the object of the novel than its subject?

3. **Ygnacio de Alfaro y Dueñas (the marquis de Casalduero):**
   Write an essay analyzing Sierva María's well-intentioned, yet rather mediocre father.

   The text initially describes Sierva María's father as "a funereal, effeminate man, as pale as a lily because the bats drained his blood as he slept" (9), who has little interest in his daughter. While he later attempts "to rectify the past and win the girl's heart" (47), R. A. Kerr makes the observation that his "lack of resolve over his daughter's incarceration ultimately costs the young woman her life" (779). After revisiting all of the references to the marquis in the novel and reconstructing both the character's biography and his psychological makeup, explain the marquis's role in the text. Do you agree with Kerr? Is the marquis merely the pathetic counterpart to his reprehensible wife, or is he more complex than first appears? For example, the text notes that, "The Marquis put his trust not in God but in anything that might offer some hope" (50). What does this reveal? On another note, given the underlying significance of his name (*casal* means "manor house," and the Duero is a river in the heart of Castile), how might he be seen as a symbol of the decline of imperial Spain?

3. **Bernarda Cabrera:** Analyze this odious, but also strangely tragic figure.

   Few of García Márquez's characters match the psychological complexity of Sierva María's mother. A strong and intelligent woman—it is she who maintains the Casalduero fortune through her "astute" (11) business sense—she is at the same time consumed by her numerous vices. Most curious of all, she fears, hates, and ultimately repudiates her own child. Reconstruct Bernarda Cabrera's biography. What do we know about her life before her marriage to Sierva María's father? How would you characterize her relationship with the marquis de Casalduero? What brings on her addictions? Most important, why does she reject her daughter? Is Bernarda Cabrera the source of her own misery, or is she also, in some way, a victim of "demons"?

History and Context

Of Love and Other Demons is a work that allows for many different interesting topics in the area of history and context. Begin by reflecting on the aspects of 18th-century Colombian history that appear in the novel. One of the most prevalent is the important role of Africans in colonial Cartagena de Indias (indeed in the entire Caribbean region). How does the text represent slavery, multiethnic society, and the survival of African culture even under an oppressive system? On the topic of oppression, a fascinating essay could be written on the novel's portrayal of the colonial Catholic Church, especially the dreaded Holy Office of the Inquisition. What was the reality of the Inquisition in Latin America, and how is that reality reflected (or perhaps altered) in the story of Sierva María's suffering? A third potential subject of a more literary nature is the intertextuality that exists between the novel and work of the 16th-century Spanish poet Garcilaso de la Vega. Who was Garcilaso, and why does his poetry play such a prominent role in the text? These are only three of the numerous topics from which you have to choose. Given that you are writing about a historical novel, almost any aspect of the story could be studied in that context. Just keep in mind that you are writing a literature paper, and inasmuch, your analysis of history always needs to return to the fictional text.

Sample Topics:

1. **Africans in colonial Latin America:** Write an essay exploring the historical reality underlying the fictional representation of Africans in the novel.

   While characters of African descent are not uncommon in the works of García Márquez (Mr. Carmichael in *In Evil Hour*; Nabo, the title character in the short story "Nabo: the Black Man Who Made the Angels Wait"; Plácida Linero, the Nasars' housekeeper in *Chronicle of a Death Foretold*), nowhere is their presence as prominent and as integral to the story as in *Of Love and Other Demons*. This significance is closely tied to the importance of Africans—both slaves and free citizens—in the cultural evolution of colonial Colombia. Should you wish to explore this topic, you will want to begin by researching the history of Africans in the Spanish Americas, especially in the Viceroyalty of New Granada. An excellent point of departure for your work is Jane

G. Landers and Barry M. Robinson's collection of essays, *Slaves, Subjects, and Subversives: Blacks in Colonial Latin America*. After having familiarized yourself with the historical background, return to the novel and reflect on the characters of African descent, how they are portrayed, and the nature of their relationship to the Europeans. How are African traditions and beliefs represented in comparison to European cultural values? What is implied by Domina de Adviento's strong bond to Sierva María in contrast to the apathy of the child's parents? In what other ways does the text comment on the virtues of the African characters relative to the Europeans? How does this reflect or repudiate the history of Africans in colonial Latin America?

2. **The Inquisition:** Explore the history of the Holy Office in 18th-century Latin America as it relates to the exorcism of Sierva María.

One of the more notorious institutions brought by the Spaniards to the Americas was the infamous Inquisition. With its mission to repress heresy, as it had in Europe, the Holy Office persecuted thousands of harmless individuals not unlike the novel's protagonist, Sierva María. Begin by researching the role of the Inquisition in colonial America (a good starting point is Clara Steinberg-Spitz's Web site *The Inquisition in the New World*), and compare your findings to the fictional representation in the text. Read carefully for all of the pertinent references. For example, consider Delaura's comment to Abrenuncio when he discovers a Latin translation of Voltaire's *Lettres philosophiques*: "'Voltaire in Latin is almost a heresy,' he said as a joke" (113). Why is a priest making a joke about the possession of a banned book by a blatantly anti-Catholic writer? What does this suggest about the reality of the seemingly monolithic Inquisition? How can it be both terrible and laughable at the same time, and what does this paradox imply about Spain's efforts to impose its cultural values on the New World?

3. **Garcilaso de la Vega:** Relate the life and work of this celebrated Renaissance Spanish poet to his fictional descendant, Cayetano Delaura.

Critics use the word *intertextuality* to describe the presence of one literary text or texts in another. Cayetano Delaura, who believes himself to be a descendant of the Castilian poet Garcilaso de la Vega and holds the writer "in almost religious reverence" (77), frequently cites his poetry at important moments. For Arnold M. Penuel, these references underscore both the young priest's humanist impulse and his desire, not for spiritual, but for romantic fulfillment: ". . . the Renaissance tradition [is] exemplified in Cayetano's enthusiasm for Garcilaso's poetry, which is a continuation of the tradition of courtly love epitomized in Petrarch's sonnets" (40). If you choose to write an essay supporting, refuting, or taking a different direction from Penuel's thesis, you will need to begin by familiarizing yourself with Garcilaso de la Vega's life and work. You might begin with Bernard Gicovate's general introduction, *Garcilaso de la Vega,* as well as with English translations of some of the original poems available through the Web page "Garcilaso de la Vega" (be sure not to confuse the poet with the Amerindian-Spanish writer of the same name, often referred to as "El Inca" Garcilaso de la Vega). Your next step will be to identify as many of the passages referencing either Garcilaso or his poetry (ideally, you would also be able to identify the specific poems cited and read them in their entirety). Why do you think the text creates the connection between Cayetano and Garcilaso? What do you know of the poet's life that seems to suggest an affinity? How do the specific verses cited relate to the events in the novel? Thinking about the concept of courtly love espoused by Garcilaso, how might it help to explain the nature of Cayetano's love for Sierva María.

Form and Genre

Essays on form and genre explore a work's relationship to accepted literary conventions. Given its setting in colonial Cartagena, one of the obvious topics you might choose for *Of Love and Other Demons* is how it correlates to the historical novel as a genre. What is a historical novel, and do its traditional features apply to García Márquez's text? Another genre issue for you to explore is the text as an example of magic realism. What is the source of magic realism in *Of Love and Other Demons*? Finally, one intriguing formal element of the novel is its use of the framing device in the form of the author's prologue. Why does García Márquez employ this device? Thinking about the general aesthetic principles and broad structures in the text, what other potential topics come to mind?

Sample Topics:

1. **Historical novel:** How does *Of Love and Other Demons* reflect or differ from the traditional conception of this genre?

   The historical novel is a genre dating back to the emergence of nationalism in the early 19th century. Writing on the origins of the genre in his seminal study, *The Historical Novel,* Georg Lukács asserts that in the "mass experience of history the national element is linked on the one hand with the problems of social transformation; and on the other . . . between national and world history" (25). How can García Márquez's novel be seen as a study of "social transformation," and in what way does it link Colombia's "national [history] and world history"? What "transformation" is taking place in the story, and how does it relate to the changing world at the end of the 18th century? Many historical novelists choose subjects still relevant to their contemporary audiences; for instance, the suffering of Quasimodo and Esmeralda at the hands of Claude Frollo in the medieval world of *The Hunchback of Notre Dame* (1831) resonated with a French public that had overthrown the reactionary monarchy of Charles X only a year earlier. What modern-day problems might García Márquez be addressing in *Of Love and Other Demons*?

2. **Magic realism:** Identify and discuss the magic realist elements in the novel.

   While not as closely associated with magic realism as other García Márquez works, such as *One Hundred Years of Solitude* and "A Very Old Man with Enormous Wings," *Of Love and Other Demons* still clearly belongs within the same genre. Before returning to the novel, begin by reviewing the constituent traits of magic realism (Maggie Ann Bowers's *Magic(al) Realism* will provide you with a basic introduction). Where in the text do you find examples of magic realism? Consider

Jonathon Handleman's description of the text's connection to the genre:

> Márquez builds a novel which is at once straightforward and at the same time utterly magical. He sets the reader up as a judge of what is real and what is not. He includes skeptical characters with a logical explanation for every event, and spiritual ones who are willing to believe any act as evidence of magic in the world (n.p.).

What do you think of Handleman's characterization of the way the text challenges the reader's perception? To which characters and which events is Handleman referring? What is your interpretation of these events? Where do you find magic realist elements in the text? Why are so many of the magical aspects in the novel associated with the African characters? Commenting on the Afro-centric influence on magic realism, David Mikics notes: "The Caribbean and Latin American mixing of cultures (African, European, Amerindian) can, then, become a source of innovation whose energy derives from the conjunctions and cross-influences of radically different modes of thought and life" (374). How might you see *Of Love and Other Demons* as an affirmation of Mikics's thesis?

3. **Framing device:** Examine the way the author's prologue affects the reader's understanding of the novel.

The opening pages of the novel describe what García Márquez alleges to be the supernatural event that would later inspire him to write *Of Love and Other Demons*. While this kind of framing device is not uncommon in narrative fiction, its function varies between texts. For Wendy B. Faris, the account of the living auburn hair flowing miraculously from Sierva María's centuries-old tomb works to provoke "hesitation" in the reader:

> We hesitate on three accounts, most important, because we wonder whether the events the novel narrates are possible and therefore could be true. That initial hesitation increases the

intensity of the two other, more pragmatic speculations about whether García Márquez actually witnessed the phenomenon, and whether the introduction is fact or fiction (19).

Do you agree with Faris's thesis? If so, what are the consequences of the reader's hesitation with regard to the subsequent story? If not, what indication can you find in the foreword that the story is to be read as either fact or fiction? Why does the text return to the framing device at the end? What might the use of framing device be suggesting about our attitude toward these kinds of popular legends?

Language, Symbols, and Imagery

Of Love and Other Demons is a text replete with interesting symbols and imagery. One of the principal symbols in the novel is found in its very title. An analysis of the metaphorical meaning of "demons" would make for an outstanding essay. Yet another image repeated throughout the story is Sierva María's hair. What exactly does it symbolize? Whether you choose one of these images or one of the many others that appear in the novel, be sure that you do not limit yourself merely to identifying or cataloging them. Interpretation requires that you offer a unified explanation—one that holds true for every reference to the symbol—of how it functions to create meaning in the text.

1. **Demons:** What or who are the demons to which the title refers?

   Demons function on both a literal and a metaphorical level in the novel. For the Inquisition and many of the residents of colonial Cartagena de Indias, demons are the satanic entities sent to corrupt humanity. As the title of the novel makes clear, demons are also impulses and passions—including love—that can possess the human mind just as much as any malevolent spirit. Asking, "What are the real demons of the title?" A. S. Byatt contends that "it is completely clear, not for the first time in Mr. García Márquez's fiction, that the real forces of destruction are the beliefs of the Spanish and the Christians" (n.p.). Do you agree with Byatt's interpretation of the demon metaphor? Is so, where do you find evidence for this reading?

Are there other demons in the novel? Are they external, internal, or both?

2. **Sierva María's hair:** What is the symbolic significance of this most frequently mentioned physical characteristic of the protagonist?

Sierva María's hair serves as both the magical pretext to the novel in the author's foreword and as the final image at the end of the story. With such textual prominence, it clearly invites a metaphorical reading. Consider the first chronological reference to Sierva María's hair, shortly after the child's birth:

> "It's a girl," said the midwife. "But it won't live."
> That was when Dominga de Adviento promised her saints that if they granted the girl the grace of life, her hair would not be cut until her wedding night. No sooner had she made the promise than the girl began to cry. Dominga sang out in jubilation: "She will be a saint!" The Marquis, who saw her for the first time when she was bathed and dressed, was less prescient.
> "She will be a whore," he said. "If God gives her life and health" (42).

How does this passage relate to the cultural conflict that exists in the text? In what way does it reflect the supernatural attributes assigned to Sierva María's hair in the prologue? Look for the other references in the text to the protagonist's hair to see if they also seem to reference these aspects of the novel. What conclusions can you draw from your findings?

Compare and Contrast Essays

Of Love and Other Demons invites any number of intriguing comparisons with other works. If you choose to relate the novel to another work by García Márquez, one possible choice would be to analyze the symbolism of disease in *Of Love and Other Demons* and *Love in the Time of Cholera*. Should you wish to compare the text to that of a different writer, think of one that seems to share one or more common traits. For example, although they are separated by more than a century and a half, there are some compelling similarities between *Of Love and Other Demons* and Nathaniel Hawthorne's *The Scarlet Letter*. With either type of essay, but especially the latter type of essay, be sure that you clearly define the aspect or aspects of the two works that merit comparative analysis. Why are the two texts relevant to each other, and what can be learned through the comparison or contrast?

Sample Topics:

1. **Disease as a metaphor in *Of Love and Other Demons* and *Love in the Time of Cholera*:** Compare and contrast the way García Márquez employs disease as a motif in these two novels.

   Acknowledging his fascination with plagues, García Márquez has stated: "Plagues are like imponderable dangers that surprise people. They seem to have a quality of destiny" (Simons 156). As with the outbreak of rabies in *Of Love and Other Demons*, the cholera epidemic in *Love in the Time of Cholera* has far-reaching and unforeseen consequences. If you choose to write this essay, your first task will be to read the latter novel, paying particular attention to each reference to disease, especially the one named in the title. How does the role of the cholera plague compare to the function of the rabid animals in *Of Love and Other Demons*? What is the definition of an epidemic or a plague? What aspects of the two novels reflect those traits? How does each serve as a metaphor for the primary relationship in the respective texts? Given that the titles of both works also specifically mention love, how might disease be understood as a symbol of that powerful emotion?

2. **García Márquez's *Of Love and Other Demons* and Hawthorne's *The Scarlet Letter*:** Write an essay comparing or contrasting these two novels about forbidden love in a puritanical colonial society.

   Nathaniel Hawthorne's classic, *The Scarlet Letter* (1850), shares numerous traits with *Of Love and Other Demons*. Both are historical novels set more than two centuries before their publication, during their respective nations' colonial period. Both focus on a forbidden love between an intelligent, promising religious leader and a young woman repudiated by her community. Both works call attention to the bigotry of that community. Each work has a powerful symbolic representation of the heroine's martyrdom (Hester's *A* and Sierva María's hair), both of which figure prominently in their tombs. Finally, just as García Márquez's novel includes magic realist elements, so Hawthorne's novel features several supernatural events. Given all these common components, would you argue that the two texts are essentially similar, or is there an important difference between them? As you read (or reread) *The Scarlet Letter,* take notes on these and other aspects of the novel that seem to be echoed in *Of Love and Other Demons.* Choose one shared characteristic, such as their common indictment of religious intolerance or the respective couples Sierva María–Cayetano and Hester-Dimmesdale, and make your argument. Do both texts represent the same timeless and universal archetypes, or are these apparent similarities actually distinct to their own historical, cultural, and literary traditions?

Bibliography and Online Resources for *Of Love and Other Demons*

Bowers, Maggie Ann. *Magic(al) Realism.* London: Routledge, 2004.

Byatt, A. S. "Of Love Possessed." *New York Times* 28 May 1995. 10 October 2008. <http://www.nytimes.com/books/97/06/15/reviews/marquez-demons.html>.

Faris, Wendy B. *Ordinary Enchantments: Magical Realism and the Remystification of Narrative.* Nashville, TN: Vanderbilt UP, 2004.

García Márquez, Gabriel. *Of Love and Other Demons.* Trans. Edith Grossman. New York: Penguin, 1995.

"Garcilaso de la Vega." *Sonetos del Siglo de Oro.* 7 April 2006. 20 October 2008. <http://sonnets.spanish.sbc.edu/Garcilaso.html>.

Gicovate, Bernard. *Garcilaso de la Vega.* Boston: Twayne, 1975.

Handleman, Jonathon. "*Of Love and Other Demons*: Review." *Literary Review.* Summer 1999. 13 October 2008. <http://findarticles.com/p/articles/mi_m2078/is_4_42 /ai_56184317>.

Kerr, R. A. "Patterns of Place and Visual-Spatial Imagery in García Márquez's *Del amor y otros demonios.*" *Hispania* 79.4 (1996): 772–80.

Landers, Jane G., and Barry M. Robinson. *Slaves, Subjects, and Subversives: Blacks in Colonial Latin America.* Albuquerque: U of New Mexico P, 2006.

Lukács, Georg. *The Historical Novel.* Trans. Hannah Mitchell and Stanley Mitchell. Lincoln: U of Nebraska P, 1983.

Mikics, David. "Derek Walcott and Alejo Carpentier: Nature, History, and the Caribbean Writer." *Magical Realism: Theory, History, Community*. Ed. Lois Parkinson Zamora and Wendy B. Faris. Durham, NC: Duke UP, 1995. 371–404.

Miksanek, Tony. *"Of Love and Other Demons." Literature, Arts, and Medicine Database*. 11 December 2006. 11 October 2008. <http://litmed.med.nyu.edu/Annotation?action=view&annid=12284>.

Penuel, Arnold M. "Symbolism and the Clash of Cultural Traditions in Colonial Spanish America in García Márquez's *Del amor y otros demonios*." *Hispania* 80.1 (1997): 38–48.

Simons, Marlise. "García Márquez on Love, Plagues, and Politics." *Conversations with García Márquez*. Ed. Gene H. Bell-Villada. Jackson: U of Mississippi P, 2006. 154–62.

Steinberg-Spitz, Clara. *The Inquisition in the New World*. 1999. 16 October 2008. <http://www.sefarad.org/publication/lm/037/6.html>.

INDEX